D-Day + 60 Years

A Small Piece of History

Jerome J. McLaughlin

authorHOUSE

1663 LIBERTY DRIVE, SUITE 200
BLOOMINGTON, INDIANA 47403
(800) 839-8640
www.authorhouse.com

First published by AuthorHouse 04/01/04

ISBN: 1-4184-0268-0 (e)
ISBN: 1-4184-0269-9 (sc)
ISBN: 1-4184-0270-2 (dj)

Library of Congress Number: 2004090871

Printed in the United States of America
Bloomington, Indiana

This book is printed on acid-free paper.

There are several people to whom I wish to dedicate this book:

My uncle, First Lieutenant Joseph Sullivan, whose loss was so profound to his family that the need to complete his story became compelling; his fiancee, Mitzy Hangarter-Coogan, who will always remain a member of our family; his immediate family at the time of his death: mother Katherine, older brother and sister Vincent and Katherine, and his loving younger sister, my mother, Dorothy. Their pain has kept his memory alive.

The World War II veterans of the 77th Troop Carrier Squadron, who were so supportive of these efforts to remember their lost brothers.

The World War II veterans of G Company, 501st Parachute Infantry Regiment, who were as proud to be brash young warriors in 1944 as they are now proud to be compassionate recorders of history.

My cousin, Glenn Kenneth Smith (1963 - 1987), who would have been this project's most ardent supporter.

And most important of all, Denise Mary Catherine Broderick McLaughlin, my bride since May 1, 1982, and the love of my life. I literally could not have completed this project but for her.

Jerome J. McLaughlin
Alexandria, Virginia
January 2004

Acknowledgments

Numerous contributors merit special mention for their help in the research and publication of this book.

Among the veterans of the 77th Troop Carrier Squadron, two men who were close to my uncle, pilot Tom Gannon and fellow navigator Earl Vollbracht, corresponded with me for several years beginning in 1984, but passed away before I attended my first 77th Reunion in 1998. I regret not having met them. Others, such as Joe Flynn, Bud Busiere, and Jesse Harrison have become, along with their wives, good friends. George Winard and Abe Friedman have gone out of their way to relate stories of the 77th and personal reminiscences of my uncle. All of these men have supported my research with their time and with the mementoes they were able to retrieve from boxes long hidden in attics and basements. Others helped with interviews and documentation, including Henry Osmer, the first squadron commander, and his operations officer and successor, Phillip "Pappy" Rawlins. Pappy's interview and his extremely well-documented, unpublished history of the squadron were invaluable. Paul Krause, Walter Lake, Gerry Mulcahy, Frank Blaisdell, and Gene Fosburg [from 435th HQ] went out of their way to assist me.

The French contingent involved refused to allow language barriers, international politics, personal crises, or the width of an ocean to stop their efforts to help with my research as well as the placement of two plaques honoring my uncle and those who died with him. Philippe Nekrassoff, a former paratrooper in the French Army and current national gendarme, played a significant role in this saga. If Philippe had not met Joe Flynn during the 40th anniversary celebration of D-Day, what follows would most likely never have been compiled. Philippe's expertise on the subject of troop carrier operations in Normandy assisted me through this project for almost two decades.

Philippe also introduced me to Michel Gaudry, a retired jazz clarinet player. Michel now lives in Normandy and works with WWII veterans, their families, and friends trying to unlock or relocate the past. Others in the French contingent include Bill and Genevieve Phillips, who acted as our translators on our first visit; Claude Dulenay, the owner of the farm on which the plaque bearing my uncle's name is displayed; and Regis and Patricia Bisset who, in addition to displaying a plaque, graciously invited twelve Americans into their home during our 2001 visit. A special thanks also to Sebastian Daher, the proprietor of *Hotel du 6 Juin* in St. Mere-Eglise, who served as a wonderful host and able translator. Nadine Hanguehard-Turmel, Philippe Nekrassoff's editor and good friend, provided translation assistance and the e-mail conduit between France and Virginia that enabled Philippe and me to communicate in hours instead of weeks.

The veterans of G Company 501st Parachute Infantry Regiment were initially involved only on the fringes of my research. Thanks to assistance from George Koskimaki, I received letters in the 1980's from Don Kane and Jack Urbank regarding the knowledge they had of the loss of my uncle's aircraft. Later Ray Geddes launched an entirely new direction for the story that resulted in this book. Don, Ray, and Jack—along with Jack's family, particularly daughters Claudia and Denise, have been major supporters. Lucien Tetrault, Don Castona, Fred Orlowski, Wilber Ingalls, and Warren Purcell contributed with detailed personal memories and pictures. A special thanks is due Cliff Marks and Art Morin, Jr., sons of G Company men who made significant contributions. Sue Kane provided several suggestions that have been incorporated in the book.

Authors Milton Dank and Martin Wolfe were helpful to me in my early research.

Some participants not part of the WWII military or citizens of France include my cousins, Katherine and Ken Smith and Margaret and Wilson Young, who have been involved both emotionally and technically. Mark Bando, the author of several excellent D-Day books, has been a major source of support. Photographs and tidbits of information he supplied are found generously throughout this book. Other contributors include Chris Wahl, a long-time friend and colleague, who translated Philippe's letters for more than a decade; Amy Whorf-McGuiggan, who contributed her Master's thesis; Art and Patti Morin and John Merkt, who made the 2001 trip to France; and Brian Williamson from the Museum of the Soldier, who contributed material on Milo Ludy. The staff at the Department of Defense Memorial Affairs Office during the time period 1981–1990 were most helpful in providing the files that I requested for review.

Others who helped have included Art Couchman, the nephew of medic Eddie Hohl, who shared the letter that his family had received from Laurence Legere in 1980. Art recounted several interesting tales concerning his search for the details surrounding his uncle's death. Ken Holmes contacted me with information about his dad, who served as a platoon leader in G Company. Ken was able to document, from his father's WWII memorabilia, that Lieutenant Luther Knowlton was seen wearing Bud Busiere's top hat while in Normandy. (Ken is a retired career Special Forces NCO; his son is the family's third-generation paratrooper.)

Others who were there when I needed help along the way include Jim Grismer, John Daley, Glenn Marshall, Maureen Rienmueller, and Scott Carothers.

I am not a professional writer. Production of this book was a labor of love. I did, however, find some fine professionals to work with me on the project. Shirley Parker and Roberto Kamide, who did the editing and graphic work, are outstanding people who made my ramblings into a product that I was proud to send to the publisher. I doubt, despite my best efforts, that this work has been completed without error. Although I did my best to ensure accuracy, any errors the reader may note are mine alone. If you would care to comment on any aspect of this book, I would appreciate hearing from you. You may contact me at: SMALLHISTORY@AOL.COM.

Frank Blaisdell
Thomas Gannon
Earl Vollbracht
George Wirtanen
JPM
MJG

Rest in Peace.

Contents

INTRODUCTION

What follows is a small piece of history. It began in 1981 as an attempt to discover what had happened to my uncle, Lieutenant Joseph J. Sullivan, who had been killed on the morning of D-Day while flying as a navigator in a Douglas C-47, dropping the 101st Airborne Division in Normandy. After years of research I was to learn what did happen to my uncle and, in 1998, to actually visit the crash site where he perished, along with nineteen other American soldiers. What happened after my visit to France in 1998 is the second story, which led to the writing of this book.

It is the story of two small groups of the young men who had been caught up in the world's largest, most horrendous war. None of the main characters had reached his thirtieth birthday; many were teenagers. The young men were members of two units of the United States Army that had not existed when the war began. Even the concept of what the units were designed to do was in its infancy when war was declared in December 1941, thirty-one months before all of the characters came together on June 6, 1944. These two units, the 77th Troop Carrier Squadron (TCS) of the 435th Troop Carrier Group (TCG) and G Company of the 501st Parachute Infantry Regiment (PIR), had been formed to participate in the liberation of Europe. Despite stunning losses, they were successful in that mission.

We are going to follow the story of two small but distinct portions of those units—specifically, the paratroopers and aircrew who on D-Day maorning flew on the three airplanes that made up B Flight of the 77th TCS, and the third platoon of G Company, 501st PIR. Most of the men on the three planes would not survive to see the dawn.

The men from G Company included Private First Class Donald Kane, a 24-year-old rifleman from West Haven, Connecticut; T/4 Raymond Geddes, Jr., a 19-year-old radio operator from Baltimore, Maryland; and 20-year-old Staff Sergeant John (Jack) Urbank, from Peninsula, Ohio. All of these men jumped into the Normandy countryside from an aircraft piloted by 21-year-old First Lieutenant Jesse Harrison, from St. Louis, Missouri.

Of the three planes in B Flight of the 77th Squadron, Harrison's was the only one to return from the D-Day drop of G Company. The other two planes, piloted by the flight leader, Captain John Schaefers, from Detroit, Michigan, and First Lieutenant James Hamblin, of Newark, New Jersey, were downed by antiaircraft fire near Picauville, France. Only three of the forty-three men on board those two planes survived. You will meet one of those survivors, and the son of another.

The center of the story that follows involves a remarkable set of circumstances linking pilot Jesse Harrison and infantryman Jack Urbank—a story that resulted in the uniting of the men from the two units fifty-six years after the several hours they had spent together in 1944, and finally, fifty-seven years later, the placement of two plaques to honor the men who had paid the supreme sacrifice just as our story was beginning.

During the course of my research I met most of the men who are quoted in the story. Some, such as Colonel Henry Osmer, I have talked with on the telephone, and exchanged countless letters and e-mails. Certain individuals stand out for what they told me, usually in private moments.

Perhaps the most personal event was related to me by Abe Friedman, the lead navigator of the 77th Squadron. At the 1998 Squadron reunion, Abe asked me if I was the first child of my uncle Joe's younger sister. When I said that I was, he smiled and said, "I remember when you were born." Joe was one of Abe's navigators, and a fellow New Yorker; the men knew each other well. Abe recounted that he distinctly remembered that when my uncle received a letter from his mother saying that his "little sister" had given birth to a baby boy, Joe had entered the Officer's Club to buy drinks for all in honor of his new nephew. I must say that it is an unusual feeling to meet a total stranger who suddenly tells you he celebrated your birth fifty-four years earlier! Abe reminded me of the event when I met him again in 2000. On both occasions we toasted the memory of my uncle.

Others told stories that were not so pleasant. George Winard told me how he had been mesmerized by the sight of my uncle's plane glowing red from the fire that started in the cockpit and worked its way through the fuselage as the plane fell toward the earth, with the apparent loss of all onboard. Several years later a group of French citizens described to a group of visiting Americans the carnage associated with the loss of the plane that had been flying next to that of my uncle.

Many of the stories that I heard told of courage, humor, and passage into manhood of the young flyers and paratroopers involved. The story of Jesse Harrison and Jack Urbank would create the bond that led to the heart of this book.

All of the events that took place from 1942 through 1945, and the final chapters, which took place from 1998 through 2001, are, together, just one small piece of history.

BEFORE

Katherine Sullivan, age 56, woke from her sleep at home in Woodhaven, Queens, in New York City. Katherine was screaming. Her daughter, in the next room, left her four-month-old son in his crib and raced to her mother. Katherine told her daughter that she had had a nightmare in which she had seen her son's plane falling from the sky in flames. Katherine's son was a navigator in the U.S. Army Air Corps, stationed in England. Everyone knew that the Allied invasion of Europe was imminent, and the Sullivan family knew that Joe would be involved. The nightmare that had shaken Katherine Sullivan, the terrible fear of a son's demise, was occurring for thousands upon thousands of other mothers around the world in 1944. Regardless of which army, or which side in the war, mothers prayed, frightened for their sons.

Katherine's daughter, Dorothy McLaughlin, had come home to live with her mother in time to give birth to her first child, a son, while her husband also served overseas. Dorothy held and soothed her mother until Katherine's shaking stopped. Then my mother returned to her bedroom, and lifted me from my crib. She wondered whether the nightmare her mother had just endured would return, and she prayed for her brother's safety in the days ahead. My mother lay down in her bed and held me as she thought how this time in her life, with her first baby only sixteen weeks old, should have been the highlight of her life. She and her husband should have been rejoicing in the start of the family they had dreamed of having. Instead, her brother and her husband were both overseas because of a war she did not fully understand. Her husband was safe, at least for the time being, stationed with the American forces occupying the Dutch Antilles Island of Curacao, near Puerto Rico. Her brother, however, was an aircrew navigator flying in C-47 troop carrier aircraft that dropped paratroopers and glider infantrymen into combat behind enemy lines. Dangerous work.

She thought how proud she was of her brother. He had been drafted in 1941 and had originally been assigned, because of his musical skills, to the band of the 22nd Infantry Regiment. After Pearl Harbor he had decided that playing the saxophone would not help win the war and had applied and been accepted for Air Cadet training. He was commissioned as a navigator in September 1943, just in time to be assigned to the 77th Troop Carrier Squadron before it departed for England.

Dorothy thought about all the stories in the newspapers, and talk among her family and friends, about the upcoming invasion. Surely it was this apprehension that had led to her mother's nightmare. As she held me in her arms, she noticed light coming in the windows. It was the morning of June 6, 1944. She carried me downstairs to the kitchen and began to heat a bottle and to make her own breakfast. She also turned on the radio. Several minutes later a news bulletin interrupted with an update of the biggest news since December 7, 1941—the invasion of Europe had begun, and was now several hours in the making. Allied forces were advancing off the beaches of Normandy. Dorothy had to sit down. Fifty years later she told me that she felt as if she had stopped breathing. Her mother's nightmare had coincided with the start of the invasion. Once again she began to pray for her brother. She could not know, of course, that her prayers were too late.

CHAPTER 1
3–6 June 1944

"June 3rd, before D-Day, Joe, Dick, and I went to the Club
and hoisted quite a few. I remember we played "Cabin in
the Sky" by Ella Fitzgerald on the jukebox over and over
again. Joe really liked that song. June 4th we were housed
behind barbed wire and everything was hush-hush. The night
of June 5th we got our briefing for the mission."

Earl Vollbracht
Navigator
77th Squadron

"I leaned down to look out the little window,
and saw a plane was on fire and going down.
You could see colored tracers everywhere.
I said, 'Christ, let's get the hell out of here.' "

Raymond Geddes, Jr.
Radio Operator
G/501

Along with the 432 C-47 transport aircraft making up seven troop carrier groups that took off for France on the night of June 5, 1944, carrying the 101st Airborne Division, the planes of the 77th Squadron of the 435th Troop Carrier Group were part of the largest invasion force ever to enter battle. The 435th was transporting the commander of the 101st Airborne Division, General Maxwell Taylor; his staff; and the 3rd Battalion of the 501st Parachute Infantry Regiment (PIR), consisting of G, H, and I Companies. The 77th Squadron was carrying a group of paratroopers with whom they had trained before coming overseas during the winter of 1943–44: G Company of the 501st PIR. The mission of the 3/501 was to defend the divisional headquarters on the morning of June 6, and then to act as a reaction force should trouble develop. {For an explanation of the chain of command structure, see the appendix, page A2.} The overall airborne plan called for the 101st to jump or arrive by glider in four different areas designated as A, B, C, and D. All four zones were located directly behind Utah Beach. [1]

Don Kane - (Rifleman - G/501): "I think it was June 4th when we were loaded onto trucks. The rear canvas was rolled down and tied for secrecy. About midnight the convoy rolled through the sleeping towns to the barbed-wire-enclosed airport."

77th Squadron Official Diary - "Shortly before 2000 [hours] on the 5th, combat crews were summoned to the Group briefing room. It was learned that the final hour had arrived, that this was not a dry run. Here crews received complete detailed instructions on the coming mission. It was revealed that the 77th would carry 215 paratroopers in the twelve C-47s, along with bundles containing rations and medical supplies. Other equipment to be carried were mortars, machine guns, bazookas, radio equipment, light guns, and ammunition. Takeoff time would be 2325 hours. On completion of the briefings, the pilots and crews went to the intelligence office and entrusted their valued possessions to the clerks to be filed away until their return. In exchange they took with them purses containing French currency and escape kits. Though visibly tense with apprehension of the hour to come, all seemed relieved as they left for their planes."

The 435th TCG sent forty-eight aircraft to Normandy on the night of June 5-6. The 77th Squadron flew twelve of those aircraftt, in four elements of three aircraft each. The element on the far left of the squadron formation was led by Captain John Schaefers. The plane to Schaefers' left was piloted by Lieutenant James Hamblin. On Schaefers' right was Lieutenant Jesse Harrison. The three planes carried fifty-one paratroopers of G Company, 501st Parachute Infantry Regiment.

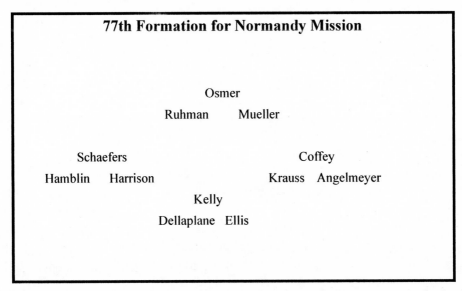

77th Formation for Normandy Mission

Osmer

Ruhman   Mueller

Schaefers   Coffey

Hamblin   Harrison   Krauss   Angelmeyer

Kelly

Dellaplane   Ellis

The aircrew in the three planes in Schaefers' element were typical of the men who made up the new concept of troop carrier aviation. They were citizen soldiers who, in most cases, had never been in an airplane prior to entering the service.

The scheduled pre-takeoff activities for the 77th called for an intelligence briefing at 9:30 P.M., with aircrew reporting to the planes at 10:00 P.M., engine start at 11:00 P.M., and takeoffs to commence at 11:30 P.M. It was estimated that flight duration from the time the squadron formed up with the rest of the 435th Group until the aircraft returned to Welford Park would be four hours and four minutes. During that time the aircraft would have flown 450 miles from England, across the Cotentin Peninsula in France, and back to Welford Park.

The paratroopers from G/501 were, in the tradition of infantrymen in all armies, very young. Many were teenagers, such as 19-year-old T/4 Ray Geddes of Baltimore, Maryland. Geddes was the radio operator for the G Company Commander, Captain Vernon Kraeger. Most of the platoon, except for some last-minute replacements, were "Toccoa men," meaning that they had been with the regiment since it had been formed at a training camp in Toccoa, Georgia, in 1942. The Toccoa men were strongly bonded as a group, in the spirit of the new airborne infantry concept of World War II. They were as well trained and prepared as any group of men the United States of America had ever sent into combat.

Henry Osmer (Commanding Officer, 77th TCS) - "I always was very concerned about our cargo; that is, the paratroopers and glider men. Some pilots flew planes with just bombs to drop, or fighters, where you were by yourself. We had living, breathing men on our ships, the finest fighting men in the world. It was our job to deliver them to the battle. That was a tremendous responsibility."

77th Squadron Official Diary - "The paratroopers attended last-minute religious services in the field while waiting for the air crew briefing to end. They clustered in small groups of their own denomination. They were seen sauntering off to the planes single file to the accompaniment of their own military band, playing a march, and their own shouts and typical GI cracks—if not gladly, sincerely wanting to go. General Eisenhower and General Brereton were on the field to see them off."

Jesse Harrison (Pilot - 77th TCS) - "Most of the pilots didn't really mix with the paratroopers. I always did. Before the takeoff I spent about three-quarters of an hour talking with Sergeant Jack Urbank and his company executive officer, Lieutenant Norman Barker. Urbank was usually a jumpmaster, and I had jumped him several times, while we were in England, and once back at Pope Field. On this mission Barker was the jumpmaster, and the three of us discussed how we would handle things. I told them that my flight engineer would be stationed at the door and would communicate any questions or orders to and from the cockpit. Mostly we talked about all the training we had been through, and that tonight was the real thing. We all agreed that we were well prepared and ready for action. When we got everyone on the plane, I made a little speech to the paratroopers and told them, 'You are going in tonight come hell or high water, and I will do my best to get you there.'"

Bud Busiere (Crew Chief, 77th TCS) - "While we were waiting to go, I got to talking with one of the paratroopers, Lieutenant Luther Knowlton. Somehow I mentioned my 'Mission Hat,' an opera hat that I took on all our flights for good luck. Knowlton asked me if he could borrow the hat for the jump. He said he would bring it back to me when they returned. I was reluctant, and figured that I would never see the hat again, but how could you say no to a guy in that situation? I gave him the hat." [2]

The paratroopers helped each other to strap on the huge amount of equipment they were to carry on the jump. When they were finished adjusting their equipment, the Air Corps personnel began to help them onto the planes.

One of the paratroopers on Harrison's plane was Private First Class Don Kane. Kane had first boarded the plane commanded by Lieutenant Jim Hamblin, but then heard his name called from outside by his platoon leader, Lieutenant Everett Crouch. Crouch ordered Kane to change planes with him so that he (Crouch) could jump with his operations sergeant, Matthew Yoquinto. Although Kane was very unhappy about leaving the men on Hamblin's plane, the squad he had trained with since basic training at Camp Toccoa, he understood that there was no question as to obeying the order.

Don Kane - "You didn't mess with Crouch. He was a good officer, but he was hard, a tough guy. He liked to practice hand-to-hand combat with the enlisted men."

Angry and encumbered with all his equipment, Kane struggled out the door of Hamblin's plane and across the tarmac. He took the last seat on the plane piloted by Lieutenant Harrison. One of Harrison's crew, probably Flight Engineer Emilio Giacomin, helped Kane aboard and tried to start a conversation. Kane was in no mood for small talk and told the man to leave him alone. Shortly after Kane sat down, the three planes started their engines and began to taxi toward their takeoff.

The sixty-four young men on the three planes, aircrew and paratroopers, were all entering combat for the first time. Most would not survive the night.

The 77th Squadron had the honor of having one of its planes, AC 42-92716, named the "Brass Hat," flown by Colonel Frank McNees and a mixed HQ/77th crew, lead the 435th on the D-Day mission. The 53rd Wing flew five troop carrier groups to France on the night of 5-6 June. The 435th would be the fifth and final group of the Wing to arrive over Normandy, and therefore face opposition from an alerted enemy.

Col. Frank McNees in the cockpit of the Brass Hat

The takeoff and assembly took place with little difficulty as the four squadrons of the 435th had been practicing this exercise regularly since their arrival in England the previous November. The 77th left its base at Welford Park on a heading carefully designed to avoid any problems with naval units mistaking the troop carriers for German bombers, as had happened with disastrous results during the invasion of Sicily the previous year. They crossed the English Channel, through various turns and course changes that were coded with the geographically American names of Austin, Flatbush, Hoboken, and Reno.

There is considerable historical documentation of the airborne operations in Normandy, along with even more speculation and comment on what happened to the troop carrier squadrons that night after they left point Reno. An unpredicted cloud bank was present right at the 1500-foot altitude at which the planes crossed the coastline. Absolute radio silence prevented the earlier groups from warning the 435th of the problem. Had Colonel McNees known of the cloud bank beforehand, he could have made a command decision to go below the clouds in order to help retain the group's formation integrity. Instead, McNees and the other pilots found themselves suddenly flying in instrument conditions and unable to see other aircraft flying only yards from their wing tips. This situation was harrowing for aircrews operating under the stress of the opening moments of their first combat experience.

Some aircraft commanders elected to go above the cloud bank, hoping to use electronic air/ground homing devices known as EUREKA-REBECCA to locate their drop zone; others elected to go below the clouds in order

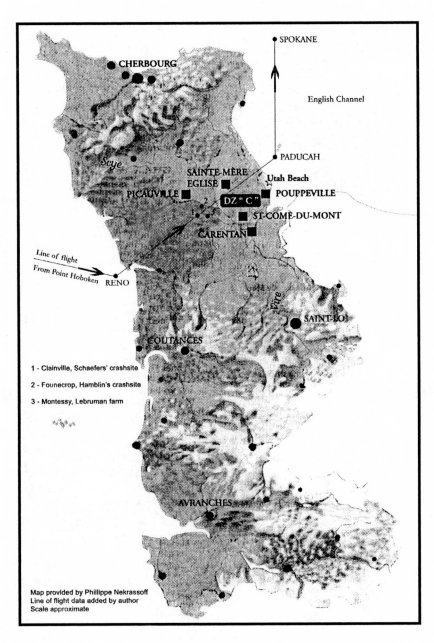

77th Troop Carrier Squadron
June 6, 1944

to be able to visually identify their drop zones. A small minority of the troop carriers held formation until they exited the clouds. The 77th was one of the squadrons that held position. During the time the aircraft were in the clouds, many squadrons lost the tight formations designed to keep the paratroopers close together when they jumped. In the case of the 77th Squadron, the intense formation and instrument training dictated by its commander, Lieutenant Colonel Henry Osmer, and carried out by his operations officer, Major Phillip "Pappy" Rawlins, resulted in a near-perfect formation emerging from the cloud bank.

Jesse Harrison - "The fog was scary, but we had trained well. I never saw Schaefers' plane while we were in the fog, but felt great that he and Hamblin and I came out of it in perfect formation. It was because we had practiced together so much."

As the 77th and their sister squadrons of the 435th continued their approach to the drop zone, using signals sent from Pathfinder troops who had landed earlier, they became outlined against the moonlit clouds above them, making ideal targets for the German antiaircraft gunners who had had ample time to prepare themselves with the passing of the troop carrier formations that preceded the 435th.

"Max Taylor, his bodyguards, his aide, and some staffers flew in the lead aircraft of the 435th Group, piloted by the group commander, Frank J. McNees. The 101st's artillery commander, Tony McAuliffe, and others flew in the second plane of that group....When the planes broke into the clear—just west of the Merderet River—the Germans were on full alert and firing." [3]

General Taylor was looking out the door of Colonel McNees' plane as they crossed the coastline. In 1984 he wrote in an anniversary editorial for the *Washington Post*, "I could see an unexpected gray wall of fog that we would have to penetrate to get to our jump zone. The fog, very thick as we entered it, caused many of the pilots to widen their formations to avoid collisions; but in so doing, they lost their directions. Not so our plane, which broke out of the fog without difficulty and brought us quickly to the battle zone. That latter was a fascinating spectacle—heavy antiaircraft fire, rockets exploding in air, and a few planes burning on the ground."

John Schaefers held his three-plane element in position to the left of Henry Osmer's as the 77th flew over the town of Picauville, near St. Mere-Eglise. Heavy antiaircraft fire caught the 77th silhouetted against the Normandy sky as they approached Drop Zone C.

Bud Busiere - "I spent most of the flight in the cockpit, as I usually did, standing between the pilots' seats. The flight over was very peaceful, as was the landfall in France. Then, all of a sudden, it was like the Fourth of July; there were tracers of every color all around us. Frank Coffey, my pilot, was like a rock; he didn't get the least bit rattled, although the copilot got very excited. As we came up on the drop zone, I went back to the cabin to kick the door bundle."

The paratroopers in the 77th planes were standing with static lines hooked up, ready to jump when the light next to the door changed from red to green. At this moment of tension, in the opening moments of combat for the 77th aircrew and the paratroopers of G Company, the German gunners of the Wermacht's 91st Division found the three planes on the left of the 77th formation.

The first plane to be hit was Hamblin's, flying on the extreme left of the formation. The plane had parapacks of equipment fashioned under the belly that were to be dropped with the paratroopers. Apparently explosives were included in the load. Hamblin's plane exploded with the loss of all on board.

Almost simultaneously with the loss of Hamblin, Schaefers' plane took two hits, in the nose and the tail.

Jack Urbank (Staff Sergeant, G/501 in a letter to the author, 1984) - "How I remember losing those planes! I was standing behind Lieutenant Norman Barker, our executive officer, Company G, when the antiaircraft fire hit the two planes. The one plane blew up in one helluva blast, killing all aboard, and the second plane burst into flame and peeled down to the ground."

Jesse Harrison (undated written statement, circa June 1944) - "When we were a few minutes from our DZ, Captain Schaefers' left wing burst into flames. I'm not sure whether the underneath of the ship was on fire or not.

We were flying about 1800 feet at 140 mph. My copilot gave me the time of 0119 that Captain Schaefers' plane caught fire; he continued on course, then peeled off and went down under me. I did not see him crash. It is possible that his paratroopers had time to jump."

Charles Word (G/501, Jumpmaster on Schaefers' aircraft, undated statement, circa August 1944) - "I, Staff Sergeant Charles F. Word...was jumpmaster of plane number 43-30734 on the night of 6 June 1944. On approach to the drop zone the plane was hit by antiaircraft fire and I was ordered by the crew chief to jump. The crew chief was in contact with the pilot by phone; when he gave the order to jump, I yelled, 'Let's go,' and jumped. To the best of my knowledge, the crew chief did not have a parachute; and, as far as I know, none of the crew got out of the plane. I landed near Picouville (sic), France."

Lucien Tetrault (G/501, first in line, behind Word, on Schaefers' aircraft; conversation with author, 1996) - "Nobody could have lived through that explosion in the cockpit. Some of our guys got hit with shrapnel through the cockpit wall, and a fire started. The plane tilted over, and guys started to fall down. My life was saved because I was standing in the doorway next to the jumpmaster, and as I started to fall my bayonet caught in the doorway. Sergeant Word yelled something and jumped; I rolled out the door as the plane began to go down."

Arthur E. Morin (G/501, undated statement, circa August 1944) - "I was jumping number 15 in a 17-man stick. The plane was hit twice by anti-aircraft fire, the first time in the radio compartment, and resulted in two casualties to the parachute echelon. The ship was on fire as a result of the first hit as well as the two men near the radio compartment door. The second hit was near the tail of the plane and baggage compartment door. Right after the first hit on the plane, the jumpmaster, S/Sergeant Word, hollered, 'Let's go,' and I bailed out, landing near Picouville (sic), France. In order to get out it was necessary for me to climb up toward the door over other members of the stick who were lying on the floor of the plane and dive out the door. The crew chief did not have a chute on, and to the best of my knowledge none of the crew members got out of the plane. Immediately after I landed, the plane crashed in flames approximately 250 yards from me and exploded." [4]

George Winard (77th - Radio Operator, letter to the author, 1998) - "I was in the (navigator's) dome of our plane (Lieutenant Mueller's aircraft; see diagram). It was like the Fourth of July with tracer bullets' flak, etc. I noted to our left that Schaefers' plane was starting to glow red from the nose back, and was in a decline—it was a horrible but mesmerizing sight. I did not see it hit the ground and never knew that anyone survived."

Ray Geddes (G/501 paratrooper on Harrison's plane) - "I leaned down to look out the little window, and saw a plane was on fire and going down. You could see colored tracers everywhere. That's when I realized that the sound of hail hitting our plane was really flak. I said, 'Christ, let's get the hell out of here!'"

The 77th was only seconds away from giving the green light for the paratroopers to exit the aircraft. Jesse Harrison, the pilot of the third plane in B element, did not give the green light to his paratroopers. Having lost the two planes on his left just seconds apart, with his plane absorbing numerous hits, Harrison dropped from the formation, dove to the right, and came back on course flying at treetop level. He sent his radio operator, Staff Sergeant Charles Darby, back to the cabin to bring Lieutenant Barker, up to the cockpit, and asked Barker what he wanted to do. The jumpmaster was emphatic: he did not want to go back to England. He told Harrison, "Just drop us!"

Harrison was unwilling to drop Barker and his men just anywhere in the black night, and made a courageous decision. He made a 180-degree turn, and returned, at treetop level, toward Drop Zone C. As Harrison had no navigator on his plane, he had radio operator Darby pick up the beam of the REBECCA system that was being operated by Pathfinders on the ground to guide planes to the drop zone. After a short interval flying on the reciprocal heading, Harrison saw the holophane lights positioned in a *T* that indicated Drop Zone C. He immediately increased his altitude to minimum jump height, 400 feet, and hit the green light switch. Lieutenant Barker and Sergeant Urbank exited with the change from red to green, followed by the rest of the paratroopers. Don Kane, the man who had not wanted to change planes, was the last man to jump. Kane landed only several hedge-rows from the battalion assembly point, while going 180 degrees in the opposite direction of the planned drop. An astonishing piece of airmanship on the part of Harrison!

Harrison's close call with the German flak as he approached Drop Zone C was not his last brush with death that night. He did another 180-degree turn after dropping Barker and his men, and set off for England on his original course. Knowing that he would have to, yet again, pass through the antiaircraft fire from the hills around Picauville, he dropped to treetop level in order to present as small a target as possible. When Harrison crossed the coast he was flying just above the water until, suddenly, a tremendous black object filled his windshield. He and his copilot both pulled back on the controls and missed by only a few feet flying into the bridge of the battleship *Texas*.

Other 77th aircraft were having similar adventures. Four minutes before reaching the drop zone, Henry Osmer's aircraft took several hits. At least one G Company paratrooper was wounded. As blood from the man's leg wound gushed onto the floor of the plane, Osmer's crew chief, T/Sergeant J.L. Coe left his position at the jump door and attempted to help the wounded man by taking him out of line before he could administer first aid. The paratrooper became irate with Coe's efforts. He told Coe that if he attempted to unhook the static line he would kill the crew chief on the spot. Dumbfounded, but realizing the paratrooper was quite serious, Coe returned to the door and waited for the green light. [5]

Henry Osmer (letter to the author, July 2000) - "As we ran in on the drop zone, my navigator, Abe Friedman, was calling out headings and time. Then he told me we were over the drop zone, and I gave them the green light. Seconds later the flight engineer, Sergeant Coe, ran into the cockpit yelling, 'They're all out, Colonel; they're all out.'"

Abe Friedman - "I recall vividly how we crossed between the Channel Islands and then came up on the mainland. The antiaircraft fire looked like the Fourth of July. Our pathfinders were exactly on target, and I picked up the beacon signal right away. Fortunately, I got the signal before we hit the cloud bank, so I was not worried at all about our course. The pilots had to worry about collision, which was our biggest problem in the clouds. The EUREKA-REBECCA system showed a 10-mile box that you navigated on, and then a five-mile box as you got closer to the pathfinders' location. The box would collapse just as you passed over the pathfinders' location. We dropped right on our pathfinders. After the drop Colonel Osmer dove so low we almost hit a ship after we crossed Omaha Beach. Osmer told me later that one paratrooper jumped from our ship even though he had been wounded by antiaircraft fire."

George Winard - "After the drop Mueller really hit the deck and took off. The ground crew found branches stuck in the wing, and we were the first plane from the 77th to return."

Bud Busiere - "As soon as the paratroopers were gone, I reached out the door to pull in the static lines, as was standard procedure; but this was not a practice drop. Coffey hit the throttles and went down even lower. I almost fell out the door. That was the last time I flew a mission without wearing a parachute."

The surviving 77th aircraft proceeded back to Welford Park. Colonel McNees and the 435th would later receive credit from General Taylor for dropping the 101st HQ, and the 3/501, in one of the closer groupings in Normandy. All of the 435th men who participated in the D-Day mission received the Air Medal for their efforts.[6]

Colonel Osmer returned to Welford and landed at 3:06 on the morning of June 6. Jesse Harrison's plane was the last of the 77th to return. Harrison landed thirty minutes later, at 3:36 A.M. A debriefing was held of the combat crews, at which time it was determined that Schaefers' and Hamblin's planes were missing. Before they went to the debriefing, Jesse Harrison and his crew counted sixty-seven holes in their aircraft from the three flights through the German antiaircraft maze at Picauville.

Jesse Harrison - "When we went to the mission debriefing, I had only one thing to report, and that was seeing both Schaefers' and Hamblin's planes being shot down. I could see those planes on fire, Hamblin's plane literally a ball of flame. I reported nothing else, and was too distressed to have a conversation with anyone."

Henry Osmer - "On the way home my crew chief told me that he thought he had seen at least one plane, from the left of our formation, going down in flames. He thought that he had seen an explosion that looked like lightning as it lit the sky. We didn't find out until later that it was probably Hamblin's plane exploding. At first I held out hope that some of the boys had survived with the help of the French, or that they had ditched in the

Channel and gotten picked up, or even landed at a different base. It was weeks until we were sure that they hadn't made it."

Earl Vollbracht - "We assumed they were all killed. I waited on the field...all night, till eight the next morning, when Operations said they knew they weren't coming back."

Abe Friedman - "I'll never forget the return from the D-Day flight. We returned very early in the morning of June 6—were debriefed and went to bed— but falling asleep was difficult, especially when looking at empty beds, feeling real low, and hearing grown men sobbing."

The two 77th Squadron planes that fell to the German antiaircraft fire crashed near each other in the area of Normandy known as Manche. Twenty-one men died in Hamblin's plane; nineteen died in the wreckage of Schaefers' aircraft. All seventeen G Company men on Harrison's plane landed safely. Among the living was Don Kane, who but for Lieutenant Crouch's fateful decision would have perished with the men of his squad on Hamblin's plane. Kane, thanks to Harrison's courage and flying skills, landed in almost the exact location as planned, and eventually joined many other G Company men at the 3rd Battalion assembly area. As the sun rose, this party, including General Taylor himself, assaulted the town of Pouppeville to clear a causeway for the advancing seaborne troops of the Fourth Infantry Division. Don Kane was among the first paratroopers to see the historical linkup of the two divisions.

The men of the 77th Squadron/435th Troop Carrier Group and G Company/ 501st Parachute Infantry Regiment had been together for several short hours as a small piece of history. In an airborne operation that history has documented as error-filled, Henry Osmer and his 77th Squadron were never singled out for the outstanding job they did that night. When Lieutenant Luther Knowlton, who jumped from Frank Coffey's aircraft, returned crew chief Bud Busiere's hat, he told Busiere that he had landed so close to the pathfinder team, in the center of the drop zone, that he could have literally touched their equipment. Further, the courageous and technically superb flying of Jesse Harrison in putting his para-troopers in the drop zone after escaping the antiaircraft fire that brought down Schaefers and Hamblin was one of the most outstanding examples of flying by a troop carrier pilot in Normandy. The twenty-one men who flew with Harrison had a particularly harrowing, and lucky, experience. It would be fifty-six years before the survivors came together again.

CHAPTER 2
77th Troop Carrier Squadron
1943–44

"By the time we got to England…
those boys could fly a C-47."

Henry Osmer
Commander
77th Troop Squadron

"It was the camaraderie that I missed after the war.
I often wished that I could relive some of those days....
The good times tend to push the bad times
from your memory as years go by."

George McDevitt
Radio Operator
77th Squadron

The 77th Troop Carrier Squadron and its parent organization, the 435th Troop Carrier Group, were activated on February 23, 1943, at Bowman Field, Louisville, Kentucky. Lieutenant Colonel Frank McNees commanded the 435th Group, and Major Henry Osmer was the Commanding Officer of the 77th Squadron.

Henry Osmer - "I interviewed virtually every man who came into the 77th. Every one! I told them that it didn't matter if you were a pilot, aircrew, a parachute rigger, or a cook. The entire mission would fall apart if every man didn't do his job. I think they got the message. They were all great boys, and they did do the job."

Henry Osmer with the 77th Squadron mascot, his dog "Pal" in 1944.

Phillip "Pappy" Rawlins (Operations Officer of the 77th, later CO) - "I graduated from flight school on October 30, 1942, in class 42-J, and was immediately assigned to the Troop Carrier School. While I was there Hank Osmer took a liking to me and kept me on as an instructor. He took me with him to be his operations officer when he got command of the 77th Squadron. I was the oldest pilot in the squadron after Hank (I had prior service in the infantry), and one day Lieutenant Foley Collins called me "Pappy." The men liked it, and they all started referring to me as "Pappy," which they do to this day."

Phillip "Pappy" Rawlins, 1945

16

Frank Blaisdell.

Frank Blaisdell (Squadron Adjutant) - "I came to the 435th Troop Carrier Group right out of OCS [*Officer Candidate School*]. They let us pick the squadron we wanted to be assigned to, and I picked the 77th because I figured it was two lucky numbers. I was one of the original men assigned to the squadron. We stayed at Bowman Field until May 1943, and then were moved to Sedalia, Missouri."

Bud Busiere (Crew Chief) - "I joined the Army on November 4, 1942, and was assigned to the 77th as a glider mechanic when it was first formed, at Bowman Field, in February 1943. The squadron only had two planes assigned to it at the time, so there wasn't much flying time for us, or even the pilots. There was a levy for C-47 mechanics right after I got there, and I was sent to the Douglas mechanics school in California. I rejoined the squadron at Sedalia, Missouri, after mechanics school, and then became a crew chief, with my own plane, when we got to Ft. Bragg. Lieutenant Frank Coffey was my pilot. We were different from the bomber crew chiefs in that we were totally in charge of maintenance, both on the ground and in the air."

Marion "Bud" Busiere, 1944.

As the squadron assembled and became larger, it was moved to Sedalia, Missouri, in May, and then to Pope Field, North Carolina, on July 1, 1943. Pope Field, adjacent to Fort Bragg, was then—and is now—the home base for aircrew in the business of dropping paratroopers. In 1943 the airborne business was in its infancy. Each airborne division was made up of several regiments. The various regiments entered combat by jumping from C-47 aircraft, or landing in gliders towed by the same aircrews. Both the paratroopers and glider men were learning their trade as the aircrew were learning theirs. During August 1943 the 77th flew around the country practicing with its airborne glider and parachute infantry in North Carolina and Georgia. The longest practice missions were flown to Palm Beach, Florida, and Puerto Rico, to practice over water operations.

Henry Osmer - "When the new pilots came to us, they were boys. They only had 200 hours in the cockpit when they got their wings. Two hundred hours! When I got my first flying job with Eastern Airlines, in 1938, I had 1350 hours, and I only qualified as a copilot, on the same airplane, the DC-3."

Jesse Harrison, 1942.

Jesse Harrison - "My roommate and I went down and enlisted in the Air Corps the day after Pearl Harbor. When we got to Texas we had to take qualifying exams to be cadets. I went to all the flight schools, and finally was assigned to the 77th, along with Jim Hamblin and Frank Coffey, when we graduated from C-47 transition training."

Henry Osmer - "We had to teach the new pilots everything! They didn't know anything about the C-47 or, for that matter, cross-country or instrument flying. We had to train them on emergency procedures and single engine operations. They knew almost nothing about formation flying. What is really amazing is that after twenty-five hours of training from us they qualified as command pilots. Then, after five more hours, they were qualified as instructor pilots. It was the requirement of the times. These boys were being rushed through a program to get the troop carrier squadrons deployed."

Pappy Rawlins - "At Pope we flew three times a day: 8:00–12:00 in the morning, 1:00–5:00 in the afternoon, and, many times, 6:00–10:00 at night. Hank wanted every pilot to have an instrument rating when we left, and every day we practiced formation flying. We were, without a doubt, the best squadron in the group; and it paid off when we got to Europe."

Bud Busiere - "When I got back with the squadron at Pope Field, we were training all the time, with both night and day operations, as well as with gliders and paratroops. We trained all the time with the 101st, who were stationed nearby at Camp Mackall. The training days were so long, and with night missions, sometimes I just slept in the plane and didn't even go back to the barracks."

In August 1943, the 77th was assigned to participate, on temporary duty, in the final week of training for a class of paratroopers going through the Fort Benning jump school. Ten planes and crews from the squadron were sent to Lawson Field at Benning for the second week of August. During the Monday–Friday period an entire class of 1200 students completed their jump qualifications, making nearly 6,000 total jumps from the 77th aircraft.

Paul Krause had this picture taken on his 21st birthday in London. Three weeks earlier he had navigated a three-plane element of the 77th TCS to Normandy on D-Day.

Paul Krause - "When I received my navigator's wings in September 1943, it was possible to volunteer for a particular type of aircraft; i.e., heavy or medium bombers, transports, etc. I had prior service as an enlisted man and had learned not to volunteer. I let the Army send me wherever they wanted. When I found myself and several others from my class [including Joe Sullivan and Earl Vollbracht] assigned to Troop Carrier, I wasn't even sure what Troop Carrier did."

On October 6, 1943, the 435th Troop Carrier Group received Special Order Number 174, notifying the group to prepare for deployment to the United Kingdom. Final processing for troop carrier groups leaving for England was held at Baer Field, Fort Wayne, Indiana. There would be two echelons traveling to England; the ground echelon would travel by ship from New York City, and the air echelon would fly the "southern route" via Brazil that was required of twin-engine aircraft without the range to fly the "northern route" via Newfoundland. The ground echelon of the 77th left Baer Field for their port of embarkation on October 13, 1943, while the air echelon remained at Baer, waiting for final maintenance to be completed on their thirteen brand-new C-47 aircraft.

The ground echelon's trip began by train, taking them to Camp Kilmer, New Jersey, where they arrived and were given medical exams, clothing issues, and a briefing on shipboard procedures. On October 20th they were taken by train to the Port of New York where, at Pier 54, they boarded a British merchant ship, the *Athlone Castle*. The men remember the ship with very negative impressions. It was overcrowded, with many of the men having to sleep in companionways, and sometimes on deck—not easy to do in the North Atlantic during October. The *Athlone Castle* departed the pier at 12:00 noon on October 21, 1943.

Frank Blaisdell - "I was the officer in charge of the ground echelon on the trip over to England. All I can say about that trip was that the crap and poker games were continuous and ferocious. The trip lasted seven days. One day there was a fierce storm, and we didn't get to eat."

Gene Fosburg, a Headquarters squadron clerk who served with the 435th from its inception until the end of the war, described the Atlantic crossing, from the enlisted man's point of view, in a letter written in 2001:

"We had to haul aboard everything we owned in our barracks and musette bags. What a shocker it was to find that we only had a cot for accommodations. There was no place to store your things but to put them in the area around your cot. The cots were three tiers high. Then we found out that you had to share your cot with another guy, and the two of you had to decide who slept when. Some of the guys had three to a cot. We heard later that the ship was 100 percent overloaded.

Gene Fosburg.

"We were assigned times to eat. The first night Ed Clark and I went to the galley and couldn't believe it. The food was English and terrible. You had to eat standing up, on tables that had a rim so that spilled food wouldn't run onto the floor. It reminded me of a hog trough. We ended up taking some bread and tea and going up on deck to eat. From then on most of our meals were K-rations or just bread and tea from the galley. The officers had a dining room and got fresh fruit with their meals. {Rank hath its privileges (RHIP) is not just a phrase.}

"We were allowed to roam the ship, and eventually we found that some guys had made themselves living quarters in what had been the ship's pool. It didn't look like anyone was going to throw them out, so several of us joined them. Later, more guys decided it was better in the pool than in the hold, and the entire area got filled.

"There were a lot of guys who became ill with dysentery and seasickness. One of our guys, Sergeant Earl Canfield, was in critical condition for most of the trip.

"Sometimes they would broadcast 'Axis Sally' on the public address system. She played a lot of good American music by Glenn Miller, Benny Goodman, and others. She would also send out propaganda that was meant to demoralize us. Rumor had it that she even mentioned the 435th on one occasion.

"One day I was standing at the very stern of the ship, watching the wake, when I was amazed to see what looked like a periscope following the ship. I ran to several of the ship's crew and told them what I had seen. They told me that it was not a U-boat, but a device that was pulled behind the ship to warn the next ship in line if they got too close during a bout of fog.

"We were happy to get off the ship when it docked in Liverpool. I will always think of that day when we finally stepped on land again. It was November 4, 1943, my 20th birthday." [7]

While the ground echelon was suffering through their trans-Atlantic experience, the air echelon was having a different series of adventures. The final work on the 77th's new aircraft included the addition of four 100-gallon "Bolero" fuel tanks in the fuselage. This gave each aircraft the ability to carry 1200 gallons of fuel, which amounted to fourteen hours of flying time at a fuel consumption rate of eighty-five gallons per hour. While the work was being completed on the planes, the flight crews were attending ground school. The curriculum was not well received by the men. It consisted of aircraft recognition checks, escape and evasion techniques, and how to behave if they became prisoners of war.

Finally, on 21 October, the planes were ready, and the squadron left Baer Field to fly nonstop to Morrison Field, Florida. The lead plane, piloted by Henry Osmer and Pappy Rawlins, left Baer Field at 9:00 A.M. and landed at Morrison seven and a half hours later. The last plane, piloted by Second Lieutenants Jesse Harrison and Charles Hazelwood, was fifteen minutes behind.

Henry Osmer - "When we got to Morrison Field, I didn't have the planes land right away. We circled the field until we had used gas from all the new gas tanks. I wanted to be sure that they all worked."

Jesse Harrison - "Somehow I ended up commanding the 13th plane of a 12-plane squadron on the trip to Europe. We were last in everything."

The 77th arrived at Morrison with the crews apprehensive about the rumored port of embarkation regulations that had filtered back from previous troop carrier deployments. The men had heard that they would have their cameras taken and their baggage searched. Neither their baggage nor their cameras were mentioned during their sixteen-hour stay at Morrison. What did happen was generally deemed positive, in that an excellent briefing was provided on what to expect on the upcoming flight to England via South America, Ascension Island, and Africa. Another excellent briefing was presented on ditching procedures for emergency water landings—a procedure that had quickly taken on new importance to crews used to flying over such areas as North Carolina, Georgia, and Indiana.

Osmer informed the flight crews that the procedure for the trip to England called for the planes of the 77th to fly in four flights of three planes, with Jesse Harrison and Charles Hazelwood following the squadron by themselves in the lucky thirteenth aircraft.

The men were told that the schedule for the ten-day trip would be as follows:

23 October	Morrison Field, Florida, to Borinquen Field, Puerto Rico
24 October	Borinquen Field to Atkinson Field, Trinidad
26 October	Atkinson Field to Zandrey Field, Dutch Guiana

27 October	Zandrey Field to Belem Field, Brazil
28 October	Belem Field to Parnamirim Field, Natal, Brazil
30 October	Natal, Brazil to Ascension Island
31 October	Ascension Island to Roberts Field, Liberia
1 November	Roberts Field to Eknes Field, French Senegal
2 November	Eknes Field to Marrakech, French Morocco
3 November	Marrakech to St. Mawgan, United Kingdom

As things turned out, the schedule was adjusted by weather on two occasions.

Earl Vollbracht - "Each of us was responsible to navigate our plane overseas—we were right out of school! We flew to Florida, then to Puerto Rico. Our plane was sabotaged, so we fell a day behind the squadron. Then to Trinidad and Belem and Natal, Brazil. Then for the big hop to Ascension Island—a little island, seven miles by 10 miles, in the middle of the Atlantic— 1400 miles, 10 hours flying. Saw German subs on the way. Everyone made it. Then to Liberia, North Africa, and Tindouf Field, and Marrakech, Morocco. Joe (Sullivan) and Dick (Tennant) and I saw each other occasionally and compared notes. The next flight was to England, around Spain off the coast of France. We saw enemy patrol bombers for the

Earl Vollbracht, 1943.

first time. It was foggy in England and everyone had a rough time getting down. We lost one plane; it crashed into a hillside."

Generally, the flight to Europe went as planned, with one tragic exception on the final leg. The anticipated stop at Atkinson Field in Trinidad was changed at the last minute when weather clearances could not be obtained, and Major Osmer diverted the squadron to Waller Field. While at Waller Field the aircraft piloted by Lieutenant Ras Ruhmann was found to have a clogged gas line that could possibly have been caused by sabotage. This caused quite a stir, and all the planes were immediately inspected for gas line problems. Notification was sent ahead to Colonel McNees, who was leading the entire 435th Group from a pilot's seat in the 76th Squadron, and back to Baer Field, where it was speculated that the sabotage had occurred.

The next several stops on the flight were without incident. When the planes arrived at Parnamirim Field, Natal, Brazil, on October 28, a layover was planned as each of the new airplanes required a fifty-hour complete inspection. Parnamirim Field was the headquarters of the South Atlantic Ferry Wing of the Air Transport Command. No leave to nearby Natal was granted to the men, but there was plenty of shopping on the base. Many bought gifts such as perfumes and leather handbags to send home; others bought themselves gaucho boots and Swiss watches, which appear in pictures taken later in England.

Joe Sullivan wrote home to his family from Natal, "If anyone had told me six or seven months ago that I'd be touring the South American jungle countries, I'd have had them examined. This has really been some experience, and I'm not kidding. I've seen more places than I ever expected to see in my life, and there is evidently a lot more coming up. Some of the places we've been through look like movie sets, and the natives could easily be Hollywood extras."

Joe enclosed a one-Reis bank note in his letter, signed by a Chinese officer he had met during his stay in Brazil, and mentioned that he had run into a high school friend doing the same route in reverse, and that "Jimmie will be stopping by to see you. We certainly had a lot to talk about, and spent several hours doing it." [8]

When the inspections of the aircraft were completed, the 77th was ready for the leg of the trip that was looked upon with the most trepidation by the crews, particularly by the newly minted navigators, the nine-hour flight from

Joe Sullivan as an Air Cadet, 1942.

24

Parnamirim Field, Brazil, to Ascension Island in the mid-Atlantic Ocean. Ascension Island measures only seven by ten miles and has no surrounding islands for use as a "diversion" landing field. Major Osmer left Natal for Ascension Island at 4:00 A.M. on October 30. The last 77th aircraft, flown by Jesse Harrison, began its flight at 7:00 A.M.

Paul Krause - "For us newly commissioned navigators, the flight from Indiana to England was our first unsupervised navigation. Until we got to Brazil the flight was made in what could be called a 'loose formation' and we brushed up on what we had learned in school. The flight to Ascension Island was something else again. Each plane was alone, and many navigation rules change south of the equator. You had to remember to change plus signs to minus in your equations, and things like that. We had to do noonday fixes and determine drift from white caps on the ocean. It was a real challenge."

All of the 77th aircraft landed safely on Ascension, nine hours after takeoff. Many of the men were surprised by the activity on the island. It had a 7000-foot runway (that ran both up and downhill, with a hump in the middle). Along with the transient aircraft flying back and forth to Europe and the United States, the island was home base to squadrons of P-39 and B-24 aircraft that hunted German submarines in the South Atlantic.

Leaving Ascension Island on Halloween, the 77th took off for a seven-hour flight to the African continent, where they landed at Roberts Field in Liberia. Their arrival in Africa was the beginning of some of the more memorable, and sometimes enjoyable, portions of the trip. The men were surprised, when they deplaned, to find that American money was the medium of exchange in Liberia. During the overnight hours drums were heard for several hours, and conversation abounded as to whether the sounds were played strictly to scare the visitors or were normal activity. Rumors also spread that some of the men had gone AWOL during the night to investigate the local culture.

George McDevitt (Radio Operator) - "Quite a few of us decided to take a trip to a native village. To get there, we had to cross a river in dugout canoes (for a small fee, of course); and when we got to the other side, the natives charged us separately for stepping from one canoe to the other (three or four canoes) to get on the shore. In the native village, they offered us some kind of native liquor or beer. I tasted it, but decided not to take too much of it. (Charles) Darby had quite a few, and passed out completely, sweating so profusely that his suntan uniform was completely soaked. Not knowing what he drank, it was hard to know what to do for him. In any event, we got him back across the river, and he was okay the following day except for a giant headache." [9]

The next stop, at French Senegal, near the city of Dakar, was, according to the 77th diary, not worth mentioning. Then things got more exciting. After takeoff from Senegal the squadron was supposed to land at Marrakech. However, weather clearances could not be obtained to fly through the Atlas Mountains, and Major Osmer diverted the squadron to Tindouf Field, in Algeria. The weather became so bad that the planes were flying in zero visibility at 9000 feet with—to the amazement of the crews—swarms of grasshoppers surrounding the planes. Tindouf Field was only a sand airstrip with a small Arab village adjoining the runway. The surrounding area was barren desert. The only Europeans in the area, other than the cadre at the airstrip, were some French Legionnaires at a small nearby fort. The men were told that the fort was 600 years old and the inspiration for the classic foreign legion story, "Beau Geste."

Despite this negative description, Tindouf was not without its positive side. That night many of the men went into the town where, according to written accounts, "amusements consisted of drinking tangy Arabian tea, while watching buxom, lithe, native prostitutes perform weird dances to the beat of a kettle drum." According to the official squadron diary, a particularly good time was had on that evening by the navigator of Major Osmer's plane, Lieutenant Morton Gladstone, and one of the plane's passengers, Lieutenant Willie Troy. Apparently the two lieutenants enjoyed themselves so much that they planned to cooperate on a book depicting the night's adventures.

The next morning, November 3, the squadron took off for Marrakech, French Morocco. Apparently Lieutenant Gladstone was feeling well enough from his night in Tindouf to navigate Major Osmer's plane with some accuracy, as the entire squadron completed the flight in three hours. At Marrakech most of the men soon realized that the adventure of their first overseas travel was about to end and the grim reality of entering a war zone was beginning. The final leg of the flight was serious business, as the 77th would leave a quiet portion of the North African Theater of Operations for the very active European Theater of Operations. A thorough maintenance check was made on all the aircraft, and in-depth briefings were conducted on what to do if their plane should be forced to land in neutral Spain on the way to England or, worse, if they were forced to ditch or land near the French coast and come under the control of German forces. Adding to the reality of a war zone, all the aircraft had to be kept under twenty-four-hour guard by the crews and passengers. Most of the men did, however, find time to have local merchants prepare Arabic name tags to be sewn above their American name tags on their leather flight jackets.

The final and longest leg of the 77th's journey to England began on November 4, from Marrakech, with Major Osmer's takeoff at 10:15 P.M. (Greenwich Mean Time). Lieutenant Harrison, still flying last in line, took off at 11:00 P.M. on the eleven-hour flight. Their destination was St. Mawgan, England. Only eight of the thirteen aircraft arrived in St. Mawgan as planned on the morning of November 5. At the time that the 77th was to arrive in England, a dense fog settled over the area surrounding St. Mawgan, and the 77th suffered its first loss of an aircraft and a life. Lieutenant Richard Burr, an aircraft commander despite being the 77th's youngest pilot at age twenty, became lost in the fog. Disregarding instructions on how to approach England, Burr flew above the fog and clouds and attempted to circle down to the airfield through a hole in the clouds. While he was descending, the fog closed in on his aircraft. He attempted to abort his descent and climb back above the clouds, but did not gain altitude fast enough, and literally flew into the side of a hill while at climbing power and a nose-high attitude. The propeller from the left engine came through the cockpit wall and killed Burr. The rest of his crew and passengers, although injured, survived the crash.

Jesse Harrison - "As it turned out, we were the last to arrive in England, by quite a long shot. On the last lap everyone got caught in a dense fog upon arrival in England. I ended up landing at Shannon Airport, in Ireland; and the entire crew got interned. We had been in Ireland for two days, and were really having a wonderful time with the local Irish military pilots, when I was called to a meeting with a Colonel Hathaway, the U.S. Air Attaché to Ireland. He asked me if I wanted to 'escape' to England. I told him that it was impossible as I had landed with less than 90 gallons of gas in my tanks and that I couldn't possibly get to England without more gas. Then he said to me, 'Suppose your tanks were filled?' I told him that under those conditions I was sure we were up to 'escaping' from our current situation.

"I thought I would sneak out in the middle of the night, and woke my crew up at 0230 hours and told them to pack their bags. We got out to the plane; and, sure enough, it was filled with gas. Hazelwood and I cranked it up and we taxied to the end of the runway. I was pretty proud of myself for doing this 'secret escape.' I turned on the landing lights and we began our takeoff roll. It was then that I found out my 'secret' takeoff was not so secret after all. Off to the right of the runway were our friends from the First Irish Pursuit Squadron, lined up and saluting.

*Lt. Jesse Harrison, passengers, and crew pose with
their Irish hosts in Shannon, Ireland. November 1943.*

*Back row, third from left: Sgt. Charles Darby, radio operator.
Fourth from left: Emilio Giacomin, Crew Chief. Fifth: Lt. Charles Sebeck,
Copilot. Jesse Harrison is fourth from the right in the back row.*

"We took off from Shannon with a destination of England, but they contacted us by radio and we had to land in Belfast (Ireland). After landing we were promptly arrested, put under guard, and shipped to London by train. It seemed that international law required that if you were released or escaped from internment in a neutral country you were supposed to be removed from that theater of operations forever. We were put up in a hotel in London for thirty days. It was a nice hotel, but we were under arrest and we were not allowed to talk to each other. I used to sit in the dining room and wave to the guys in my crew—but no talking. Finally after thirty days they told us we were free to go. None of us understood what was going on, and it was clear that the brass in the 77th didn't know either, so we pooled our money and stayed in London for several days before we reported back to the squadron."

The 77th air echelon arrived in England (except for Harrison) on November 4, 1943. The *Athlone Castle* had delivered the ground echelon to Liverpool the day before. The entire squadron was reunited at Langer Airdrome, near Ramsbury, several days later. The group spent Christmas at Langer, where they frequently bought fresh rabbit meat from 101st Airborne Division poachers operating in the game preserve next to the base. There was still some moving about to be done, and the 77th finally found their permanent home, in Welford Park, near Oxford, on February 8, 1944.

Henry Osmer - "By the time we got to England, most of the pilots had between 1200 and 1500 hours in their log books. By then those boys could fly a C-47."

After the arrival at Welford Park, an intensive training period began for the 77th. Day and night parachute drops were conducted, as well as low-level maneuvering of three-plane flight elements as low as 250 feet. After considerable practice the 435th Group learned that they could take off or land fifty-four C-47's on one runway in fifteen minutes, one every fifteen seconds. Much of the flying was dangerous, with unexpected circumstances raising the stress levels of the young flight crews.

Pappy Rawlins - "The 435th was an elite group, and within the group the 77th was an elite squadron. We emphasized formation flying. I would lead practice missions with my copilot flying the plane while I stood in the navigator's dome with a portable microphone and headset. I would yell at the pilots, 'Close in, close in.' The pilots of the 77th could really fly formation. I also made sure that every power pilot got to fly a glider at least once. I wanted the power pilots to know what it was like for those guys they were pulling through the sky. Some of our power pilots ended up with quite a few hours in gliders before the full complement of glider pilots arrived. Copilots also had to qualify as command pilots as soon as possible."

Jesse Harrison - "I must have accumulated one hundred hours in the gliders. Most of the other pilots only did minimum time, but I loved them. It was a real challenge to plan your approach knowing that you had to do it right the first time."

Joseph Flynn, 1943.

Joe Flynn (77th Pilot) - "One night we had a practice night drop on the Salisbury Plain, near Stonehenge. We took off and joined up in a V of Vs. Then thick fog moved in on us. We flew the drop successfully because Salisbury was above the level of the fog. After the drop the problem was that Welford Park was too closed in for us to return.

"Looking for another place to land, our flight leader, Captain John Kelly, discovered the English trying to assist some Spitfire fighters in landing near the city of Bath. They concentrated searchlights, creating a bright spot on top of the fog above the center of their airfield. In addition, they fired red rockets up through the glare. We located the lights and rocket fire, and then all nine planes from our squadron landed safely by tuning to Kelly's radio and descending through the fog until we found the English field's outer circle lights. The Spitfires never made it, their pilots parachuting after pointing their planes out to sea when their fuel was almost gone."

The 77th squadron history states that, during late January and early February 1944, the 77th spent time working with British Airborne forces. The final portion of this project included a mass parachute drop (*Exercise Cooperation*) in which 687 British paratroopers were dropped by the 435th, with twelve 77th aircraft participating by dropping 170 British troopers.

Early February also saw the 77th experimenting with the new radar-based EUREKA-REBECCA pathfinder system for locating drop zones in the dark. REBECCA was a transponder, operated by pathfinders on the ground, that sent signals to the EUREKA set aboard the incoming aircraft. Major Osmer flew the test mission with a borrowed crew and got unsatisfactory results. In a simulated drop situation, the navigator, Lieutenant Joe Sullivan, and the EUREKA operator, Lieutenant Adrian Laboissioniere, determined that an actual stick of paratroopers would have landed mostly in a nearby river. Three passes were made at the DZ, with each pass having identical results. It was finally determined that the radar was improperly calibrated, and the crew returned to Welford Park. The results of this experiment would have major implications for the 77th in Normandy.

Some of the experiments during this period were not as technical as the EUREKA tests. Considerable "research" went into how to drop supplies to the airborne forces. Flights were made with packages designed to drop K-rations in large containers, but without parachutes; the food was crushed and the idea scrapped. Another idea called for tracks to be installed inside a C-47. The tracks would carry carts packed with supplies that were run out the door more quickly than crewmen could push out bundles. This idea was also deemed unacceptable. New ideas were constantly being tested as this new form of airborne warfare began to mature.

Joe Sullivan, standing on right, with the second of three crews he served with in England. Standing at left: Lt. George Batz (co-pilot) and Capt. John MacDonald (pilot). Kneeling at left: S/Sgt. Paul Taub (radio operator); at right: T/Sgt. Michael Planchock (crew chief). The entire crew survived the war with the exception of Sullivan.

Abe Friedman (Navigator, 77th TCS) - "I remember that we did so much low-level flying as we trained that we were told that the farmers from the area around Welford Park complained that the planes were scaring the cows into aborting their calves."

After five months in England, the 77th Squadron had bonded as a military unit. Many of the men were becoming good friends. Joe Sullivan wrote to his family on March 16, 1944: "I am sending some pictures. The one is of my CO, Major Osmer, who is a peach of a guy—lives in Jackson Heights. He said he would sign the picture, but that 'your folks will probably pity you working for such a mean looking guy.' He may look mean, but he's anything else but. The other picture is of him and two of my best friends in the squadron, Captain 'Pappy' Rawlins and Captain John Kelly. Pappy has his nickname due to the fact that he has two little daughters. The other picture is of Tom Gannon, who was the other pilot with our crew on the trip over—he has his own crew now. He's a special pal over here, and we are getting to be known as the 'Shanty Irish Twins.' Tomorrow we'll really howl 'cause it's St. Patrick's Day and we have to live up to our reputation.' "

The "two Irish Joe's," Joe Flynn and Joe Sullivan, in London; May 1944, less than a month before D-Day.

Jesse Harrison - "During February or March I got a pass for London. When I had returned I found that someone had painted a half-naked woman on the nose of my plane, along with the name *Urgin Virgin*. Over the next few weeks both Colonels Osmer and NcNees told me that the picture and name had to go. I didn't agree. I guess it wasn't a major issue with them because nothing had

The aircraft that Jesse Harrison flew across the Atlantic and to Normandy, shown with Charles Darby's artwork.

been changed when I flew the plane to Normandy on D-Day. The picture and name were still on the nose when another pilot flew it into the side of a hill several months later. It wasn't until after the war that I learned that my radio operator, Charles Darby, had been an artist before he was in the service. I think he was the culprit."[10]

New York Times, Mar 5, p. 44. Row 1, left to right: in flight gear-Capt. Pappy Rawlins (77th TCS operations officer), Capt. Seymour Malakoff (75th TCS operations officer). Third row, far right: Capt. Abe Friedman. Partially hidden by Friedman, Lt. Joseph Sullivan.

On May 10 Joe Sullivan wrote to his mother asking her to find a copy of the March 5, 1944, *New York Times*, as it had pictures of a 77th Squadron officers' briefing that had taken place at Welford Park. He told her, "If you look close, in one you can see me sitting in the third row back. First row: Captains Rawlins, Malakoff, and Smith. Second row: Lieutenants Collins and Beyer; and in line with Curtis and Collins is old JOE. I just happened to pick up the paper while I was sitting in the Red Cross in London, and there I was."

On May 15, as the training for D-Day neared completion, the 77th stumbled into what might have become a major disaster for both the troop carrier and airborne forces. During a practice night jump, the 435th's flight plan called for the planes to circle near London before beginning their run to the drop zone at Salisbury Plain. What almost caused a major calamity was that the German Luftwaffe had chosen the same airspace for a bombing raid on London that night. Suddenly the 77th pilots, and their 101st Airborne passengers, found themselves with the dual problem of avoiding midair collision with the Germans, and British antiaircraft fire.

Don Burgett from the 506th PIR related his firsthand version of what happened that night in his book, ***Currahee! A Screaming Eagle at Normandy***:

"The takeoff was easy, and our flight of ships formed in the English skies. We flew for almost two hours, circling over the English countryside. I looked out of the port and saw the dark shadow of another C-47 ghosting alongside us in the black skies. Suddenly tracers lanced through the air between us and them. Antiaircraft shells started bursting in fiery, short-lived flowers through our formation, sending hot ragged steel seeds screaming outward to tear into the soft skins of our ships. The ship rocked and bounced under the impact of the exploding shells while we hung on to the safety straps of our bucket seats, wondering what the hell was going on." [11]

Joe Flynn - "One night during training the flight path of our large formation was just east of London. A German air raid was in progress as we were passing. The searchlights and antiaircraft guns following the Germans came up to our formation. Colonel McNees radioed to confirm that our flight path had been communicated to the antiaircraft crews. The lights targeting the enemy above us went through the formation, making things as light as day. The flak stopped when it got close to us, then began again when the lights reached the other side of the formation. When the lights came close to us my pilot, George Callicoatte, told me to cover my eyes; and when it got dark again, he ordered me to take over, as he was now pretty blind. The practice mission continued as planned."

Abe Friedman - "We were briefed for a mission where we were going to do a night drop with some Polish paratroopers on the Salisbury Plain. The Colonel was away at the time, so I was flying with Chisholm's crew. There was heavy, low cloud cover, and the briefing officer told us it was 'visibility unlimited' by order of the commanding general. We took off, and at about 2,000 feet we did come out to absolutely clear sky. We headed south and, all of a sudden, near London, we are in the middle of British antiaircraft fire. It seems we had flown into the middle of a German air raid. We headed west and finally got to Salisbury Plain. Now the problem was that we had a language problem with the paratroopers, and they didn't want to be dropped into the clouds. I don't know how they worked that out, but they did jump. Then things got worse for us; we couldn't get down through the clouds. We ended up landing at a British field in Wales that had sent up shafts of light into the clouds. Some of the guys landed in Ireland. Jesse Harrison cut his engines back and flew in circles until morning, when he was able to land at Welford Park. The miracle was that we didn't lose a plane that night."

The weeks before D-Day were very busy for the 77th. One of the biggest events was a full dress rehearsal for the invasion code-named EAGLE on 10-11 May. The entire 101st Airborne was dropped by the 50th and 53rd Wings of Troop Carrier Command from 432 aircraft and fifty-five gliders.[12]

The buildup of troop carrier units for the D-Day invasion would continue until shortly before the invasion began. Because the 77th arrived in England seven months prior to the invasion, they had adequate time to train for their mission. (The 77th's successful drop, among many squadrons who misdropped their paratroopers on D-Day, attests to the training that took place.) There were fourteen troop carrier groups available for duty in England on June 6, 1944. Each group had four squadrons of twelve planes each to fly the invasion mission and several spare aircraft assigned to each squadron that would be used to make up for combat losses.

Historian Clay Blair, in his biography of Mathew Ridgeway, estimates that on June 5 the availability of C-47 aircraft to Troop Carrier Command had been so increased by last-minute ferry flights from the United States that there were about 100 more aircraft available than were crews to fly them. Moreover, as each squadron had been increased in size, the shortage of ground crew became quite serious. [13]

77th Squadron Diary - "Thursday, June 1, 1944, the long-awaited order came from the 53rd Wing Headquarters; the 435th area was closed with barbed wire, admittance limited to special passes issued to certain operations and intelligence personnel working on the briefing. At 10:00 A.M., June 2, power crews, less crew chiefs, were briefed. The briefing was conducted by Major Frank M. Bradbury, Group Intelligence; Lieutenant Clifford, Navigation; and Captain Rawlins, Operational Aspects. Rawlins was on loan for additional duty from the 77th to Group Operations. All information pertinent to the initial mission—a paratroop drop—was briefed, except the precise time. All personnel briefed were then restricted to the barbed wire compound. Despite the extremely crowded conditions and quarters therein, morale was high. Navigators had been issued maps, and one navigator was assigned to each three-plane formation. During the night of June 3, invasion markings were painted on all aircraft and gliders. The markings consisted of five alternating black and white stripes around each wing and the fuselage, just in front of the tail section. Camouflage nets were used to cover the aircraft and gliders from enemy aerial observation, or from spies on the ground, until time for the mission.

"The invasion of Normandy was imminent!!! This is what we had been created for, and the reason for the intensive training undertaken with the airborne. Now it was no longer a question of *whether*, but one of how soon we face the enemy?"

Bud Busiere - "The job of painting the invasion stripes on the planes was done by the crew chiefs and the mechanics. After that I had to supervise the preparation of the door bundles that would go out before the paratroopers. There was an awful lot to do."

Joe Flynn - "On June 5th, late in the afternoon, we went to Mass in a day room. About 9:00 P.M. (Double British Summer Time) we received the final briefing and went to our planes. We were much surprised to see the invasion markings for the first time. The planes were all marshaled on the runway, nested, so to speak, for the takeoff. The weather was marginal. My crew drew an assignment as one of the replacements, if any plane was faulty. We were not needed. As you know, Schaefers' plane and the others did not return."

The 77th Squadron would lose twelve men (including three glider pilots) killed in action before they completed their D-Day combat missions in Normandy.

*Captain John Schaefers (standing, center) with his original crew.
Copilot Eugene Timmons (standing, left) was transferred to another crew
prior to D-Day and survived the war. Navigator Richard Tennant
(standing, right) was a classmate and good friend of Joe Sullivan.
Tennant volunteered for Pathfinder duty in March 1944 and left the 77th
TCS, resulting in Sullivan replacing him on Schaefers' crew. Tennant also
survived the war. Radio operator David McKenzie (kneeling, left) and
crew chief Melvin "Blackie" Isserson (kneeling, right) were KIA on June
6, 1944, with Schaefers.*

CHAPTER 3
G/501 – 1943/44

"If the 501st had been just an ordinary regiment, half the men would have been muttering about the 'brutal treatment' by the commanding officer, but they were airborne...."

Maxwell Taylor,
from Clay Blair's
Ridgeway's Paratroopers

"One thing about the airborne, nothing happens slowly. We were just flying along nice and peaceful, and then we were in the war."

Donald Kane
Rifleman, G Company
501st Parachute Infantry Regiment

Col. Howard Johnson,
Commander 501st Parachute
Infantry Regiment [Mark Bando]

The 501st Parachute Infantry Regiment (PIR) was formed as an independent unit, at Camp Toccoa, Georgia, in November 1942. The regiment was commanded by Colonel Howard R. Johnson. Johnson was a colorful character who later became an icon of airborne history despite what became an abbreviated combat career.

Maxwell Taylor remembered Johnson in this way, "He was tough—very, very tough. He'd begun his military service with two years at the Naval Academy (class of 1927), then resigned to take a commission in the Army. He was an All-American collegiate boxer. He'd made I don't know how many parachute jumps—more than 100, I think. He wanted the 501 to win the war all by itself and worked his troops awfully hard."[14]

Laurence Critchell, who served as an officer with the 501st, published the definitive history of the regiment in 1947, entitled *Four Stars of Hell*. In that work, he described Johnson's formation of the 501 as follows:

> "Johnson's brilliance as a tactician remained to be seen. But nobody denied his extraordinary influence on the men. They were reporting to him by the hundreds, all volunteers, fresh from civilian life. He and his officers interviewed them all, rejecting three for each one they accepted. Were they physically fit? Were they mentally alert? Were they aggressive? Could they kill? Johnson wanted killers; he wanted to fight force with greater force; he wanted a regiment that could be fused into a single weapon.
>
> "He himself led the men on the morning runs. He could run farther and faster than most of the youngest of them. He was the friend of anyone who could bite his teeth and go on until

he was blind. The utmost, the impossible: those were his goals. So violent was his hatred of cowardice that his voice rose to a scream whenever he encountered it, as he did sometimes at the training towers. He asked his men to do an extreme of endurance that made those who failed hate him. To those who succeeded, he was the symbol of their success. Bookkeepers, ironworkers, bank clerks, farmers, bricklayers, plumbers, dishwashers, college graduates, ex-criminals—these were his raw materials. And he was hammering them into shape to the whisper of a distant drum."

As the 501st formed, so did G Company. One of the officers who met Johnson's demand for aggressive and fearless leadership was the company's commander, Lieutenant Vernon Kraeger, from St. Louis, Missouri. He personally selected the men of his company, as did the other company commanders. Among those Kraeger selected was Raymond Geddes, recently graduated from high school in Baltimore, Maryland; Donald Kane, a 22-year-old part-time college student and factory worker from Connecticut; Donald Castona, age 22, from the state of Washington; Jack Urbank, a 20-year-old farmer from Ohio; and the required "guy from Brooklyn," Fred Orlowsky.

Raymond Geddes, 1943.

Ray Geddes - "I enlisted on December 11, 1942, and was sent that day on an Army bus to Fort George G. Meade, Maryland, where they did the usual things to enlistees. After several days there, some of us were put on a train to Camp Toccoa, Georgia. The camp consisted of tarpaper shacks called *hutments*. I was put in a casual company until I could be assigned.

"The bunks were covered with a mattress only, no blankets. It was so cold there. I remember one night sleeping (or trying to) fully dressed between two mattresses. I was then assigned to the third platoon, Company G, Captain Vernon Kraeger, CO, for parachute infantry basic training. They ran us everywhere, trying to separate the men from the boys. First thing in the morning we would fall out and the regimental commander, Colonel Howard R. Johnson (we called him 'Old Jumpy'), would holler, 'Who's the best?' and we would holler back, 'We are!' We wore plastic regimental insignia buttons on our Class A uniforms, which we called 'We Are' buttons. The chow was pretty bad. I ate a lot of Hershey bars, but it all must have done some good because I went from a skinny 133 pounds to 170 pounds of muscle. There was seldom any toilet paper; we preferred the *Atlanta Constitution* to the *Atlanta Journal* because it was softer."

Don Kane - "I enlisted in the paratroops in December 1942, at Fort Devens, Massachusetts. They sent me by train to Camp Toccoa, Georgia. The camp was a bunch of one-story shacks that each held about half a platoon. We did our basic training as a unit. Each morning we began with calisthenics and rifle drills; then after breakfast we were taken on a five-mile run led by Colonel Johnson, up Currahee mountain, where everyone threw up their breakfast. I learned not to eat breakfast, and saved myself from getting sick. I remember that there was no rifle range at Toccoa, so we did our weapons training and final qualifications at the Clemson University range."

Donald Kane, pictured as a veteran of the Normandy campaign, 1944.

Don Castona - "I enlisted in April of 1942, in Seattle. I went to basic training at Camp Roberts, in California, with other parachute volunteers and officer candidates. I got to jump school in the fall of 1942, and then spent a month in commo school. I reported to G Company in December 1942, at Toccoa. One of the first people I met was Colonel Johnson. He was riding his motorcycle, and he let me know who he was in no uncertain terms."

Fred Orlowsky - "I enlisted in June of 1942 and was sent to basic training in South Carolina. I wanted to get into the paratroops, so after basic training they sent me to jump school. Then I was sent to Camp Toccoa, and did basic again, with the guys from G Company."

Fred Orlowsky, 1945

Don Kane - "G Company had spirit right from the beginning. Sometime during basic training a goat showed up in camp, and became the company mascot. The goat was named Geronimo, and seemed to spend a lot of time hanging out around the mess hall. There were no moves to get rid of him, and he later made the trip with us to jump school. Although I never witnessed it, I understand that he came up only several jumps short of receiving his wings." [15]

Ray Geddes - "There were several times during basic training that I thought my career in the airborne had come to a close. One day, at Camp Toccoa, I was crossing the compound and passed a man wearing no insignia whatsoever. I thought this was a little strange, but paid no attention as I hurried on my way. What a mistake! It was Colonel Johnson. He gave me quite a chewing out for not saluting. Over the last 55 years I have thought of several great comebacks I could have delivered to the colonel at that time for his being out of uniform, but as a terrified 18-year-old I was speechless, thank God. My second incident was during a morning run when I fell out with a pain in my side. This was a serious sin. Later that day I was called to the orderly room to report to the First Sergeant. I had planned to tell him 'No excuse,' and hope to get another chance. At the very last second I lied and told him I had been up all night with diarrhea and vomiting. The lie saved me. If I had told the truth I would have been shipped out and probably would be telling stories about the artillery today."

The new airborne units in 1943 took their basic training by regiment. When the basic training portion of the 501st training was completed, the entire regiment departed for jump school at Fort Benning. Critchell described it as follows: "The parachute school was, perhaps, the only school that was tougher than legend reputed it to be. Physically, it was the American equivalent of the British commando school, differing in that it was more concentrated—it lasted only four weeks. Discipline was severe. The treatment, both for officers and men alike, was snarling in its animality. An

G Company recruits during basic training at Camp Toccoa, Georgia, 1943. Raymond Geddes is standing in center of back row. Lying prone with rifle is Matthew Yoquinto. It was the decision of Lt. Everett Crouch to change aircraft in order to jump with Yoquinto that saved Donald Kane's life on D-Day [Geddes]

unofficial policy of pushing men until they broke and qualifying those who didn't made the parachute school something that most graduates remembered afterwards with mixed feelings of pride and revulsion. Colonel Johnson's men skipped the first week, known as 'A' stage. Physically they were tough enough. As a matter of fact, they were so accustomed to pushing themselves beyond the limit of endurance that for the next two weeks of school they had (to the annoyance of the instructors) a good rest. They learned for the hundredth time how to tumble, how to jump off the 40-foot towers, how to make a good exit from the dummy planes. It was old stuff. The 250-foot 'free towers,' certainly the largest Army teaching aid in existence (and a showplace...for visiting dignitaries), were a new experience. But the men were mostly waiting, marking time, for the payoff: the jump from a flying plane."[16]

Fred Orlowsky - "When we were done with the airborne basic training, the whole regiment went off to jump school. Those of us who already had our wings were kept at Toccoa to do KP and guard duty."

Future paratroopers marching past "hutments" at Camp Toccoa [Mark Bando]

<u>Don Kane</u> - "We finished our basic training in April of '43, and those that were left went off to jump school at Fort Benning. We had followed the 506th at Toccoa, and we followed them through the course at Benning. One thing that we were particularly proud of was that, thanks to Colonel Johnson, we were in such good physical shape when we got to Benning that we were able to run the training cadre into the ground. They decided that we didn't need the first 'conditioning' week, and we went right into week two of the four-week course."

Kane continues, "The towers were tough. The Mock Tower was a simulated exit door from an airplane. It was 32 feet high, and you jumped in a regulation parachute harness attached to a cable, and then rode the cable to the ground after the simulated exit and opening shock. Many guys couldn't do that tower. They immediately disappeared and we never saw them again. We packed our own chutes for our first jump. After that the riggers packed them for us. Some of the cadre told us, 'Don't worry, you could stuff one of these things in a barracks bag and it would open.' We weren't that confident. Everyone was nervous about packing that chute. To make it worse, as we worked in teams to pack the chutes, the last team to finish had to sweep out the hangar when they were done, so there was pressure to hurry with the packing."

Wilber Ingalls , 1945.

Wilber Ingalls - "We worked in teams of three men to pack our chutes. The first time my team took an hour and a half to pack our three chutes. Finally, we could do all three in fifteen minutes."

While the 501 was going through jump school some of the men, including Ray Geddes, were astonished to see a special visitor quickly pass through their training area. President Roosevelt made a tour of Fort Benning in April 1943, and visited the packing sheds as G Company was preparing their parachutes for their first jump.

On April 10, 1943, while in his second week of jump school, Don Kane wrote to his girlfriend, Sue Richards (now his wife of more than 50 years), "Another thing I have never said much about was a paratrooper's wings. As much as he prizes his boots, his wings are even held in higher esteem. The girls also like the wings. There have been many cases where some girl gets an unsuspecting victim and plies him with liquor and sweet words. The next morning the poor boy wakes up wingless."

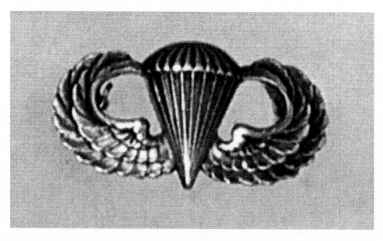

U.S. Army paratrooper insignia (wings).

46

While in his final week of jump school, Don wrote to Sue:

"I made the first jump Monday afternoon. While waiting to be called to get my chute I managed to work myself into such a state that every time one of those big transports would gun their engine I would jump off the ground. Finally with ten thumbs I put on my chute and waited in line for a plane. By this time my stomach was just so much lead. My mouth was entirely empty of saliva and my heart was beating like a triphammer. We circled the field once. Then the jumpmaster said 'Stand up.' I staggered to my feet; 'Hook up,' and then, 'Stand in the door,' he said. I was second in line. Then suddenly I was outside the door and dropping into space. I heard a loud bang and felt a hard jerk. Looking up I could see that beautiful white silk. Below me the houses, roads, and cars looked like something a little boy had made in a sandpile. I hollered like an idiot and waved to the fellow nearest to me. It seemed a long time before the ground came any nearer to me; but when it did, it came fast, and hit me in a very ungracious manner.

"Today I made two jumps in less than an hour. I remember more of each one. I have just about ruined the little picture you sent me, for it was with me on all the jumps. Now as I sit here it does not seem possible that I have jumped from a plane, but I guess it is true."

Some of those who had survived the many rigors of both Toccoa and jump school towers did not make it through the ultimate test of Jump Week. All of the men of G Company have stories of men who froze when it came their turn to jump, or refused to stand up when ordered to prepare for the jump. If the "refusal" froze in the door, he was pulled aside by the jumpmaster. Those who remained in their seats were simply left sitting until the plane landed. If there was a particularly compassionate jumpmaster, the man might be asked if he wanted a second chance to jump, and if he said yes, the plane was taken around for a second run. Some men did take this opportunity, if offered; most did not. As was the case with the men who refused to jump from the towers, these men were gone from the post in hours.

Ray Geddes - "I remember, on one jump, when the command was given to 'stand up,' one guy did not. The jumpmaster came over and said something to him. The guy was looking at the floor, and he shook his head. The jumpmaster patted him on the shoulder and went back to his duties."

Don Kane - "Colonel Johnson, I believe, was already jump-qualified when we got to Benning. He jumped constantly. He would land, get another chute, and then join another stick and jump again. The guys nicknamed him 'Jumpy Johnson' because of this. That was one thing I liked about the airborne. The officers and men did everything together. There was only one way to get back to the ground, and that was to jump."

Col. Howard Johnson in parachute gear [Mark Bando].

Johnson was reputed to have made more than 100 parachute jumps by the time the 501st deployed for Europe. As his men made their qualifying jumps, he made as many as six jumps a day. His constant participation is remembered to this day among 501 veterans as having had a major effect upon the morale and spirit of the regiment. Asked once for the reason that he jumped so often, Johnson remarked that he was working to overcome his fear of parachuting. [17]

Something of a spectacle was made of Johnson's "hundredth jump." He jumped along with several other officers and enlisted men, with expectations that there would be a photographer recording his successful landing. It took a total of three jumps on that day for the colonel's "100th" to be recorded for history. [18]

Don Kane - "After jump school we went to Camp Mackall in North Carolina for more infantry training. (Mackall, we were told, was the name of the first airborne trooper killed in the war. He was with the 82nd Airborne in North Africa.) We were allowed to go to Charlotte on a pass. There was a division of Filipino soldiers in town at the same time. It wasn't long before one of our guys started a fight, which resulted in a major riot. The 501st was thrown out of Charlotte and told we were not welcome to return. Some major got us lined up the next day and gave a speech in which he said that paratroopers had to have many things to be good at their jobs, but brains was not one of them. We never saw him again. Personally, I think Colonel Johnson loved it that we had been thrown out of Charlotte for fighting." [19]

Jack Urbank, 1944.

Jack Urbank - "By the time that we got to Camp Mackall, Lieutenant Kraeger had been promoted to Captain. For some reason we were all required to walk a measured mile and count the number of steps we took. Kraeger asked me how many steps were in my mile. I told him I had taken 1,758 steps. That night at Retreat he told the whole company that Sergeant Urbank obviously could not count, and that after Retreat he and I would be walking the course so that I could see how many steps it took to walk a mile. We had just started when he realized what the problem was. He was a small man, and had a 30-inch step. My step was more than a yard long. The next morning at formation, he told the men what had happened. From then on I had the nickname 'Route Step'."

G-Company photograph, at Camp Mackall, 1943. [R. Geddes]

Ray Geddes - "When we arrived at Camp Mackall I was assigned (as radio operator) to Captain Kraeger, whom I liked; and my good friend from radio school, John Berlin, was assigned to Lieutenant Gielow, whom I liked even more. I tried to get Berlin to switch, but he wouldn't. If he had switched, I would have been on his stick (at Normandy) and he on mine. Now his name is on the 'Wall of the Missing' in the cemetery above Omaha Beach. I have thought of that many times over the years."

Jack Urbank - "While we were at Camp Mackall we made a practice jump with Lieutenant (Jesse) Harrison as our pilot. They were experimenting with a new audible buzzer that would go off at the same time as the green light. A piece of tape on the side of the plane started to vibrate, and I mistook that for the sound of the buzzer, and, as jumpmaster, led my troops out the door right over the town that was the 'target' for the operation. We were supposed to land seven

G Company mortar squad, L-R: Lt. Norman Barker, Joe Garcia (KIA), F.K. Morrison, Jack Urbank, Clarence Klopp (KIA); July 1943. [J. Urbank]

miles away, walk to the town, and then 'take' it. The mistake caused my squad to miss the march and gave us time, about two hours, to sit around and wait for the rest of the company to show up. We spent our time eating sundaes and drinking soda from the local drugstore.

"Finally they staggered in after seven miles of North Carolina 95-degree heat and humidity. I had cut my chin when I landed, and that night Captain Kraeger asked me, kidding, if I had gotten the cut from being belted by one

These two photos were taken on July 23, 1942, when Jack Urbank jumped his stick prior to reaching the drop zone. It was the ninth jump for the G-501 men, the first of four they would make with the 77th TCS. The picture on left (L-R): Jesse Harrison's crew chief, Emilio Giacomin, along with G-501 troopers Clarence Klopp and Joseph Garcia. (Klopp was KIA in Normandy, where he also jumped from Harrison's aircraft.) Picture on right: Eugene Morrison boarding Harrison's plane for the same jump. (Morrison was KIA in Normandy on Captain Schaefers' aircraft.) [J. Urbank]

of my troops because I had jumped them in the wrong place. I told him how I got it, and Kraeger laughed and agreed that my men could hardly be mad, with my mistake saving them from a seven-mile hike."

Lieutenant Nathan Marks – (*Portions of Nathan Marks' letters to his wife Eleanor were made available to the author by their son, Clifford Marks, of Seattle, Washington. Lieutenant Marks was killed by a sniper in G Company's first combat on the morning of June 6, 1944.*)

Nathan Marks and wife Eleanor, 1943. [C. Marks]

September 27, 1943, Tennessee maneuvers. "This last week was a rugged one. Although we haven't jumped yet, we really have been moving. We are being used for shock troops and have moved around so fast that even our own general has a hard time keeping track of us. There is no doubt about it: that 501 can out-march and out-fight any regiment down here.... We've been eating, marching, fighting, and sleeping in mud for a week. Damn annoying to say the least. If anyone tells you your husband isn't fit to sleep in a pig pen you tell them they're wrong. Cause he is! Spent Wednesday night in one."

Don Kane - "While we were in Tennessee I almost got court-martialed, or worse. We were at the live fire range one morning, and that afternoon we were doing some kind of simulated tank attack. They had real tanks to use against us. We were to fire blanks at the tanks as they came across a field with infantry supporting them. One of the guys in my squad passed out from the heat, and when they took him away in the ambulance they left his rifle behind. For

Medics attend to the G/501 soldier who collapsed during the Tennessee maneuvers, resulting in Don Kane being nicknamed "Killer." [Mark Bando]

some reason, I will never understand why, I picked up the guy's rifle, and when the exercise started I decided to use his M-1 to fire at the tanks. Well, the 'attack' starts and I let loose with this guy's rifle. He had not unloaded it from the morning exercise, and I was firing live ammunition. The officers went crazy!! From that day on the guys called me 'Killer' Kane."

Jack Urbank - "There was an episode that happened while we were training, after jump school. The daughter of some local farmer had gotten a little too 'friendly' with one of our guys, and she was in the family way. They made the whole company walk past her and her father so they could pick the guy out. The first time she couldn't identify anyone, so we had to do it again. She couldn't identify anyone the second time either. Finally they got an idea, and had the officers walk by her. Sure enough, she found her man!!!"

Apparently the 3rd Battalion commander, Julian Ewell, had a special feeling for those men who felt it necessary to fill their canteens during a hard training day. Two stories follow:

Ray Geddes - "When we were on the Tennessee maneuvers I had yet another run-in with the powers that be. John Berlin, my good friend and

Julian Ewell (Mark Bando)

fellow G Company radio operator, and I were out in the woods one day and found ourselves out of water. I guess they had told us that we couldn't take water from the local streams for some reason or another, and that all water in our canteens had to have halazone tablets added to make sure we wouldn't get sick. Anyway, John and I found a stream and filled our canteens with water. We added the halazone tablets and then turned around to return to the road, and who is sitting there, all by himself, but Colonel Ewell. We flat out couldn't believe it! We pled our case, but it was no use. He offered us the choice of a summary (low level) court-martial on the spot, or a more formal court-martial later on. What choice did we have? We took the summary, and as I remember, I didn't get a good conduct ribbon, and they might have taken some money away. Thus, I have the distinct honor of having been personally chewed out by Colonel Johnson and court-martialed by Colonel Ewell, and still remained a member of the regiment. Not many men can make that statement."

Fred Orlowsky - "While we were on maneuvers I took the canteens for about five guys down to a creek and filled them with water. I was walking back up the hill and who should I run into but Colonel Ewell. He tells me I am about to be court-martialed for obtaining 'unauthorized water.' What was I going to say? He fined me two days' pay. When I got out of the Army the guy doing my records noticed that the pay had never been deducted, and asked if I wanted to file an appeal or forfeit the money. I didn't file."

Don Kane - "During the Tennessee maneuvers we made a night jump. We didn't realize it then, but it was supposed to duplicate what would happen on D-Day. We flew out over the Atlantic, and then in over the coast to jump. We were in the air for over three hours. As I recall, it was a good jump. As we marched up the road to the airport the day of the jump, I noticed some men cleaning out a drainage ditch by the side of the road. As we got closer, I recognized that they were German POWs. These were the first Germans I had ever seen. All of us stared at them, and they stopped working and stared back at us. Needless to say, the entire company marched by them head up, chest out, just like passing in review. I couldn't help thinking, *You bastards are safe and sound in Tennessee, and I have to go to war.*"

After the Tennessee maneuvers of 1943, the 501st was given leave over the Christmas holidays. When talking to many of the men today, it is interesting that they all seemed to have had the same reaction to that leave. They were anxious to get home and see their families—most had not been home since they had enlisted in late 1942—and show off their new jump boots and wings. However, after they got home they found that they were uneasy in the presence of their families. The strange feeling that they describe is one unique to the situation: they were engaged in the single most exciting experience of their young lives. They were strongly bonded to new friends whom they had not known when they left home, and they knew that they were going to go to war with these men. It was time to get on with what was to come, and sitting at home with the family was delaying what had to be done. The men returned from their Christmas leave and were told that their wish to "get it over with" was being granted with the opening of the new year.

The regiment moved by troop train on January 2, headed north for a destination that was kept secret. Ray Geddes, nineteen years old, vividly remembers the train stopping at Pennsylvania Station, in Baltimore, his home town. He got off the train as it sat in the rail yard, and looked at the city skyline, wondering what his parents were doing, and wishing he could contact them. The train continued up the northeast rail corridor to Massachusetts, where the regiment was finally quartered at Camp Miles Standish, outside Boston. They remained in camp, enduring bitter cold weather and a great deal of snow, while they were entertained with USO shows and hatched plots for a last AWOL adventure into Boston before they departed. Fear of a "desertion in the face of the enemy" court-martial assured that none of the AWOL plots ever came to fruition. Finally, on January 18, 1944, the regiment was moved out to Boston, where they boarded the troop transport, *George W. Goethals.*

The men remember that there was an attempt by the officers, at first, to conduct organized activities on the ship, such as calisthenics. This was quickly abandoned with the rolling of the ship and heavy spray and icy wind crossing the deck bringing about the reality of losing men overboard. So many men were seasick with the North Atlantic weather that organized activity eventually was completely forgotten, and the men were left to spend time on deck, or below, as they wished. Gambling was the main form of entertainment.

Ray Geddes - "The North Atlantic Ocean in January is something I will always remember! The ship pitched and rolled for almost all of the twelve days it took to make the crossing. When you looked at the other ships in the convoy they would roll over so far that you could see the red paint on their bottoms."

The men were fed two meals per day, morning and evening. They ate them standing up, at chest-high "tables" that had rims to prevent their trays from falling off when the ship rolled. The only showers were salt water, and cold. Soap would not make a lather. Most of the men were so sick that the taking of showers almost ceased. Further, the toilets were also operated with sea water, and the rolling of the ship would result in surges of water backing up into the latrines. None of the men from G Company speaks well of the trip across the Atlantic on the good ship *Goethals*.

Warren Purcell - "I joined the 501 as a replacement, in January 1944, at Camp Miles Standish, just before the regiment boarded ship for England. The final rosters for the ship had been made up by the time I was assigned, and I got put in a compartment with a group other than G Company. Finally an announcement came over the ship's loudspeaker, telling me to report to the G Company compartment. They were really mad, and wanted to know where I had been for the last three days. I told them I had been on the ship, like everyone else."

Warren Purcell, 1943.

After landing at the Firth of Clyde, in Scotland, the regiment was moved by troop train to England. The 3rd Battalion ended up in Lambourne, a small village about fifty miles west of London. Many were quartered in stables. Warren Purcell and Ray Geddes shared a stone stall that had previously housed a horse.

The 501st arrived in England as an independent regiment. Soon after their arrival they were attached to the newly formed 101st Airborne Division as that division's third Parachute Infantry Regiment, joining the 502nd and 506th parachute regiments. The fourth regiment in the 101st was the 327th Glider Infantry.

After their arrival in England, G Company and the rest of the 501st began an arduous training program. During March a demonstration jump was made for General Eisenhower and Prime Minister Churchill, with the 101st Commander, Maxwell Taylor, escorting the honored guests. The 3rd Battalion was not included in the jump, and the men were lined up in company formation to witness the jump and be inspected by the visitors.

Ray Geddes - "We were standing at attention on a hillside, watching the jump, and were mesmerized as we saw a 'streamer' (a parachute that had failed to fully deploy). I was in the front rank and clearly saw Eisenhower, Churchill, and General Taylor. They were being escorted by Colonel Johnson. As all the brass walked by, some poor bastard in the rear rank wanted to see the big shots, and kept jumping up and down to get a better look. Johnson, and probably all the other big shots, saw this guy. After the inspection Churchill had the men break ranks and gather around so he could make a speech. I don't remember what Churchill said, but after he and Eisenhower left, Johnson raised hell trying to find the guy who had been jumping up and down in the rear rank. Of course, he never found out who it was, but he made many dire threats and was absolutely livid."

Lt. Nathan Marks
[Mark Bando]

Nathan Marks wrote to Eleanor on March 29, 1944, "I guess you know that we put on a big jump and a big show for Winston and Ike—Old Winston didn't even as much as glance at the colonel, but walked right over to the junior officers (me and the likes of me) and looked us over from head to toe—he appeared very interested, even asked some questions. Ike looked bored and didn't say a damn word!"

Don Kane - "Sometime in the spring they gave us a break from all the training, and we got a pass into London. I stayed with a couple of other guys at a Red Cross hotel, and we were very impressed that we were given rooms on the top floor, with a terrific view. Then we found out that the Germans were still bombing London, and if you got hit on the top floor you were a goner....Like most young soldiers we were looking for two things: liquor and women. I met this girl who was a 'Piccadilly commando.' She

Bill Burns (KIA Normandy), Don Kane, and Don Castona on leave in London, shortly before D-Day.

56

told me that her husband had been killed at Dunkirk. Later on I found out that all of them had lost their husbands at Dunkirk—it was the standard line. When we got back to the trucks to return to Lambourne there were so many drunks who had passed out that they stacked them like cordwood in the truck beds."

Nathan Marks wrote to Eleanor on April 10, 1944, that it wasn't only the enlisted men from G Company who were having a good time on leave. "Wonder of all wonders," he wrote, "Kraeger has a girlfriend in London, and apparently he's nuts over her! When he doesn't get off she comes down here to see him. We tease him till he's miserable."

Marks also mentioned the training regimen the men were going through. "The colonel is around all the time now, raising hell and 'whipping us into shape.' We stay out in the rain and mud and live off K-rations, march our feet off, and in general get the hell worked out of us."

A great deal of research had gone into finding a training area in England that could be used to simulate both the landing beaches and the area in which the airborne drops would take place during the invasion. The search yielded an almost perfect situation. The area was called *Slapton Sands*, and it very much resembled the beach and rear areas of the secret Utah Beach landing site. Most important for G Company were the two bridges at Slapton Sands that resembled the causeways that the 101st was tasked with seizing in order to allow the seaborne forces to exit the beach. Along with the rest of the 101st, G Company "seized" the two bridges over and over again as they rehearsed for D-Day. The first time they went to Slapton they arrived by truck. Later, when troop carrier aircraft became available, they made actual jumps into the area. The final dress rehearsal was conducted several weeks before D-Day, on May 11-12, code-named *Exercise Eagle*. [20]

Finally, with the end of May, the time for training had ended. On June 4th, after several days of low activity, the men of G Company were told by Captain Kraeger to pack all of their belongings in barracks bags for storage at Lambourne. They boarded trucks and were driven to Welford Park Airdrome, home of the 435th Troop Carrier Group, where they would live in tents until the start of the invasion.

After G Company arrived at Welford Park, now classified a "marshalling area," they were quarantined. Military policemen guarded the perimeter of the camp, and once admitted, no one was allowed to leave. The men learned that the mission of G Company, along with the rest of the 3/501, was to land with and protect the Division's command element, and then to become General Taylor's division reserve and reaction force. After the briefing the men were more or less on their own. According to Critchell, there were none of the usual duties assigned for KP or menial details. The men talked, speculated, cleaned weapons, talked to their God, and packed and repacked their equipment. They were ready to go. [21]

During the afternoon of June 5, Captain Kraeger held a final briefing with the men of G Company. We can only assume that he was disappointed that the 3rd Battalion was detached from the rest of the 501 and assigned to a "reserve" role for the opening of the invasion. Kraeger was aggressive and anxious to prove his worth in combat; certainly he did not want to be far from the center of the action in the largest invasion in history. He could not know how history would play out, and that G Company's mission would drastically change as the fog of war would place them in position as the only infantry soldiers available to General Taylor when he would personally direct an attack to clear one of the important exits for the seaborne forces from Utah Beach. After landing in Normandy, Kraeger would become enraged at the losses his company had suffered with the downing of the two 77th Squadron planes; but surely he would later be gratified that his company would make history by linking up with the seaborne invasion forces coming off Utah Beach on D-Day morning.

As Kraeger finished his briefing, he told the company that in the event that he was wounded or killed, it was the duty of each man in G Company to carry on to the best of his ability in the coming combat. One of the young troopers at the briefing, a red-headed Irish teenager named Mike Reiley, answered the captain by piping up, "Oh sir, don't say anything like that." Kraeger laughed and told Reiley that he was flattered to see that the young soldier was so concerned for his captain's safety. Reiley brought the house down with laughter as he replied that it wasn't the captain he was concerned about, but that "I'm jumping right behind you, sir, and if they get you, they might get me!"

Jack Urbank - "June 5th, I recall bad rainy weather. Our stick waited on the tarmac next to the plane. Men played poker and shot craps until one or two fellows had all of the money. We sharpened our bayonets, trench knives, and hunting knives until you could shave with them."

On the evening of June 5 Colonel Johnson called the 3rd Battalion together. Men who were there describe him as being in an even more agitated state than normal. This was the epitome of his military career, and the absolute high point of what he had done to create the 501. His high-pitched voice was louder than the men had ever heard him speak. He told them he was proud of them, that he had confidence in them, that they were proven fighters. "Tonight," he yelled, "you'll be fighting Germans! Are you ready?" The men answered with a loud roar. He told them that the practice was over and that what would happen in the next few hours would be "written in history." Then he made a statement and a demonstration that would forever carve for him a place in airborne folklore. He pulled his trench knife from its scabbard and screamed so loud that every man present heard him say, "I swear to you that before tomorrow night, this knife will be buried in the back of the blackest German in Normandy!" His men, driven to a fever pitch by his excitement yelled back at him. He had convinced them that they were the best fighting men in the world, and in his final before-battle speech, had made them as psychologically ready for war as he possibly could. [22]

Ray Geddes - "June 5th, it was on. It must have been late afternoon when we were marched out to where the planes were waiting. One thing that still stands out clearly in my mind: our regimental commander, Colonel Johnson, formed us up and made his famous 'knife in the back of the blackest German' speech. (It is in the history books.) Then he did something else I will never forget. We walked past him and he shook the hand of every man in the battalion. We then marched off to the planes."

Don Kane - "Before we began to put our equipment on, Colonel Johnson gave his famous speech where he said that he was going to put his knife in the back of the 'blackest German in France' before daybreak the next morning. What the history books don't tell you is that in the middle of the speech, when he went to pull his knife out of the scabbard, it got stuck. He had a hell of a time getting it out. It was really funny."

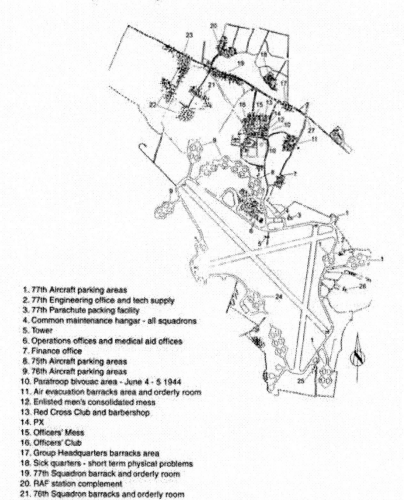

WELFORD PARK AIRDROME
Home of the 435th Troop Carrier Group
D-Day Marshalling Area For 3rd Battalion, 501st PIR.

1. 77th Aircraft parking areas
2. 77th Engineering office and tech supply
3. 77th Parachute packing facility
4. Common maintenance hangar - all squadrons
5. Tower
6. Operations offices and medical aid offices
7. Finance office
8. 75th Aircraft parking areas
9. 76th Aircraft parking areas
10. Paratroop bivouac area - June 4 - 5 1944
11. Air evacuation barracks area and orderly room
12. Enlisted men's consolidated mess
13. Red Cross Club and barbershop
14. PX
15. Officers' Mess
16. Officers' Club
17. Group Headquarters barracks area
18. Sick quarters - short term physical problems
19. 77th Squadron barrack and orderly room
20. RAF station complement
21. 76th Squadron barracks and orderly room
22. 78th Sqaudron barracks and orderly room
23. 75th Squadron barracks and orderly room
24. Service group hangar and parking
25. Communications section office and repair shop
26. 3rd air cargo work area
27. MP station at gate

Each paratrooper was expected to carry more than 100 pounds of equipment. For reasons that remain unclear to the men of G Company, even today, each man wore long underwear and a heavy OD uniform under their jumpsuits. The jumpsuits were impregnated to resist gas, and therefore did not "breathe." They were remarkably hot. After donning his uniform, each man added ammunition for his weapon, grenades, and rations to the many pockets of the uniform. Then each put on his web harness, to which he attached more ammunition, a canteen, shovel, first-aid kit, sidearm, bayonet, and a musette bag, in which he stuffed personal items such as extra socks, underwear, cigarettes, and in many cases, yet more ammunition. The men strapped gas masks and trench knives to their legs or boots. Some men carried bandoleers of ammunition slung over their shoulders; others had binoculars, antitank mines, or radios. Some had extra leg packs of TNT or ammunition for mortars or machine guns. These packs were designed to be released on a rope during the descent in order to hit the ground prior to the paratrooper's landing. Then came the main parachute and its harness.

Weapons (mostly M-1 rifles or carbines) were carried in one of two ways. The first option left the weapon fully assembled, and jammed inside the main parachute's "belly band" with the butt of the weapon facing upward. The second option was to put the disassembled weapon in a storage container called a Griswold bag, which was also secured inside the band that crossed over the jumper's midsection. When the weapon was secured, an uninflated life preserver was put over each man's head, and then the reserve parachute was attached to the front of the parachute harness. With the addition of the traditional steel helmet, with a special chin strap to avoid loss of the helmet from the opening shock of the parachute, each man was ready to go. [23]

Ray Geddes - "I had four or five hand grenades, a full cartridge belt of ammo, an SCR536 radio, an M-1 rifle in a Griswold bag, musette bag, canteen, gas mask, first aid pouch, entrenching tool, bayonet, and heaven knows what else. They also made us wear, in addition to GI shorts, long underwear and ODs under the impregnated jump suit. The next morning, the first opportunity I got, I cut off those damn long johns."

Finally, the waiting was over. As the paratroopers finished putting on their equipment, the aircraft commanders told the jumpmasters to begin loading the paratroopers onto the planes.

George Koskimaki, General Taylor's radioman, described the takeoff from Welford Park: "At 2245 hours, our plane began moving down the runway, gathering momentum rapidly, and gently lifted from the concrete surface. The rest of the planes in our serial followed at seven-second intervals until the entire (435th) group was airborne.

"Our plane (Colonel NcNees) served as the point for the serial...wing lights were on and it was a beautiful spectacle to behold through the open doorway." [24]

Don Kane - "I don't remember much about the flight over. It seemed like it took forever for the planes to form up after the takeoff. It was very quiet on our plane. Most of the guys seemed to be buried in personal thoughts. What I remember most was how angry I was because I wasn't with my friends from the third squad, after all the time together since Toccoa."

Jack Urbank - "I remember standing in the door looking out and seeing all the ships in the Channel. No conversation—just hearing the loud droning of the engines of all the planes and seeing their blue-green running lights and red exhaust from all the planes' engines. We hit the coast—enemy territory—greeted by a fog bank and enough antiaircraft fire to walk on."

Fred Orlowsky - "On the way over I looked out the window and saw all the ships. Then we got over land and it started. As I looked out I thought I saw a haystack on fire; when we got closer I saw that it was one of our planes that had been shot down."

Ray Geddes - "For me, until the flak started, the trip over was quiet. Mostly we dozed. [25] Finally someone said, 'We're over land.' I looked out the door. It was sort of moonlit haze. Shortly thereafter the red light came on and the drill started. 'Stand up! Hook up!' The plane started bouncing around, which it had not been doing before. We also heard explosions, and it sounded like hail inside the plane. Someone hollered, 'Those guys are on fire!' I leaned over, looked out the window, and could see bits of wreckage as that plane was going down. I did not see it crash. The plane to its left exploded. (I found that out in November 1999.) Some of us called, 'Let's get out of here,' or words to that effect. The green light came on and we jumped into hazy moonlight. The opening shock was terrific; it was so powerful that I lost my radio and my watch stopped. While in the chute, I could see a farmhouse, and then I landed. I was in the harness so tight I could not get out. Fortunately the only other living things in that field were cows. I reached for the knife attached to my boot—gone— ripped off, I guess, by the opening shock. I finally cut the leg straps by using the jump knife.

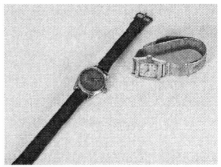

Watch on left is a U.S. Army radio operator's timepiece issued to Ray Geddes. The opening shock of his parachute stopped the watch at 1:24 A.M. on June 6, 1944. He later used the watch on the right, taken from a German corpse, to keep his radio log.

"After getting out of the harness, I assembled my M-1 rifle and moved off, trying to find someone. There was a lot of noise, but I was alone. Finally in the moonlight, I saw some helmets. I gave one click on the 101st recognition signal (a toy cricket), and waited for the reply (two clicks). None came. I clicked again and again. I was just about ready to throw a grenade; and then, thank God, I saw the shape of the helmets. As you can guess, there was some cursing, but they said they didn't hear me. We assembled and moved off. I found out later we landed in Drop Zone C, exactly where we were supposed to be, one of the few units in the whole U.S. Airborne part of the invasion to land correctly."

Jack Urbank - "I went out the door as second man, behind the G Company executive officer, Lieutenant Barker. I landed in a cow pasture. There was shooting going on all around us, so I couldn't stand up. Tracers were going right over my head. The first thing I did was take out a white phosphorus grenade and put it next to me in case any Germans showed up. After I got out of the harness I began to crawl to my equipment bundle with the mortar and ammunition in it, but the bundle had tape on it that glowed in the dark and the Germans were shooting at it. There were cow pies all over the field; I was a mess. I found Frank Morrison lying in the field. His parachute had malfunctioned, and both of his legs were broken. He wasn't going anywhere, but he told me to go on, he would take care of himself. [26]

"When I finally got out of the field, I met Don Castona. We used our crickets to identify each other. I said to him, 'Do you think we should attack those machine guns?' He said, 'Hell no!' Then the craziest thing happened. We were looking right at each other, and I said, 'Let's go to the right.' We did. He went to his right; I went to mine. He didn't get back to the Company for two days. I finally found three of the guys from my squad: Paul Hellinger, Howard Lewark, and Lester Senter. I led them into a wheat field as I knew there wouldn't be any mines there because the wheat would have to be harvested. We hid in a ditch with three guys from the 508th (82nd Airborne) until the sun came up at 5:00 and we could see what was going on."

Don Castona - "I was G Company communications sergeant, and went with Lieutenant Barker, who was our executive officer. I was the third man in our stick (behind Urbank). It was my responsibility to release the equipment bundles when the light went on. I did release them when we got to the DZ. Then the pilot, Lieutenant Harrison, told Barker that he was going low to evade the antiaircraft fire, and we flew out over the water. Harrison asked Barker if he still wanted to jump, and Barker told him to drop us anywhere, as long as it was in France. We went back over land flying in the opposite direction.

"When we jumped we were going very fast. We were being fired at on the way down; it was a low jump and there were tracers all around us. I don't know how they missed me. I had to struggle to get out of my chute as a machine gun was firing right over me. After I assembled my M-1 rifle I decided to leave my musette bag with the chute and prepared to fight to get the hell out of that field. I saw another trooper coming out of the dark. The sign/counter-sign was 'Flash/Thunder.' The other guy said, 'Thunder,' and I said, 'Is that you, Urbank?' It was Urbank. I suggested that we attack the German machine gun with grenades. He talked me out of it. [27]

"Then we agreed to take off and meet at the corner of the field to our right. Something got confused because it was a couple of days before I saw him again. When I couldn't find anybody in the corner of the field, I decided to follow a road. I went quite a ways without seeing anyone; then a German patrol came along and I hid in some brush and stayed there until daybreak.

When the sun came up I saw some troopers in the distance and ran over to join them. It turned out they were from the 82nd. I wanted to leave to find our guys, but there was a lieutenant leading them, and he ordered me to stay. I was not happy. I was with them for two days; then I got to the coast road and hitched a ride to Omaha Beach, and to G Company. I was saddened to see how many weren't there."

Don Kane - "The antiaircraft started and it looked like the Fourth of July. The plane began to rock violently, and as I looked out the window the plane next to us went down slowly. We were standing up with a red light; we did our equipment check, and then we were out the door. I was the last man in the stick. The opening shock was tremendous. I had to climb the risers to stop oscillating, but when I saw the tracers coming near me I spilled air to drop more quickly. As usual, I landed in a heap. I was alone in a small field. The first thing I did was take my trench knife and put it in the ground next to me; then I undid my harness and assembled my rifle. I ran to the edge of the field and jumped into a trench. Almost immediately I heard someone coming through the hedgerow. I was trying to hold my rifle and work that cricket at the same time. Impossible. It turned out the guy was one of our medics. We talked for a while and then heard the trumpet that we had been told would be used for the battalion assembly signal. We walked toward the sound, and then saw a flashing light that identified the assembly point. I will never understand why the Germans didn't get that light."

Warren Purcell - "We must have had too many guys on our plane, or too much equipment. When the red light came on and we stood up, there wasn't enough room for all of us in the cabin. I was last man in the stick, and one of the crew had to open the door at the bulkhead and let me get on line by standing in the cockpit. I couldn't see the door and the green light. When the green light came on, the crewman told me, and then added, 'It's 1:22; good luck to you!' I told him, 'Good luck to you guys, I hope you make it back!' Then I went through the cabin and out the door with the other guys. I landed all by myself in a field surrounded by hedgerows. They told us that we should never use the gates in fields like that because the Germans would watch the gates. I tried to get out of the field through the hedge and fell in the ditch that was in front of it. I had a terrible time getting out of the ditch with all my equipment on. Finally I just walked down to the gate and used it. There was a guy coming down the road, and I clicked my cricket. He returned the signal and we started talking. He was out rounding up as many men as possible. He told me that the assembly point was two fields away on the same road. I reported to the field and there were officers everywhere; I counted three generals. I was sent out to a corner of the field with one of those thunder whistles, with orders to keep blowing the whistle. I said I would do it as long as the guy who gave me the order would tell me when everyone was leaving so I wouldn't be left alone."

Fred Orlowsky - "I landed in a field with Walter Turk. His risers had smacked him in the back of the helmet and he was unconscious. Later on he told people that I saved his life because he was out of it. I didn't save his life, I just took care of him."

As the men of G/501 searched for each other in the darkness of the Normandy countryside, the survivors of the 77th squadron followed their planned course back to Welford Park. Jesse Harrison trailed the squadron by approximately thirty minutes, because of his detour back to the drop zone. On the ground the G Company men were starting forty-two days of combat before they would be relieved and return to Lambourne. Before being pulled out of Normandy on July 17, 1944, G Company would suffer eighty-five percent casualties in killed, wounded, and missing, returning to England with twenty-four men out of the 130 who jumped on the morning of June 6. Luther Knowlton was the only G Company officer remaining on duty. Captain Kraeger had been evacuated with two wounds on June 7, and Lieutenants Marks and Crouch had been killed. Don Kane had been wounded on June 8th in fighting for St. Com du Mont near a location that would later become famous as "Dead Man's Corner," but not seriously enough to be evacuated. Others, such as Jack Urbank, Fred Orlowsky, and Warren Purcell, had endured the entire campaign without a scratch. Urbank, as the senior NCO left with the company, had become a platoon leader, commanding only seven men. Many of the wounded and missing, including Captain Kraeger, Art Morin, and Lew Tetrault, would later rejoin the company. Others, such as Ray Geddes, who had lost an eye from a shrapnel wound at "Dead Man's Corner," were alive but would never return to the company. Many others, including the thirty-one G Company men who were victims of the antiaircraft fire over Picauville, were lying in temporary graves scattered throughout Normandy.

CHAPTER 4
Normandy 1998

"Jerry, here is where your uncle died."

Philippe Nekrassoff
June 24, 1998

"The experience in that field touched me
deeply. It is reassuring to know that we
of World War Two are remembered,
the dead and the living."

Donald R. Burgett
Letter to the Author
August 19, 1998

I moved to Washington, D.C., from my original home on Long Island, in November 1980. One of the goals that I set for myself when I arrived in the Capital was to use the government archives to develop a family history, and to settle a mystery that had started the year I was born.

When John Schaefers' plane was shot from the sky in the opening hours of D-Day, one of the nineteen men who lost their lives was my uncle, Schaefers' navigator, First Lieutenant Joseph J. Sullivan. Joe was the only one of the men on Schaefers' plane who remained MIA when the war in Europe ended eleven months later, in May 1945. In 1946, one year after the end of the war, he was declared as having officially died on June 6, 1944. However, he remained classified as Missing in Action, since his remains had never been located.

No more information was forthcoming on Joe until 1948, when my grandmother received a letter informing her that Joe was buried in a temporary military cemetery in Belgium. The letter asked whether she wished Joe's final interment to be in a permanent cemetery in Europe, or at the cemetery of her choice in the United States. This letter came as quite a shock to the family and resulted in a flurry of correspondence between my grandmother and the government about what had transpired between 1944 and 1948. My cousin, Katherine Smith, remembers the receipt of the letter as "the first time I ever saw adults crying," a sobering moment for a nine-year-old.

The responses my grandmother received from her letters never answered her questions; rather, they continued to request her decision on where Joe should be buried. Finally, she asked that he be returned to the United States, and he was buried near his New York City home, in Cypress Hills Military Cemetery, on June 14, 1949. At that point attempts by the family to find out what had happened to Joe ceased for thirty-two years.

Upon the death of Joe's brother, Vincent Sullivan, in 1972, I received a shopping bag full of letters. The bag contained literally every letter that Joe had written to the family from the time of his being drafted, in 1941, until June 3, 1944, when he was sealed into his station at Welford Park, waiting to take off on his first, and final, combat mission.

It was the June 3rd letter that I placed next to the phone when I began calling various military offices seeking information. After just a few calls, I obtained the number for the Military Records Center in Suitland, Maryland.

Using the return address of Joe's 1944 letter, I explained that I was looking for any information relating to circumstances of his death. A very cooperative voice at the other end of the line asked for my telephone number and agreed to check the records. The telephone rang one hour later, and an odyssey began that would last through the millennium!

The researcher who returned my call told me that he had looked up Missing Aircrew reports, using my uncle's serial number, and had found an entire folder of material, including eyewitness accounts of the loss of his plane. The next day I was at the Records Center when they opened for business. The folder of original materials was waiting for me to read. I was stunned by the wealth of information it contained.

There were original statements made by the jumpmaster, Sergeant Charles Word, and by a private, Arthur Morin, as well as statements by Lieutenant Jesse Harrison and his copilot, who were in the plane next to Schaefers'. There was also a manifest of all the men who had been on the plane when it was shot down, and their status as of October 1944. The statements all said essentially the same thing: the paratroopers in the plane were standing and crowding the doorway in anticipation of their arrival over the drop zone, which was only a few miles away, when the plane was hit with antiaircraft fire in the cockpit and the tail. Word and Morin had apparently been the only survivors. There was no more information.

I talked to the researcher who had helped me, and asked where I might find more information. He directed me to the Department of Defense Memorial Affairs Division, in Alexandria, Virginia, and the Albert F. Simpson Historical Center at Maxwell Air Force Base in Alabama.

I contacted Memorial Affairs; and, again, the response was most positive, indicating that they would need several weeks to retrieve Joe's file. They soon sent a postcard asking me to contact them and inviting me to visit their facility to review the file. I was at their office two days later and was amazed to receive a file several inches thick. I was given work space and access to a photocopy machine, and I spent the next several hours utterly astounded at what I found. My emotions ranged from shock to frustration to elation as questions were answered and much of the mystery of what had happened between 1944 and 1948 was revealed in the contents of the file.

The story that evolved was this: John Schaefers' aircraft crashed on the farm of a Mrs. Simone in the hamlet of Clainville, outside the village of L'Angle, in the commune of Picauville, France. The morning after the crash (on June 6), Mayor Touraine, from L'Angle, formed a burial party who gathered what they believed to be all the bodies of the men killed in the crash. They buried the men next to the wreckage, in the rear of Mrs. Simone's home. The file also revealed that a third paratrooper, Lucien Tetrault, had escaped from Schaefers' plane. The story then took a three-year pause.

On July 18, 1947, Lieutenant James A. Hoover was leading a U.S. Army graves registration team, searching the Picauville area in an attempt to solve several MIA cases. Paul Macomte, a local farmer, directed them to the crash site on Mrs. Simone's farm. Lieutenant Hoover's team then began to search the wreckage of the plane. Their report states that Joe's remains were located in the front of the wreckage, with identification confirmed through dog tags and an ID bracelet that were inscribed with his full name and serial number. The report ends with an official form listing July 19, 1947, as the day that Joe's remains were forwarded to Neuville-en-Condroz Temporary Military Cemetery in Belgium. The next item in the file showed that Joe was buried in a temporary grave at Neuville on September 15, 1947; a delayed letter was sent to his mother, dated January 15, 1948, asking her decision on Joe's final grave site. No explanation of the circumstances were included with the form letter.

I remembered the stories of how everyone in the Sullivan family had been taken aback by the arrival of the January 1948 letter. It had been the first notice that Joe's remains had been located, four years after his death. The letter stated that Joe was buried in Belgium, which was yet another mystery surrounding his death. My grandmother's letter in reply was the next item in the file. She asked for an explanation of the circumstances of Joe's buriel in Belgium and the determination that the remains in the grave were that of her son. She also asked for time to decide if Joe should be moved from his temporary grave in Belgium to a final site in Europe or to United States.

Then I began to read the final item in the file: It was an original letter addressed to my grandmother from a Major Richard B. Combs of the U.S. Army Quartermaster Corps. That letter was dated March 10, 1948, and contained the general circumstances surrounding the recovery of Joe's remains in Normandy and his burial in a temporary military cemetary in Belgium prior to the family's decision on the location of his permanent resting place. The letter asked for an immediate decision on where Joe's final grave should be located. The original letter was paper clipped to several carbon copies. I stared at the letter for several minutes before realizing the obvious - the letter had never been mailed to my grandmother! Because of a clerical error, this letter explaining what had happened to my uncle, along with the carbon copies, had been in this folder for almost forty years. My grandmother spent the rest of her life trying to find out what had happened to her son, and I was sitting in the Memorial Affairs office with the official answer to her questions in my hand.

I do not know how long I sat reading and re-reading that letter. Finally I took it, and the letter written by my grandmother, and copied them. Then I put the file back together and returned it to the Memorial Affairs secretary. It had been quite a day.

From the Simpson Center I received the microfilm history of the 435th Troop Carrier Group and the 77th Squadron. While the entire roll had only one reference to Joe, when he flew as the navigator with squadron comman-der Colonel Henry Osmer on a EUREKA-REBECCA practice mission, it told a complete story of what the unit had done, from activation in 1943 un-til the end of the war when it was deactivated in the United States as their deployment to Japan was ended with the dropping of the atomic bombs.

After reading all of this material, I had the general story of what had happened to Joe, and the sequence of his service until the time of his death. But I was not satisfied. I had gotten the bug that must attack many researchers; I had to find more details!

I had learned an important lesson—persistence pays off! In August 1984 I saw an Author's Inquiry in the Sunday *New York Times* from a Milton Dank. Dr. Dank had been a glider pilot in the 91st Squadron of the 439th Troop Carrier Group, and was requesting information from other troop carrier veterans for a book he was writing. I wrote to Dr. Dank, asking if he could help me locate veterans of the 77th Squadron. His reply enabled me to obtain the addresses of ten 77th Squadron members, and I mailed letters to each of them.

Three of the ten men called me the day they received the letters. Joe Flynn, a pilot from California, had been one of Joe's best friends. Abe Friedman, a fellow New Yorker, had been the 77th's lead navigator and, as such, had worked closely with Joe. Tom Gannon, a pilot from Ohio, was the most elated about getting my letter. He and his wife, who had been a flight nurse in England, both had been close to Joe, who was to have been their best man when they were married several months after D-Day. Tom received my letter the week of their 40th wedding anniversary.

Eight of the ten men to whom I wrote eventually contacted me. Many sent pictures and letters describing the activities of the 77th and personal reminiscences about Joe. The most touching and poignant messages came from Earl Vollbracht of Canton, Missouri. Earl had gone through navigator's school with Joe and had Joe as his best man when he was married just prior to the 77th Squadron's departure for Europe. Earl described how, when he returned from the D-Day mission and learned that Joe's crew was missing, he had gone out to the Welford Park runway and waited for several hours, praying that the plane would return, only to learn from an operations officer that during the mission debriefing it had been confirmed that Captain Schaefers' plane had gone down.

I now had a very detailed description of what Joe's life had been like prior to his death, the circumstances of his death, and the missing pieces of the mystery of what had happened after he died. I put these facts together in two versions of the story. One version I sent to my brothers and cousins—all of Joe's nieces and nephews. The other version I prepared for all of his friends from the 77th Squadron who had been so kind to give me the details. None of the men of the 77th had ever known what happened to Joe and the other members of his crew, and they wrote that they were grateful to be given the details. I thought that in 1984, forty years after Joe's death, the story was over. I was wrong.

During ceremonies in Normandy for the 40th anniversary of D-Day, Joe Flynn met a French policeman and ex-paratrooper who was starting research on a book about troop carrier planes that had been shot down in Normandy dropping the 101st Airborne Division. This Frenchman, Philippe Nekrassoff, kept in touch with Joe Flynn as he worked on his book, and eventually Joe suggested that Philippe contact me for information on my uncle's plane. I got a letter from Philippe in June 1990, and Phase II of my D-Day research began.

I shared all of my material on Joe's plane with Philippe, and volunteered to use the resources I had located at Suitland and the Memorial Affairs Division to help him locate additional information. During the next seven years I did research for Philippe on six different crews. On one occasion I was able to document the names of a flight crew and paratroopers who were all lost in a crash in the small town of Magneville. The official documentation was the last information needed to erect a stone monument and hold a ceremony honoring all of the men on the plane. I was invited to the 1992 ceremony by the Mayor of Magneville, but was unable to attend. I did, however, continue to do research for Philippe, and we corresponded regularly.

From the time that I first learned where Joe's plane had crashed, I wanted to visit the crash site. In my mind I imagined that the location was now probably covered with a condominium community and there would be no one in Normandy who even remembered the event. Another mistake on my part. After several aborted attempts I finalized plans for my wife Denise and me to visit Normandy, with Philippe, in June 1998. I could not have begun to imagine the plans that Philippe had put in motion to make this a once-in-a-lifetime experience. Nor did I realize that immediately after my trip to France, Joe Flynn would add another, and, *perhaps*, final chapter to my odyssey.

Denise and I arrived in Paris on June 20, 1998, and spent two days visiting the city. On June 22 we finally met Philippe, when he and his good friend, Eric Brassard, picked us up at our hotel and drove us to Normandy. On the way we stopped for lunch in a small town and met two of Philippe's friends, Bill and Genevieve Phillips. Bill was to be our interpreter for the trip. He is an expatriate American who arrived in Normandy on D+6 as a captain on the staff of Eisenhower's chief engineer. He has lived most of his life in France ever since, mainly because he met Genevieve there.

We had a wonderful lunch in a small restaurant, and then proceeded to the U.S. Cemetery at Omaha Beach. As Bill described the cemetery to us, we were amazed to learn that he had been one of its builders; in fact, he had been offered the job of the first site manager when the cemetery was dedicated.

We went to the information desk and asked for a printout of the graves for the 77th Squadron, 435th Troop Carrier Group, and quickly were provided with a list of where every man from the 435th was buried in the various European military cemeteries. We then visited the graves of Thomas

Ashworth from Massachusetts, the copilot on Joe's plane, David Mackenzie from Detroit, Michigan, the radio operator, and crew chief Melvin Isserson, another New York City native.

From the cemetery Philippe took us to Point Du Hoc, site of the famous U.S. Ranger attack up the steep cliffs, and, finally, to Utah Beach, where we stood with Bill as he explained that the road we were standing on was the same road on which he had walked up from the beach as a young captain fifty-four years earlier, almost to the day.

Finally, we traveled to St. Mere-Eglise, where we would stay during our visit, and settled in a small hotel named *Hotel du 6 Juin.* That night we had dinner in the town square, looking at the steeple of St. Mere-Eglise from which 82nd Airborne trooper John Steele had hung for hours on D-Day

Gravestone of Thomas Ashworth, John Schaefers' copilot.

Gravestone of Melvin Isserson, John Schaefers' crew chief.

morning, watching the battle for the town go on under his feet—a scene that almost everyone has seen depicted in the movie *The Longest Day.*

After a much-needed night's sleep, we gathered for breakfast the next morning and met another man who was to play an important part in our visit. His name was Michel Gaudry. Michel is a retired musician who now "works" full time with returning veterans and relatives who visit Normandy. He is a man of great humor and extensive knowledge of the events of D-Day and the Normandy countryside. He also speaks excellent English.

Hotel du 6 Juin, St. Mere-Eglise

After breakfast Michel took us into the town square of St. Mere-Eglise. As we stood in the square he gave us a description of the events that had

occurred on the morning of June 6, 1944, around where we were standing. It was exciting to hear the story of John Steele as we looked at the actual church tower from which he had hung by his parachute shrouds. Michel pointed out to us the locations where various members of the 82nd Airborne had landed in and near the square. In most cases he told us stories of each of the men as the men themselves had told the stories to him.

We learned from Michel that Steele, who is now deceased, had visited the town on several occasions after the war. Further, we learned that, although the movie depicted him as hanging directly over the square, he had, in fact, been hanging from a spire that did not face directly over the square. It is most likely that, because he was facing away

Church spire in St. Mere-Eglise.

75

from the actual combat in the square, he lived to be cut down by German soldiers after the end of the opening engagement. While each of Michel's stories would have been interesting to hear in any location, to hear them in the midst of that town square was absolutely thrilling to this history major.

After Michel's tour of the square, we went to the church and met three more very interesting people. Outside the church were Mark Bando, Ed Benecke, and Don Burgett. Mark is the author of several books, including *The 101st Airborne Division at Normandy*. When I first read his book I was surprised to read a description of the events surrounding the men who had escaped from Captain Schaefers' plane. I had contacted Mark, through his publisher, and we had become friends via the telephone.

Don Burgett, a veteran of all the 101st's major battles in WWII, had published his first book in the 1960's. It was entitled *Currahee!* and depicted his role in Normandy with A Company of the 506th PIR.[28] The third

Town Square, St. Mere-Eglise, June 24, 1998. L-R, Michel Gaudry, Philippe Nekrassoff, Ed Benecke, author, Denise McLaughlin, Genevieve and Bill Phillips (with friend).

member of the group, Ed Benecke, had served with the 101st in the 377th Parachute Field Artillery Battalion. Ed had done his fighting in Normandy as an infantryman, as only one of the eight pack howitzers belonging to the 377th that were dropped on D-Day ever got into action. What Ed did have with him when he landed was his camera, a camera that he carried from Normandy until the end of the war. Much of Ed's wartime photography has become the basis for Mark's books.

Ed and Michel told us a story that had Ed misty-eyed. The story related to a picture that Ed had taken shortly after dawn on June 6, of a family hiding in a ditch outside of St. Mere-Eglise. Michel had placed a copy of the picture in the local newspaper several weeks earlier, asking if anyone could identify the family. The young girl in the picture, now 65 years old, contacted Michel and said that she and her cousin were the children in the photograph. Michel and Ed had met the woman the previous day, and Ed had photographed the cousins in the same ditch, 54 years after the original picture.

Photo taken at dawn on June 6, 1944, by Ed Benecke. Right to left: Paulette Roger, her cousin Bernard Berlot, Bernard's mother (who had been wounded), and Bernard's father. The remaining men were field hands on the Berlot farm [Michel Gaudry].

After hearing Ed's story, and introducing everyone, Philippe organized our group for the trip to the location where Joe's plane had come to rest. We drove out through the streets of St. Mere-Eglise into the Normandy countryside, past the massive hedgerows that had played such a major part in the fighting, and arrived in the town of Picauville. Outside the town we

Michel Gaudry photographed Paulette Roger and Bernard Berlot along with Ed Benecke at the location of Ed's D-Day picture on June 24, 1998. [Michel Gaudry].

stopped at the farm that in 1944 had been owned by Mrs. Simone. The present owner (Mr. Claude Dulenay), had bought the farm in 1964. He met us and unlocked the gate to the small pasture where the plane had crashed. After all the years of research, wondering, and stories, it evoked mixed emotions for me to walk on the actual ground where Joe and the others had died. Philippe showed us the precise location where the wreckage had been, and I learned for the first time that the plane had been upside down when it came to rest. He pointed out the area where the mayor and the local farmers had buried all of the men except Joe, and the location, in the adjacent field, where the body of copilot Thomas Ashworth had been found.

*Dulenay farmhouse and field where Schaefers' plane came to rest,
taking off the tops of the trees on the left.*

We talked for a while, and the conversation stopped. On impulse, I asked that we remember that nineteen young men had met their death in that field and that honoring the sacrifice they had made was the reason we were assembled there. Thanks to Mark, we have a videotape of Philippe's description of the site and what was said in memory of the men who died there.

Our adventures with Philippe, Eric, and Michel were far from over. The next stop was the crash site of the plane that had been next to Joe's in the 77th Squadron formation. That plane had been piloted by Lieutenant James Hamblin. We were visiting the site in the hamlet of Founecrop to video the details for Don Kane. I had become acquainted with Don during my early research after the president of the 101st Airborne Division Association had sent me Don's name as someone who had been a member of G Company. Don's squad had been assigned, prior to takeoff, to jump from Lieutenant Hamblin's plane. At the last minute Don had been pulled off of that plane by his platoon leader, Lieutenant Everett Crouch, and had transferred to the next plane in line, piloted by Lieutenant Jesse Harrison. All of the men on Hamblin's plane, including Lieutenant Crouch, were killed when antiaircraft fire caused the plane to explode. Don had been unable to make the trip with us, and asked that we bring back pictures of the site where, but for the last-minute whim of his lieutenant, he would have perished with the others.

After leaving the Hamblin crash site, we embarked upon one of the most interesting parts of our trip. Three men had escaped from Captain Schaefers' plane before it crashed: the jumpmaster, Staff Sergeant Charles Word; Private First Class Lucien Tetrault; and Private Arthur Morin. Tetrault and Morin had landed on a farm owned by the Lebruman family near the hamlet of Montessy. Tetrault had landed in a tree next to the barn; and Morin, who had jumped only seconds before the plane crashed, had landed next to a pond that was used to feed the Lebrumans' animals. Charles

Barn on the Lebruman farm in which Art Morin and Lucien Tetrault took refuge on the morning of D-Day.

Lebruman, age 23, had found both men, and hid them in his father's barn. Charles had decided that while history was going on all around him, he was going to participate in the action. Before the night was over he and his brother-in-law had, in addition to hiding Tetrault and Morin, also visited the site of the crash at the Simone farm, which he described as an immense fire next to the house. To this day he cannot believe that the house was not destroyed in the fire.[29]

Philippe had arranged for us to meet Charles Lebruman and his daughter on the farm on which the Lebruman family has lived for several generations, and where he had hidden Arthur Morin and Lucien Tetrault on D-Day morning. Charles turned out to be a shy and pleasant man. He and his daughter, Gilberte Richard, a nurse at the Picauville hospital, met us in the front yard of their home, a large one by local standards, and showed us to the barn where Charles had hidden the paratroopers. Bill Phillips was our translator and Philippe videotaped the entire visit.

My wife Denise and Gilberte, sharing a professional background of nursing, hit it off well, and after we went through the barn, Gilberte told us several family stories relating to D-Day. One story involved her mother, who entered the barn as part of her morning chores on June 6, and was shocked to find one of the paratroopers, wearing his combat garb, complete with face camouflage, milking a cow. Not having been told that the men were hiding in the barn, she fled to the house in panic. Gilberte also showed us the tree in which Lucien Tetrault had landed. (It is

Lucien Tetrault's parachute hung up in the tree in the left of the photo. This picture was taken from the door of the barn in which Tetrault and Morin were hidden by Charles Lebruman.

interesting that, to this day, the family refers to Tetrault and Morin by their first names, Lucien and Arthur. Apparently they had never learned the men's surnames. The Lebrumans had gotten along quite well with the paratroopers, perhaps because, ironically, both men had French-Canadian backgrounds and were able to converse in French.)

Gilberte Richard and her father, Charles Lebruman outside the barn in which Mr. Lebruman hid Lucien Tetrault and Arthur Morin, Sr. in 1944.

Charles had several pictures in his house of soldiers he had met during the war, and I presented him with a framed copy of Joe's graduation and commissioning picture from navigator's school. Chris Wahl, a friend from Alexandria, Virginia, who translated Philippe's letters for me, had prepared a brief narrative on my uncle's life, which was attached to the back of the picture.[30]

We all returned to St. Mere-Eglise that evening exhausted from the day's events. Little did we know that the following day would be equally exciting.

The next morning Philippe and Eric took us on a tour of the area in which Joe's plane had crashed in order to show us the bigger picture of what had happened on the morning of June 6. An important event of the story, which I only vaguely understood before the visit, was that while only forty-two of the 821 troop carrier planes that delivered the American airborne forces on D-Day were actually lost in combat, a significant number of those forty-two were lost in the area immediately around Joe's crash site. The reason for the heavy losses in the Picauville area was simply the fortune of war. On the night of June 5, the German 91st Division had parked their vehicle-mounted antiaircraft guns on several hills outside the town. The hills happened to be on the edge of the airspace designated for the aircraft dropping the 101st. The Germans may well have been surprised by the first serial; but as circumstances show, they were more than ready when Colonel Osmer and the 77th Troop Carrier Squadron arrived overhead. John Schaefers' plane, along with Jim Hamblin's, was flying on the extreme left side of the 77th Squadron formation. Philippe showed us the valley that was the 77th's path to Drop Zone C; he then took us to the hills where the antiaircraft guns had fired on the planes. We could see the location of both crash sites from where we stood on the hill.

From the antiaircraft site Philippe and Eric took us to a most amazing place, a memorial site that almost no visitors to Normandy ever get to see. Another troop carrier aircraft, apparently brought down by the same anti-aircraft unit that hit the 435th, was from the 441st Troop Carrier Group. As with Hamblin's aircraft, there were no survivors. It had come down in a forest located between two large estates.

Driving down a private road, we arrived at a memorial site erected by the families who own the land. In an open area in the middle of dense woods is a polished stone memorial with the names of all the men who perished in the crash. On either side of the memorial are the French and American flags. The flags are raised and lowered every day by the families who own the land. This beautiful memorial is maintained to the standards of a fine public memorial you would see on the Mall in Washington, D.C.

Philippe and Eric led us into the woods behind the memorial and we visited the actual crash site. Unlike the location of Joe's crash, a field in the middle of a working farm that has been gone over many times with metal detectors, this private place was almost virgin territory. While there were no large parts of the aircraft on the ground, we easily found parachute buckles and cords, ammunition magazines, and even a rotted gas mask. The forest was eerily quiet, the only direct sunlight coming through the break in the trees caused by the crash. Philippe cautioned us to be careful not to step into foxholes that remain on the site next to the location of the crash. He told us that the holes had been dug by men of the 506th Parachute Infantry Regiment, who had fought in these woods in the weeks following D-Day.

As I write this narrative, several years later, I remember those few minutes as both a very exciting and somewhat haunting experience.

Philippe had two more special events for us in Normandy. Ironically, he did not know the significance of one of them. That evening he took us to the home of Michel Mourocq and his wife Odile. Michel, the mayor of Magneville, and his family welcomed us and several other friends into their

Private memorial at the crash site of Eugene Henning's C-47 from the 441st TCG.

home, a castle—portions of which date back to the time of William the Conqueror—a castle that even today has a totally functioning moat!

The reason for our visit was not, however, the castle. Approximately one half-mile from the castle is the crash site of another troop carrier plane. In this case the plane was from the 95th Squadron of the 440th Troop Carrier Group; and, again, all on board had been killed. Many people in the village who saw the plane crash believe that, at the last moment, the pilot, First Lieutenant Roy B. Pullen, had swerved to avoid the village. This location is

Stone monument located in Magneville.

also marked with a stone monument inscribed with the names of all the men killed in the crash. Philippe wanted me to see the site because I had been responsible for providing Mayor Mourocq with the documents that verified the names inscribed on the monument.

The next day, June 25, brought about the event for which not even Philippe was prepared. He had accounted for thirty-seven of the forty-two planes that had been shot down dropping American airborne forces on D-Day. Despite his efforts in France, and mine in the U.S., we had not been able to find any information relating to the fate of the aircraft piloted by Captain John B. McCue from the 100th Squadron of the 441st Troop Carrier

Group. Both Philippe and I believed that the plane had been hit after McCue had dropped his paratroopers, and then crashed into the English Channel as he tried to return to his base in England.

Just prior to our trip to Normandy, Michel had received information regarding remains of an aircraft in a bog located outside the town of Carentan. On the afternoon of June 25th, Michel picked up Philippe, Eric, and me; and we drove to the outskirts of Carentan and into the bog. It was approximately a mile wide, and several miles long, filled with waist-high grass and gullies that were three to four feet deep. The Germans had flooded the area in June 1944 to prevent its use as a drop zone for allied paratroopers.

Michel parked his car, and we walked to the area that his contact had indicated might have been a crash site. Eric led the way with a metal detector. A quarter of a mile into the grass Eric began to get readings on the detector and Philippe began to dig. Soon an area twenty to thirty feet around was identified as having strong metal reports. Philippe began to find fist-sized pieces of aluminum, several of which were covered on one side with U.S. style green (olive drab) paint. We had definitely located a wreck site. Because the single trowel we had was not worth the title of *shovel*, we decided to come back the next day with serious digging implements.

The next morning we had several shovels to work with, and Eric had discovered an even wider area that reported metal beneath the surface. The digging on this day was even more productive. Almost an entire glass window, of the type that ran down each side of a C-47, was found. Another window was found that had a latch attached to it, and a rubber grommet surrounding most of the clear plastic. Several switches, with wires attached, were also found. We all agreed that we had probably found materials that had once been in the cockpit of an airplane.

While we were discussing what we had found, from across the bog came a four-wheel-drive vehicle with a young policeman at the wheel, and an older man sitting at his side. The policeman helped the man from the vehicle, and they walked to where we were working. The conversation that followed was truly amazing, even to me; and I was only getting portions of it when Michel remembered to translate. The story that emerged was that the man was asking if we were there because of the plane crash. Well, you can imagine the reaction to that question!! He then confirmed our hopes when he told us that, as a young man, he had watched, from his family farm on the hill adjacent to the bog, as a plane crashed on the morning of June 6, 1944. The next morning the man and his brother had rowed a small boat out to the crash site to inspect the wreckage and had removed the tail wheel with the hope of using it in some way on the farm. He said the tail wheel was still in his barn. So, the mystery of 38th plane had been solved, and I had the

John McCue and crew;
100th TCS, 441st TCG.

astounding luck to be with Philippe, Eric, and Michel when it happened.

When the man left we all piled into Michel's car and drove to Carentan, where we celebrated with several bottles of beer at a sidewalk cafe. The perfect finish to the trip of a lifetime.

After returning to the U.S. I began gathering my thoughts about the trip. I decided to call Joe Flynn and tell him what we had done. Joe was very glad to hear from me, and added yet another chapter to my odyssey. He told me that the rolls of the 77th Squadron were getting smaller as the years progressed, and that the final reunion of the Squadron was scheduled for two months hence, in San Antonio, Texas. He asked if I would like to attend. How could I say no?

Joe put me in touch with the reunion organizer, Paul Krause. Paul lives in Fort Worth, Texas, and I called him to make arrangements. He told me that he remembered my Uncle Joe well, as they had gone through navigator's school together and had been assigned to the 77th Squadron on the same set of orders. He also told me he had read a detailed article that I might find interesting on what had happened to Joe's plane. He had found the article when visiting a WWII glider museum, and he stated that he planned to take us to the museum during the reunion. He said, "I have the article right here," and then he laughed. "Oh," he said, "You wrote it." It was a copy of my original research that had been published as an article in the March 1993 issue of *Air Classics* magazine. Paul and I talked for some time and I anxiously looked forward to meeting him and his colleagues, including the men that I had received letters from or read about in Joe's letters home to the family.

The 1998 77th Squadron reunion, Ft. Worth, Texas. L-R: Joe Flynn, author, Paul Krause.

Despite a very busy schedule involving a wedding in Savannah that same weekend, I arrived in San Antonio late on the night of August 14, and met Joe Flynn and his wife Halmar the next morning at breakfast. Joe brought me into the dining room of the hotel and began to introduce me to his colleagues from the 77th. I met Colonel Phillip "Pappy" Rawlins, the operations officer of the 77th on D-Day, who later became the squadron commander; Frank Blaisdell, the squadron adjutant; and Abe Friedman, the 77th's lead navigator. I was saddened to learn that Tom Gannon had passed away before I was able to meet him.

That afternoon we visited the glider museum, where it was interesting to see an immense photograph of the entire 77th Squadron—several hundred men—lined up in front of a C-47. Abe Friedman and several of the other men spent a long time looking at the picture, and while they could identify many of the men in the picture, they could not find Joe. That evening there was a very nice dinner, during which I was formally "inducted" into the 77th, followed by a get-together in the hospitality suite.

Late in the evening, when the crowd was breaking up, I sat and talked with George Winard. He had been standing in the navigator's dome of his plane during the action over Normandy. George described to me that his terrifying first moments in combat had been vividly illustrated as he watched the two planes on the left of the formation hit by antiaircraft fire. He told me that he watched as Schaefers' plane started to glow red from the nose back, and as the plane dropped away, the glow began to move down the cabin toward the tail. It had been a horrible but mesmerizing sight. While this eyewitness description was not pleasant to hear, it, along with Lucien Tetrault's firsthand description from inside the plane, gave the true story of what had happened to Joe and the others.

The next morning, after saying my good-byes, I felt that my odyssey was finally over. From April 1981 until August 1998, I had solved a family mystery, made many new friends, and, I hoped, helped to preserve the memory and honor of the sacrifice made by my uncle and the men who had died with him. Satisfaction from my accomplishments, I had yet to learn, was to be short-lived. Events were unfolding that would take the search for the facts surrounding my uncle's death to an entirely new level.

CHAPTER 5
Jesse and Jack

"I have waited 56 years to see this man.
I am not going to wait one minute longer."

Jesse Harrison
Penninsula, Ohio
April 29, 2000

"All my life I had been hearing about
the burned pilot: and, suddenly,
I was talking to him on the phone."

Denise (Urbank) Coy
Towson, Maryland
April 15, 2002

Jesse Harrison and his wife Sheila arrived in Peninsula, Ohio, on April 29, 2000. Jesse had driven to Ohio from Connecticut to see a man who had helped him in his darkest hour, more than a half-century earlier. That man was John "Jack" Urbank. The two had last met when they had been young men practicing the art of war. Jack had been a paratrooper, a sergeant, commanding a mortar squad. Jesse had been a lieutenant, an aircraft commander, who dropped airborne and glider infantrymen behind enemy lines. Both men were now fifty-six years older, Jack suffering from Parkinson's disease, Jesse waiting to see if he would have to undergo his second heart bypass operation. Despite their health concerns, both men were invigorated by the fact that they had, through the most remote circumstances, regained contact with one another.

As the Harrisons approached the Urbank home, Jesse's wife Sheila was afraid that they were arriving too early and the Urbanks might not be ready for them. She suggested that they stop, and delay their arrival. Hours later Sheila would tell Jack's daughter that when she suggested stopping, she had watched tears well up in Jesse's eyes. He had replied, "I have waited fifty-six years to see this man; I am not waiting a minute longer." They didn't stop.

Jack and Jesse first met, in 1943, with hurried professional introductions when the 77th TCS was assigned to Pope Field, adjacent to Fort Bragg, North Carolina, to provide aircraft for practice parachute jumps and glider operations.

Jack was a sergeant and a jumpmaster in G Company of the 501st Parachute Infantry Regiment. The job of the jumpmaster—which required attending a special certification school—is to have the final word on releasing paratroopers out the door of the aircraft. Jumpmasters and aircraft commanders have a touchy relationship. The pilot can certainly fly the airplane as he wishes, but the paratroopers will not exit the plane until the jumpmaster is assured that all is in order. During the early days of airborne operations, many pilots had little or no contact with their jumpmasters, by design. Many jumpmasters did not care to have any unnecessary contact with pilots. This was not the case with Jesse Harrison and Jack Urbank.

It becomes apparent when you meet both men that each leads by example and takes his responsibilities seriously. Both are gregarious men who love to engage in conversation. The luck of the draw put Jack and Jesse together on July 23, 1943, at Pope Field. Jack put his men on board Jesse's plane; they flew to the drop zone, and Jack led them out the door for the practice jump. The two men had then, literally, gone their separate ways.

The next time they met, both men had traveled with their units to the United Kingdom—Jesse by air, Jack by ship. By rare coincidence Jack served on two occasions as the jumpmaster on Jesse's aircraft during practice parachute jumps as the two units practiced for the planned invasion of Europe. They recognized each other from Pope Field, and the friendship between the pilot and the infantryman grew. Then, on June 5, 1944, Jesse and Jack found themselves standing outside the *Urgin Virgin* preparing for the ultimate test of all the training and practice that had gone into their preparation for the Allied invasion of Europe. This time both men knew there was a great deal riding on their efforts. There would be no debriefing of the exercise to correct errors and plan for more practice. The debrief of this mission would be recorded in the history books.

Previous chapters record what happened on that mission. Jesse and Jack were both fortunate to survive the trials of Normandy. Jesse, with an amazing bit of flying, dropped Jack and the other G Company paratroopers in the center of their drop zone and returned to England with the *Urgin Virgin* full of holes. Jack landed in the midst of German machine-gun fire and crawled off the drop zone to survive a month of combat in which G Company suffered eighty-five percent casualties.

The next mission for G Company and the 77th Squadron did not follow previous history and link the two units. Operation MARKET-GARDEN, the airborne invasion of Holland, was part of British General Bernard Montgomery's plan to end the war with a push into northern Germany. That operation placed G Company with another troop carrier unit. The 77th dropped the 502nd PIR rather than the 501st. Neither Jack nor Jesse would finish this assignment with his unit. Instead, the two would meet in a hospital in Southampton, England.

Jack was sent back from Holland with a serious skin infection, but not because he had gone to the medics with his problem. Colonel Julian Ewell, the regimental commander, had noticed that Jack's hands were in such bad condition he could not pull back the bolt on his M-1 rifle for inspection.

Ewell personally ordered Jack to report to the medics for treatment. The medical staff was not able to help Jack, and he was passed up the line until he reached Southampton, under the care of skin specialists who were able to cure his infection. He had several ward mates in the hospital, whom he describes as "five pilots who were there as psychos and two guys with venereal disease." Finally, another man was brought into the ward; he was also a pilot. That man was the only one of the group who had a private room. The reason for the special accommodations was that the pilot had been seriously burned. He was close to death, and the stench of his burns was too offensive for a shared room. That pilot, unknown to Jack, was his friend Jesse Harrison.

Jesse had arrived in the hospital on September 25, directly from combat in Holland. His luck for flying through antiaircraft fire, as he had three times in Normandy, had finally run out. He had not been flying *his* C-47, the *Urgin Virgin*, on September 19, 1944. The *Virgin* was beginning to show signs of wear from the hard flying she had done since Jesse had picked her up fresh from the factory a year earlier. All of the training with gliders had bent her frame and her doors could no longer be shut with a glider in tow.

September 19, 1944, was the third day in a row that the 77th Squadron flew a mission in support of MARKET-GARDEN. Because of the *Virgin*'s problems, Jesse had received a brand-new airplane, serial number 42-16030, while the *Virgin* had been reassigned to a replacement pilot and left behind at Welford Park. Jesse and his crew were towing a glider full of men and equipment from the 101st Airborne's 327th Glider Infantry Regiment. The glider was piloted by Flight Officer Reimer Pederson of Seattle, Washington. While the airplane had changed, the same crew flew with Jesse that had been with him in Normandy: Copilot Philip Sebeck, Flight Engineer Emilo Giacomin, and Radio Operator Charles Darby.

The 77th departed Welford Park under the command of Colonel Osmer at noon on the 19th with fifteen aircraft and gliders, carrying elements of the 327th and twenty-two tons of supplies. They were scheduled to release their gliders over the landing zone three and a half hours later, with an estimated return to Welford at approximately 5:00 P.M.

Several miles from Landing Zone W, Jesse's new aircraft was hit by antiaircraft fire. Sergeant Giacomin came to the cockpit and told the pilots that the plane was on fire. Jesse made the same decision over Holland that he had made the previous June in Normandy; his first loyalty was to those who had been entrusted to his care for delivery to the battlefield. He would not release his glider knowing that those men would have to land in German territory. While Jesse kept his position in the 77th's formation, the fire in the back of the aircraft worsened.

Charles Darby (from his official statement, circa 1 October 1944) - "Just before the LZ we got hit. Wisps of smoke started to come through the floorboards. Sergeant Giacomin then went up front and yelled to the pilots that the ship was on fire.... All this time the glider was still on, and the ship was holding straight and level.... The plane was getting very hot, the floor was red, and flames were growing rapidly toward the rear. I jumped, and Sergeant Giacomin came right after me."

Jesse Harrison - "When the fire started coming up through the floorboards—about five minutes after Giacomin told me we were on fire—I had Darby and Giacomin jump. My thoughts were to get them [the glider] to the landing zone, and, if possible, bail out, or ride the plane down if I got too low. I had Sebek stay to take airspeed and altimeter readings, as we were slowly losing power and altitude. I had instructed Sebek that when we hit 400 feet he was to bail out, which he did, just before we reached the landing zone. When I knew the glider had been released, I put the plane on autopilot and started for the rear door with my parachute in my hands. I got the left side snapped on but could not see [in the smoke] to snap on the right side, so I returned to the cockpit to get it fixed. As I left the cockpit the second time, I looked at the altimeter and it read 300 feet. I rushed to the rear door and jumped. The chute opened just before I hit the ground. My plane actually hit the ground before I did. I received second- and third-degree burns from head to waist."

Witnesses to Jesse's odyssey reported that the fire trailing the plane had become so heavy that just before Flight Officer Pederson cut the glider loose, the flames were trailing the plane by several hundred feet, as measured by the 300-foot glider connection. When Jesse landed, after a very short time in his parachute, he was in a heavily wooded area adjacent to glider Landing Zone W, near Zon, Holland. [31]

Despite his serious burns, Jesse Harrison was a lucky man. Two priests, who apparently had some knowledge of medicine, saw him land and came to his aid almost immediately. They cut his parachute into strips and wrapped his burns in the silk to protect him from infection. They hid Jesse until darkness, and then contacted the nearest American unit and told them of the airman's plight. Several troopers were sent to the location and carried Jesse back to their medical collection area. There it was obvious to the medics that Jesse would die without better help than they could provide in front-line conditions. They also knew that evacuation would be very difficult.

Jesse was put in an ambulance and driven from the collection point to a field hospital. In the course of the journey, the ambulance had to cross multiple canals, which involved troopers placing heavy timbers over the narrow canals and the driver being able to keep the ambulance on the tracks to avoid falling into the canal. The ambulance crew helped to carry Jesse into the hospital, and told him that they had taken German fire during the evacuation, and that he was a very lucky man—again—as bullets had passed through the walls of the ambulance only inches above his body.

The field hospital was able to stabilize Jesse's condition, and he was marked for transportation directly to the United States, where burn wards and plastic surgeons could care for him. His first stop was an Army hospital in Paris, where the doctors reevaluated his condition and determined that he was too weak to survive a trip across the Atlantic. Instead, he was sent to the U.S. Military Hospital at Southampton, England.

<u>Jesse Harrison</u> - "I was in pretty bad shape when I got to Southampton. After I was there a while, a guy came into my room. He said he had seen the name on the chart and came in to ask if I was the same Harrison that had dropped him in Normandy. I was hardly able to see anything, and asked who he was. He said he was Jack Urbank, from G/501. From then on he came in a couple of times a day to talk to me. Nobody else would come into the room except the nurses because my burns smelled so bad. I was in and out of consciousness as I was losing fluids faster than they could put them into me. Jack would come in and encourage me not to give up; he told me that I'd soon be flying again. I don't know how many times he was in there with me. I have no sense of time during that period, but whatever time he spent with me, it was a major part of my recovery."

Jesse Harrison and Jack Urbank
before a map of the D-Day invasion.

Jack Urbank had offered friendship and warmth to a man whom he had only known in the past months through coincidence. The man was near death, and Jack's words had helped to ensure Jesse Harrison's survival to become a husband to Sheila, a father, grandfather, and a great-grandfather.

As Jesse struggled to survive, Jack was healed of his infection and discharged from the hospital in time to return to G Company before its departure for the Battle of the Bulge. Over the next fifty-six years Jack Urbank would often wonder what had happened to Jesse Harrison. He mentioned it often enough to his family that the "burned pilot" became known to each of them as a mystery, and part of the lore that Jack had passed on to his family about his World War II experiences. Over the years Jack stayed in touch with many members of G Company and contributed generously with his time and memorabilia to assist historians and authors who wrote about the airborne infantry portions of the European war.

The Harrison family, living in Connecticut, had no mysteries to ponder regarding Jesse's experiences in the war. He did not share those experiences. He did not maintain contact with friends from the 77th Squadron and was not a member of any veterans' group. He had no contact with any historians. He did stay in the Reserves, and remained on flight status until the mid

1960's. What Jesse Harrison did do during the half-century after the end of World War II was never to forget Jack Urbank. Many, many times he wondered what had happened to the airborne sergeant who had played such an important role in his recovery. He often thought of the inspiration that Jack had given when it would have been so easy for him to give up. Like many others in similar situations, he often had these thoughts, and then he put them aside to deal with the immediacies of life as he and Sheila raised a family and dealt with day-to-day issues.

All of this changed on October 14, 2000. On that day Jesse's telephone rang, and on the other end of the line was a man named Ray Geddes. "Excuse me, but are you the Jesse Harrison that dropped paratroopers in Normandy on D-Day?" Geddes asked. Jesse was stupefied. "Why, yes, I am," he answered; and before he could ask whom the voice belonged to, Geddes went on, "Then why were we going so fast, and why were we so low?" The conversation that followed lasted more than an hour. Ray introduced himself as one of the paratroopers from Jesse's plane, and went on to say how he had gotten Jesse's telephone number through the efforts of another man who had jumped from the *Urgin Virgin*, Don Kane, when they had met at the 2000 reunion of the 501st Parachute Infantry Regiment.

Jesse was overwhelmed by this call linking him to the past, and he couldn't stop talking to Ray Geddes. He learned that the connection that had them on the telephone together had been my research in finding the circumstances of my uncle's death. Jesse told Ray that he had known my uncle, but they had never flown together and were only acquaintances. He also told Ray that he was unaware of my efforts to find out what had happened to my uncle. Finally, and most importantly, he stated that he had returned to Welford Park from Normandy with sixty-two holes in the *Virgin*, and that they were going low and fast to avoid the German antiaircraft fire that had destroyed the two aircraft piloted by Schaefers and Hamblin.

Ray Geddes - "Jesse told me what he had done to avoid the antiaircraft fire that got the other two planes. By flying low and fast he had saved our lives. I'm glad we finally got together. The speed and height of that jump had been making me really mad for over fifty years."

Jesse did not tell Ray about the 180-degree turn he had made that night. He wasn't trying to hide anything from Ray; he just never told anyone that story. The men talked about many things that they had both experienced on the night of June 5-6, 1944. Finally, Jesse paused and asked Ray if he knew what had happened to Jack Urbank over the years. Not realizing the importance of this question, Ray simply stated that he knew Jack lived in Ohio and had attended several 501 reunions. For Jesse Harrison it was as if a bolt of lightning had hit him—now he would be able to get in touch with Jack! He asked if Ray had Jack's address, which Ray did, from a 501 veterans publication.

Jesse Harrison - "Ray found Jack's telephone number for me. That same afternoon I called Jack. When he answered, I said, 'This is the guy that dropped you and your stick in Normandy.' Jack replied, right away, 'Jesse Harrison, how are you?' Then he proceeded to tell me he was still mad that I had dropped him in a cow pasture because he had gotten covered in manure after he landed, and had had to wear that same uniform for six days until he could get it changed. We talked for over an hour, about everything imaginable. I asked if he knew the names of the men that were on the plane with us. He was able to name nine or ten. As luck would have it, his daughter Denise was there, and I got to chat with her for a moment, as well as Jack's wife, Edna. Denise told me how she had been hearing about me—'the burned pilot'—since she had been a child. She gave me directions to Jack's home in Peninsula, and we made arrangements to visit."

L-R: Edna Urbank, Jesse Harrison, Jack Urbank. April 30, 2000.

When the Harrisons pulled into the Urbank driveway, both Jack and Edna were sitting on the front porch waiting for them to arrive; there was no worry about arriving early. There was much handshaking and hugging, and almost immediately the two veterans and their wives were sitting at the Urbanks' kitchen table with pictures and other WWII mementos spread out between them. As the men talked, Edna asked Sheila to come see the room in which the Harrisons would be staying.

Sheila had been nervous about staying in the Urbanks' home, as she was uncomfortable away from her own house; but now she was overwhelmed by what the Urbanks had prepared for them. The guest bedroom had been completely redone for the arrival of the Harrisons. Today Sheila Harrison refers to the room as "Sheila's room," as it was painted and decorated specifically to make her visit comfortable.

Dinner that night was a grand affair with the Urbanks' children and grandchildren gathered at the house. What the Urbank children remember most about that evening is the obvious joy their father and Jesse felt at being reunited and the enormous warmth that Sheila Harrison brings to any gathering.

The next day Jack suggested they call another man who had jumped from Jesse's plane in Normandy: G Company's communications sergeant, Don Castona. A portion of that conversation jolted Jesse Harrison. Castona was, it turns out, the only paratrooper in the rear of the plane, with the exception of Lieutenant Barker, who realized that the plane had turned around after diving away from the antiaircraft fire and the falling wreckage of Hamblin's and Schaefers' planes. Castona asked Jesse, "Why were we going the wrong way?" Jesse then told the story to Don and the others in the room for the first time about his decision to make a 180-degree turn and drop his paratroopers in the original drop zone. Other than the crew that flew with him that night, Colonel Osmer and the intelligence officer who debriefed the mission, no one had ever been told that story before. [Jesse would later learn that Colonel Osmer and the intelligence officer had been much impressed with what he had done that night. But, as is often the case with complicated bureaucracies, recognition would be a long time coming.]

After a three-day visit, the Harrisons said their good-byes to the large Urbank family and returned to Connecticut. Both Jesse and Jack were filled with happiness, not only at renewing their friendship but also in learning that the other had survived and prospered since the dark days when they last had met. The two vowed to keep their friendship alive in the months and years to come, a vow they continue to keep.

CHAPTER 6
June–September 2000

"He wrote to me for 16 months, and then
the letters stopped, in September 1944.
After a while I figured he must have found
someone else. Then I got a letter; it was
written by a nurse because Jesse's hands
were burned so bad."

Sheila Harrison
Baltimore, Maryland
June 5, 2000

"I knew that he had jumped in Normandy.
Every day I would wait for the mailman.
Finally, some time in July, the mailman came
running down the street as I was leaving the house;
he was waving 30 V-Mail letters from Jack."

Edna Urbank
Baltimore, Maryland
June 5, 2000

After returning from my 1998 visit with the men of the 77th and their families, I wrote the story of the trips to France and San Antonio. I sent that story to my family, the people who had been so nice to us in France, and to several of the 77th men who had requested copies, as well as to Don Kane. At the end of that work I had mentioned that I wondered if the story was finally over. It wasn't.

Don Kane took his copy of my story to the 1999 reunion of the 501st Parachute Infantry Regiment in Green Bay, Wisconsin. This was the first 501 reunion that he had attended. While renewing friendships that were a half-century old, he showed the story to several of his G Company comrades. One of the original Toccoa men, Ray Geddes, was intrigued, particularly because he had been harboring a wish for fifty years. He wanted to talk to the pilot of the plane from which he and Don Kane had jumped in Normandy. He wanted to know why they had been going so fast and low when they jumped.

Don called me when he got back from the reunion and told me about Ray Geddes; he also said that Ray would be contacting me. Several days later a letter arrived from Ray. I called him and we started what has become a wonderful friendship. He talked about his inability to remember who had been on the plane with him when he had jumped in Normandy. He also told me how he had been wounded on June 8th while working a radio for his battalion commander, Lieutenant Colonel Julian Ewell. He said he had been one of the first D-Day wounded to return to the United States. After a month in the hospital in England, he had been flown back to Mitchell Field on Long Island, arriving on July 11, 1944.

Eventually our conversation turned to his half-century wish to talk to the pilot of his plane. He was harboring "50 years of anger" as to why the plane had been going so low and fast when they jumped. The high speed of the plane had led to an enormous opening shock that was so strong it stopped his government-issue radio operator's watch at exactly 1:24 A.M. I told Ray that I very probably could get him in touch with the pilot, Jesse Harrison, since Joe Flynn had mentioned Harrison in a recent e-mail.

I contacted Joe, and he sent me Jesse Harrison's telephone number and address in Connecticut, which I sent on to Ray. Several nights later Ray called me again. He had talked with Jesse for more than an hour. He told me that on several occasions the conversation had become very emotional for both men. And, of course, he finally found out why the airplane had been flying so low and going so fast.

Ray and I began talking by phone several times a week regarding his getting in touch with Jesse. Now Ray wanted to meet with Jesse and with Don Kane to talk about the several hours that they had spent together fifty-six years earlier.

I was hesitant about Ray's idea. My interest in the subject had been limited to discovering what had happened to my uncle, and that job had been accomplished. I was also very busy at work, and with family commitments, and didn't know if I had the time, or inclination, to get involved in this meeting. Then a new story, not the mystery that had encouraged me to research what had happened to my uncle, but an amazing story of coincidence and brotherhood, began to emerge.

The new story began this way: Don Kane's circulation of my research had encouraged Ray Geddes to contact me, in the hope that he could contact the pilot who had flown them to Normandy. I had facilitated that contact, and Ray was now in regular contact with Jesse Harrison. Then Jesse took the story one step further—a step that would result in another quest to complete a story involving many men, not only from the 77th Troop Carrier Squadron, but G Company of the 501st Parachute Infantry Regiment as well. As Jesse Harrison and Ray Geddes exchanged e-mail and telephone calls, it soon came out that Jesse had a half-century-long wish similar to that of Ray.

Jesse told Ray the story of how he had nearly died from burns received when his plane had been shot down on the third day of the MARKET-GARDEN campaign in Holland. He told Ray that, as he lay close to death in an English hospital, he had heard the voice of a man that he had met several times in the past, both in England in 1944 and back in the United States during 1943. The name of that man was Jack Urbank, from G Company, 501st PIR. Jesse asked Ray if he had known Jack Urbank, and if he knew where Jack was today. Ray replied, "Yes;" he had known Urbank, and he was sure he could find Urbank's address from material he had brought home from the 501st reunion. Through a disjointed series of events, a new and exciting story linking G/501 with the 77th TCS was about to emerge.

A gathering of Ray Geddes and Don Kane from G/501, Jesse Harrison from the 77th TCS, and myself soon began to come to fruition. It was decided that we would all get together at Ray's home in Baltimore. A date was agreed upon that worked with everyone's schedule, and most certainly was the most appropriate, June 5-6, 2000—fifty-six years to the day since Jesse had dropped Ray and Don in exactly the right place, while going the wrong way, through a barrage of German antiaircraft fire.

While plans for our getting together progressed, other events were occurring that would eventually affect our meeting. The first, and most significant, was the trip that Jesse and Sheila Harrison took to Ohio to see Jack Urbank and his family. The second event was a telephone call I received during April from Art Morin, Jr., the son of the man who had made the miraculous escape from John Schaefers' plane.

It started with an e-mail from Mark Bando in which he told me that he had come across information that Art Morin was from the Boston area, and that he had found several men with that name during a quick Internet search. He thought I might be interested. I certainly was interested. I found the three addresses and sent out postcards. Several days later Art Morin, Jr. called me. He told me that his dad had died in 1995, but that in his later years he had shared with his son many of the stories of his time with the G/501. Like Don Kane, Art Morin, Sr. was one of the few men who had jumped in Normandy and was still serving with the company at the war's end. Art Jr. obviously had tremendous respect for his father, and for what he had done during World War II. When I told him that some of his father's comrades would be getting together in Baltimore, and invited him to attend, he said "yes" even before he knew the date. Art and his wife Patti were added to the list of those who would meet in Baltimore.

The list of attendees continued to grow. For several years Ray had been in touch with Warren Purcell, the man with whom he had shared a horse stall at Lambourne. Warren, Ray told me, was not a man given to traveling, but Ray was determined to try to have Warren attend.

As the day of the get-together approached, Ray contacted me with the news that Jack Urbank would also attend. The visit from Jesse had been so helpful to Jack's morale that two of his children, daughter Claudia and son David Vernon Urbank (named after Jack's good friend from G Company

David Mythaler, and their revered company commander, Vernon Kraeger), would bring their father and mother to Baltimore to meet with us.

It was during this period that the idea of this book began to form. The story of Jack Urbank and Jesse Harrison had somehow kindled my interest beyond the story of my uncle. While the research for Joe's story had been done out of a personal desire to solve the mystery of his death, many who had read or heard Joe's story had stated that it was more than one family's story; it was a story that others could relate to with interest.

I began to realize that when the years of research on what happened to Joe were combined with the story of uniting Jesse and Jack, I had much more than a simple bit of family research. This was truly a story that many families, particularly those with World War II veterans, might want to hear. The idea that others might be interested was magnified just before I left for Baltimore when an envelope arrived from Joe Flynn. He had forwarded a copy of the latest column he had written for his local newspaper. The column, dated June 6, 2000, told the story of what would be happening in Baltimore on June 5-6. Joe related the story of his friendship with my uncle Joe, and how my search for the circumstances of his death had resulted, so many years later, in the reunion in Baltimore. [32]

When I got to Baltimore on June 5, I registered at my hotel and drove to Ray Geddes' house. This man had become a good friend during the previous year; we had talked on a regular basis; but we had never been in the same room together. Ray welcomed me to his home, introduced me to his wife Shirley, and proceeded to take me on a whirlwind tour while he asked questions about how we should manage the meetings over the next two days to allow me to get as much information as possible for this book. After several hours of good conversation, I left Ray's home to return to my hotel and change clothes for dinner.

When I arrived back at the hotel, I saw a sight that made me smile. A gentleman of the correct age to be a World War II veteran was standing in the middle of the lobby doing absolutely nothing. On his head was a hat that read, "101st Airborne Division - - W.W. II." I walked over to the man and asked if he were a friend of Ray Geddes. He smiled. "Well, I know him," said Warren Purcell, lately of G Company, 501st Parachute Infantry Regiment, "but I never liked the guy." We laughed and I saw that the G

Company veteran, who had survived 150 days of combat without a scratch, was a man with a great sense of humor. "I knew if I stood here long enough someone would come along," he told me.

Soon others arrived: Don Kane and his wife Sue; then Warren's wife, Madeline. Next I heard a deep voice say to me, "Is this the guy I have been talking to on the phone for the last few months?" It was Jesse Harrison, a man I had been hearing about, reading about, and talking to on the phone for almost twenty years. I knew that this was going to be a great occasion. Next Ray showed up, and we departed for the restaurant where he had arranged for us to have a private dining room. When we arrived we met the Urbank family, Jack and his wife Edna, and their son and daughter, David and Claudia. Art and Patti Morin arrived just as we did, to fill out the group.

The next thirty minutes were a blur to me as the men from the 501st saw each other, in some cases for the first time in fifty-six years. I introduced myself to the Urbanks and the Morins. A waiter took drink orders, and the group sat down at a table arranged in a large square.

Small stories and further introductions were shared back and forth over the table, and the opening of our small reunion remained rather unorganized and full of laughter as those at the table got to know each other or, in the case of the 501 veterans, renewed friendships. Soon our waiter announced that a buffet was being served in the next room, and we all went into the main dining room to get our meal with other hotel guests. When we had finished eating, the group had become more interested in each other's stories, and only one story at a time was being told. All the better for a writer to listen to what was being recounted.

Ray Geddes brought up the subject of G Company's first combat as a unit. That engagement had taken place on the morning of June 6th, after sunrise, with an attack on the town of Pouppeville. Many D-Day histories tell the story of Pouppeville because it was the scene of the first major linkup between the forces that landed on the beach and the airborne forces. In fact, Lieutenant Luther Knowlton, a platoon leader from G Company, had made the contact when he shook hands with a Fourth Division tank commander coming up from Utah Beach. It was also the engagement of which General Taylor was later quoted as saying, "Never have so few been led by so many."

At Pouppeville the men from G Company saw their first serious combat, and lost friends for the first time. Three of the men in the room—Don Kane, Ray Geddes, and Warren Purcell—had participated in the fight at Pouppeville, and the men spoke of the events in that fight for some time.

They discussed how the company had been on the road entering Pouppeville when they met a German patrol leaving the town. A brief and violent firefight had followed, in which Captain Kraeger and Corporal Virgil Danforth had led a charge that killed all of the Germans. Several minutes later a sniper had shot Major Laurence Legere, the assistant division operations officer, in the leg. Legere fell in the road writhing in pain. Ray Geddes told how he had jumped into the ditch next to the road after Legere was hit. Ray remembered that when he turned to look behind him in the ditch, he had seen medic Eddy Hohl return to the road to assist Legere.

Ray Geddes - "I still get mad when I think about what happened to Hohl. Legere was yelling in pain; and Hohl went right out there, as he was trained to do, wearing a big red cross on his helmet and another on his arm. The sniper fired again, and Hohl just sort of did a somersault. He never said a word. I called out to him to see if he was all right, but he never answered. I hope someone got the bastard that shot him. There was no doubt that he was shooting at a medic." [33]

There was more general discussion about the assault on the town. The men mentioned the bravery of Virgil Danforth, who received a Distinguished Service Cross for his actions at Pouppeville, and the deaths of other men in those first hours of combat—friends such as Eddy Hohl, Earl Williams, and Luther Gulick, as well as Lieutenant Nathan Marks.[34]

There was also some humor in the stories that came out about the battle at Pouppeville. Jack Urbank, who had not rejoined the company until June 7th, told us that when he did return everyone was telling a story about Ray Geddes that would become legendary in G Company. According to Jack, with no denial from Ray, when the shooting had ended and the German prisoners were locked in a barn for safekeeping, several of the men were assigned various chores to "clean up" after the action. Ray, having no radio to operate, was assigned to collect and stack German weapons. He found the detail to be a good one, as he was a gun collector and familiar with various weapons. Finally, without thinking of the implications, he decided to test one of the German rifles by firing it at some decorative ironwork on top of the building that had been the German headquarters in Pouppeville. Standing in the courtyard, Ray took aim and fired, then looked around and realized he was the only man still standing. He had sent most of his G Company comrades, not to mention several battalion and division level officers, all diving for cover with that single shot. Although neither Ray nor Jack went into detail about what followed, it was clear that 19-year-old T/4 Geddes had been in serious hot water with everyone from Captain Kraeger to General Taylor.

Don Kane told a similar story on himself that had taken place slightly before Ray's fiasco. While he told the story as a humorous anecdote, it could have had serious implications. Don had found, and was inspecting, an abandoned German machine gun emplacement near the German headquarters. The gun had been abandoned by its crew and was in perfect working order. Across a field directly adjacent to the town Don spotted some Germans making their escape. He jumped behind the machine gun and started shooting at the running soldiers. Just like Ray, he had failed to anticipate the reaction of his comrades. After he stopped firing he heard shouting coming from nearby. The yelling was from an American paratrooper with a grenade in his hand. Hearing the German gun go into action, the paratrooper, who was unknown to Don, had begun to creep up on the emplacement with a grenade to eliminate what he was sure was Germans firing at the American troops entering the town. Only because the paratrooper had looked before throwing the grenade had Don avoided being wounded, or possibly killed, by one of his own.

Warren Purcell followed with a story about finding a sheepskin flying boot lying on the ground at the edge of Pouppeville. Thinking how unusual it was, he had walked over to investigate. When he had leaned over to pick up the boot, he found that it still had a foot in it.

At this point someone asked how many men were still with the company when they were pulled from combat on July 16, 1944. Jack Urbank remembered that there were seven men in his platoon. (As the ranking NCO left in the company, and only one officer present for duty, Urbank had become an acting platoon leader.) Warren Purcell believed that when they walked down to Utah Beach to get on the LST that took them back to England, Lieutenant Luther Knowlton was acting commander of

G Company, which consisted of twenty-four men. The company roster on June 5th, according to Jack Urbank, had 119 enlisted men and NCO's and approximately eight officers.

One of my goals for the meeting was to hear from the wives of the men what their views had been of the war and their men who were fighting that war. Amazingly, all of these veterans had been married to their wives for more than fifty years. Most had been married to, or dating, the woman with whom they sat at the table that evening when they had left for Europe. Each woman at the table seemed anxious to tell her story.

Edna Urbank –"I first met Jack on the school bus when we were freshmen in high school. He told his friends, 'That's the girl I'm going to marry,' but I didn't like him at all. He was always after me for a date, but I always refused. One year, on Valentine's Day, he ran up to me in the hall at school and gave me a bag of peanuts with a poem. The poem said, 'I tried to date you, but you're unkind, so nuts to you my valentine.' Well, we graduated from high school without ever having gone out on a date. He knew that I loved Persian cats. One day I came home and my mother was holding a Persian kitten. I said to her, 'Has Jack Urbank been here?' The answer was *yes*. He had walked seven miles to deliver that cat. Then he came by the house with flowers. I finally had to go out on a date with him, and we started going to the movies on Thursday nights. He didn't have any money, so we just smelled the popcorn, but it was fun.

"Then it all changed. We went on a midnight cruise on Lake Michigan with my sister and brother-in-law in the summer of 1941, and I fell in love with him. Then the war started, and we got engaged in 1942, on his first furlough. We got married in 1943, right before he left for England.

"He wrote every day until June of 1944, and then I didn't hear anything for a month. I knew that he had jumped into Normandy, and every day I would wait for the mailman. Finally, some time in July, the mailman came running down the street to my house just as I was leaving—he had 30 V-mail letters from Jack in his hand!! Jack got home on Christmas Eve, 1945. My brother and sister-in-law took me down to the train station, and when everyone got off he wasn't there. Then the conductor said that a second section of the train would arrive in a few minutes. He was on the second train, and he looked so terrific, that soldier with the scarf around his neck!" [35]

107

Jerome J. McLaughlin

Shirley Geddes – "Fortunately, I did not know Raymond while he was overseas and in harm's way. I have always been thankful for that. I was a Western Union telegraph operator, and worked at both Penn and Camden stations in Baltimore. I did not meet him until early 1945, after he had become a military policeman in the city. MPs were posted at the various railroad and bus stations because there were so many servicemen traveling. Many of the military men would stop at our counter to send or receive money or messages. Sounds antiquated doesn't it? But that is the way it was during World War II. There were times when I was very busy and times when we had nothing to do. Of course, I would talk to the MPs when I wasn't busy—they had wonderful uniforms. One of the MPs whom I liked was Raymond. One thing led to another, and we started dating. We were married in 1950 during his junior year at the University of Maryland."

Sheila Harrison – "Jesse had flown his plane up to Connecticut to work with the people who made the gliders. He was in town for several weeks, and one night he showed up in a bar that my girlfriends and I used to go to after work. He was quite dashing, a pilot and everything, and the first night he paid for cab fare for all of us when it was time to go home. We began to see each other almost every night. When Jesse had to leave, he told me that he would fly his plane over the house and wave good-bye to me. He did as he promised and wiggled the wings as he flew over. I remember that my father said to me, in his Irish brogue, 'Tell that young man to be more careful; I thought he was going to hit the house.'

"He wrote to me for 16 months after he left. The letters stopped in September 1944. I figured he had found someone else because it was so long without hearing from him. Then I got a letter. It had been written by a nurse. Jesse's hands were so burned that he couldn't write. He came to Connecticut at the beginning of March in 1945. I met him at the railroad station. He was covered in bandages, and his hair had turned white—he was only 22. We were married two weeks later, on St. Patrick's Day. We had only spent a month together in all that time. We've done okay for a Southern Baptist and a Northern Catholic."

Madeline Purcell - "In 1941 I was attending Meredith College in Raleigh, North Carolina. I met Warren and his brother, who were going to North Carolina State, at the Presbyterian church. Warren was only there until April, when he left to join the Army. I stayed in touch with his parents during the war, and visited them several times in Petersburg, Virginia, while I was in graduate school. Warren came home from the war in December 1945, and we started dating. We didn't correspond at all during the war, but got serious after he came home. We were married in August of 1947."

Sue Kane - "I met Don just around my 19th birthday, in 1941. It was a blind date. He was 21 and going to school at night while he worked in a factory. When he showed up he had blond hair, was good-looking, and funny. I was in junior college and living at home. There was an instant attraction and we started dating regularly. We went dancing almost every Saturday night. I graduated and took a job in a bank. I hated it. It was so boring, and there was a whole world out there. Then Don decided to go into the service before he got drafted; that was in December of 1942. I decided that I was going to do something also, so I enrolled in an engineering program at Penn State that trained women to be assistants to engineers. We hadn't made any commitments when he left, but we both knew that when he came home we would get married. He went to his various training camps, and I ended up at the Curtis Wright plant in Buffalo, New York, where we made P-40's and C-46's. I remember that they rang the church bells in Buffalo on June 6th, when the invasion started. Then Don's letters stopped for a while. He finally came home in December of 1945. We got engaged at Christmas and married in March of 1946. Then we moved to Vermont where Don was accepted to the University's School of Engineering."

Art Morin spoke for his parents and told their story. Art Sr. met his future bride, Pauline O'Connor, when they both worked at the Whitin Machine Works in Whitinsville, Massachussetts. They married in 1948, and Art Jr. was born in 1949. Art Sr. later went to work for General Motors, and retired at age sixty-five with thirty-seven years of service. Art told us his dad was a strong union man, and had been offered several management jobs, always turning them down to remain with his union. Art Jr. grew up in a home that his father purchased in Milford, Massachusetts, after going to work with GM. He told us how his father had been

Art Morin, Sr.
Paris, 1945.

109

diagnosed with cancer in October 1995, and had died four months later. He paused briefly, obviously choked with emotion as he discussed his father with us, a group of strangers. He began again, and told us that his mother was still living, and that he and Patti had been blessed with two children of their own. Later, in a private conversation, he made it even more evident how close he and his father had been, describing how they would meet at the Milford Veterans Club after work and share a beer before going home for the evening. He also described how his father had never discussed his WWII experiences until the last few years of his life. The intimacy and importance of those talks between father and son have become a treasured memory for Art.

Art's moving story was followed by a silence, broken by Jesse Harrison, who brought up the subject of the date and hour on which we were meeting. Jesse then addressed the group, with great feeling, apparently brought on by Art's comments, about being in the same room with some of the men he had dropped into the Normandy countryside fifty-six years previously, to the day. He believes that none of the aircrew from the 77th Squadron, or even the 435th Troop Carrier Group, ever had contact with anyone whom they had dropped in Normandy, and certainly not in a reunion such as that in which we were gathered.

<u>Jesse Harrison</u> - "Fifty-six years is a long time to wait to find out what happened to the guys who jumped with us in Normandy. Many times we would wonder, 'What ever happened to those guys? What was it like when they landed?' Of course, when I did find out what happened to you guys, all I heard was that all of you wanted to kill me for not slowing down when I gave the green light."

Jesse's last statement got a good laugh from the group. By now, of course, everyone had heard the story of how Jesse had probably saved many lives in his reversal of course and second trip through the antiaircraft fire. He reminded the group that he had come home with more than sixty holes in his plane, and that they were the lucky ones, as the two other 77th crews in their flight, and most of their complement of G Company men, had perished in that terrible firestorm over Picauville.

There was a pause in the conversation after Jesse finished. Then Ray Geddes reminded us of the amazing feat that Jesse had accomplished fifty-six years earlier, "You realize," he said, "that we were among the lucky ones who came down in the right spot; not many can say that."

Finally the group admitted that it was time to retire for the night. After several private conversations, as mentioned above, I went back to my hotel room and began to record notes on the night's discussions and listen to the tape recording that I had made of most of the discussion that took place during dinner.

Warren Purcell in his WWII uniform. Picture taken in 1995.

Late the next morning we gathered at Ray's house and had what developed into a "show and tell" session, with each veteran showing off memorabilia that he had brought along. The highlight was clearly Warren Purcell, who brought an original 1943 jumpsuit, which he proudly proclaimed still fit him. [36]

More discussions ensued as the day progressed, the most important of which would have significant implications for all of us. Sometime during the day it was mentioned that it "would be nice" if plaques could be placed at the Normandy crash sites where veterans in the room had lost friends from the 77th Squadron and G Company. Jesse Harrison even began to entertain the idea that perhaps the company for which he had worked might produce the plaques. Further, Jesse returned to the subject that he had brought up the night before: that this was probably the first time that 101st soldiers had gotten together with the pilot who dropped them in Normandy. He invited all of the 101st men present to join him and Sheila at the 435th reunion to be held in Arizona the following September. Jack Urbank and Ray Geddes immediately took Jesse up on this offer with the promise that plans would be made over the summer. The group returned to the hotel in the afternoon and then gathered for a final meal together at the hotel that evening.

While we were waiting for the others to come down from their rooms, I spent some time in the hotel lobby talking with Warren Purcell. He began to discuss with me the advance on Pouppeville. He vividly remembers that Major Legere was advancing on the road with the lead men in the column. Many of the published reports on the Pouppeville action describe how Legere was wounded in the leg and fell in the middle of the road. As Ray Geddes had described the night before, Warren remembered that medic Eddy Hohl ran to Legere and began to assist the wounded man. Almost immediately a sniper shot Hohl through the chest, a mortal wound. Warren was in the ditch farther down the column from Legere and Hohl and watched the events unfold.

Warren added to the Legere story by telling me that after Kraeger's charge across the road, he began to move down the ditch until he was opposite Legere. Despite the fact that most of the Americans had advanced beyond that position, a German machine gun began to rake the area. The fire was so intense, Warren told me, that branches were falling on him from the trees next to the ditch. He noticed that Legere was still alive and gesturing to him. The major had tied a rope around his arm and threw the other end to Warren, who pulled Legere into the ditch. The major was in great pain and still bleeding. Warren opened the major's first aid kit, which had been attached to the netting on his helmet, and proceeded to give him a shot of morphine and bandage his wound. When he was finished, he wished Legere good luck and continued down the ditch to catch up with his comrades. [37]

Much of the material from Warren Purcell and Jack Urbank that appears in this book emerged that evening, as I spent time with both men and they talked about special incidents that they felt the need to emphasize. Warren spoke of his feeling like the "law of averages" was haunting him as the war continued and he was one of the few survivors who jumped in Normandy and remained with the company. Even more, of those veterans left, he was one of only a few who had not been wounded in some way. Jack related his landing in the field at Normandy, among the cow pies and beneath the German machine gun fire. He told the story—his version—of meeting with Don Castona in the dark and suggesting that they "go to the right."

Back Row, L-R: Art Morin, Jr., Pat Morin, Warren Purcell, Don Kane, Shirley Geddes, Ray Geddes, Jesse Harrison, Claudia Urbank, author, David Urbank.
Front Row, L-R: Madeline Purcell, Sue Kane, Sheila Harrison, Jack Urbank, Edna Urbank.

As we left the hotel that evening, there were extended good-byes and promises to keep in touch. I was probably the quietest of the group, as the enormity of what had occurred suddenly began to take effect. As I drove down I-95, returning to my home in Alexandria, Virginia, I was proud of my part in reuniting these men and providing the opportunity for their families to meet men about whom they had been hearing for years—especially in the case of Jack Urbank and Jesse Harrison. There had been some truly happy people at Ray Geddes' Baltimore reunion.

The second thought that dominated my thinking for the remainder of the trip home was the idea of the plaques. After almost twenty years of research and closure on the subject of what had happened to my Uncle Joe, now it seemed that possibly there would be another chapter to the story. I began to think about placing a plaque in Mr. Dulenay's field with my uncle's name on it. I thought of my grandmother, and how proud she would have been to see Joe remembered by the next generation with a monument that would last for generations to come. Even before I got back to Alexandria, I knew that I had to do whatever it took to place a plaque on Mr. Dulenay's farm and another at the farm where Jim Hamblin's plane had come down. I did not have to wait long to find out that I had a strong and willing accomplice in my quest.

Three days after my return from Baltimore, I received an e-mail from Jesse Harrison. He had wasted no time upon his return to Connecticut in contacting friends to have the plaques made. I was amazed as I read his e-mail. This was really going to happen!!! I called Jesse and we talked about what to do next. We agreed to make the format of the plaques a group project, and Jesse sent out an e-mail to everyone who had been at the Baltimore re-union, asking their opinion on what the plaques should look like. At the same time I mailed Jesse copies of the official Missing Aircrew Reports for both the Hamblin and Schaefers aircraft to ensure that all of the appropriate names would be on the plaques.

During the next week we agreed, after much cyber discussion, on several important facets of the plaques' format. We decided on the wording of the statements that would be at the top of the plaques and agreed to list the 77th men by crew station, as had been done in the Missing Aircrew Reports, and the G Company men by rank vice the alphabetical listing on the MARs, for visual reasons. We all were very much in agreement that the plaque at the Schaefers' crash site, on Mr. Dulenay's farm, should include the names of the three survivors.

I talked with Jesse on the Fourth of July, and we finalized details for him to have the plaques produced. I was amazed when he contacted me on July 14 to tell me that the plaques were finished. Attached to the e-mail was a picture of the plaque with my uncle's name on it. He told me he would bring both plaques to the 435th Reunion the following September. [38]

As the summer progressed the group continued contact via e-mail, and plans for the 435th reunion to include 101st Airborne troopers who had jumped from Jesse's plane in Normandy began to get around among the troop carrier veterans. Pappy Rawlins was writing the 77th Squadron newsletter at the time, and he sent out the summer edition, which included all the details of the upcoming reunion and mentioned that several of the paratroopers from Jesse's plane might be making an appearance at the reunion. The ex-commander of the 77th realized the implications of such a reunion of paratroopers and troop carrier crews. After the usual amount of changed plans and decision-making, two G Company men, Ray Geddes and Don Kane, were able to attend the 435th reunion. Jesse contacted Pappy Rawlins, and both men were sent invitations by the former Squadron

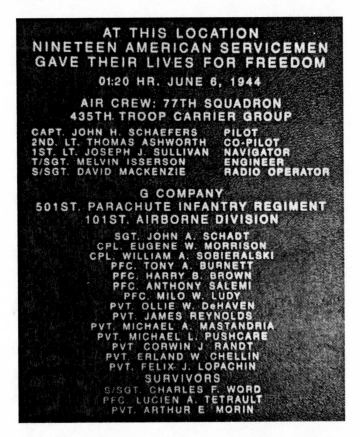

AT THIS LOCATION
NINETEEN AMERICAN SERVICEMEN
GAVE THEIR LIVES FOR FREEDOM
01:20 HR. JUNE 6, 1944

AIR CREW: 77TH SQUADRON
435TH TROOP CARRIER GROUP

CAPT. JOHN H. SCHAEFERS	PILOT
2ND. LT. THOMAS ASHWORTH	CO-PILOT
1ST. LT. JOSEPH J. SULLIVAN	NAVIGATOR
T/SGT. MELVIN ISSERSON	ENGINEER
S/SGT. DAVID MACKENZIE	RADIO OPERATOR

G COMPANY
501ST. PARACHUTE INFANTRY REGIMENT
101ST. AIRBORNE DIVISION

SGT. JOHN A. SCHADT
CPL. EUGENE W. MORRISON
CPL. WILLIAM A. SOBIERALSKI
PFC. TONY A. BURNETT
PFC. HARRY B. BROWN
PFC. ANTHONY SALEMI
PFC. MILO W. LUDY
PVT. OLLIE W. DeHAVEN
PVT. JAMES REYNOLDS
PVT. MICHAEL A. MASTANDRIA
PVT. MICHAEL L. PUSHCARE
PVT. CORWIN J. RANDT
PVT. ERLAND W. CHELLIN
PVT. FELIX J. LOPACHIN
SURVIVORS
S/SGT. CHARLES F. WORD
PFC. LUCIEN A. TETRAULT
PVT. ARTHUR E. MORIN

Commander. Along with their wives they became, according to Pappy Rawlins, the first paratroopers who jumped in Normandy to attend a troop carrier reunion along with the pilot who dropped them!

I flew to Tuscon on September 15 and was happy to be met as a familiar face by the men of the 77th and their wives on this occasion. Again I met the group at breakfast, and was immediately shaking hands with Abe Friedman. George Winard and his wife Mikki asked me to have breakfast with them, and others stopped by to say hello as we ate. It felt wonderful to be remembered and so well received by the 77th family. Ray, Don, and Jesse had arrived with their wives the day before and had already been adopted by everyone from the 77th. The three were constantly in conversations with their long-ago troop carrier colleagues, comparing notes on the days they had been together in 1944. Over and over one of the 77th veterans would say to me, "We never knew what happened to those guys." Don and Ray were certainly the center of attention at this reunion.

The night of my arrival each of the squadrons in the 435th had a private dinner. It was easy to see why the reunions were now being run as Group vice Squadron affairs. In the two years since I had last been with the 77th, the numbers had dwindled. Pappy's briefing on the State of the Squadron verified that the men who had served with the 77th more than fifty years earlier were all too rapidly becoming frail and unable to travel, or worse. Those of us in the room—half the size of the '98 reunion, listened as Pappy read letters from friends who could not attend, or from spouses and children who were informing the group that their loved one had passed away.

After the correspondence portion of the Squadron's business meeting, Pappy asked that Jesse address the group. Jesse told them how he had spent fifty years suppressing his memories of D-Day and his portion of the war through September 1944, in Holland. He explained that this was the first reunion of the Squadron that he had attended, and that circumstances, starting with his call from Ray Geddes, and followed by his meeting with Jack Urbank in Ohio and the mini-reunion in Baltimore the previous June, had inspired him finally to meet with his comrades in arms fixty-six years after they had last been together. Jesse spoke very eloquently about how good it felt to be among his comrades again, and of how glad he was to have in the room two of the men who had jumped from his plane. He then introduced Don and Sue and then Ray and Shirley. They stood to receive applause from the group.

435th TCG 2000 Reunion.

Back Row, L-R: Don Kane, author, Sheila and Jesse Harrison. Front Row, L-R: Sue Kane, Ray and Shirley Geddes.

Pappy asked Don and Ray if they would like to address the group. Both of the paratroopers mentioned how honored they were to be invited to the reunion. After the remarks and dinner had been completed, I was approached by a man who introduced himself as Bud Busiere. Bud reminded me that at the '98 reunion we had spoken, and that I had given him a picture of the headstone at the Normandy cemetery of the flight engineer from my uncle's plane, Melvin Isserson. Bud told me that he was greatly interested in what I was doing, and asked that I not hesitate to call upon him for any help he might give on the book. Further, he told me that he was interested in traveling to France when we put the plaques up at the crash sites. I took his name and telephone number and promised I would be in touch. Little did I realize at the time that Bud would be the only veteran from either the 77th or G Company able to make the trip.

Later that night there was a combined social for all the 435th squadrons, and I took Bud up on his request to participate. We sat on the hotel patio while the socializing went on around us, and he talked to me and my tape recorder about his time in the 77th and his friendship with "Blackie" Isserson, who had died with my uncle on D-Day.

I also was able to sit down, in a quieter atmosphere, with the man who has always been the heart of the 77th Troop Carrier Squadron, Colonel Phillip "Pappy" Rawlins. Much of what you have read in this work about the Squadron has come from the men who provided their personal remembrances of their time in the 77th. Everything else came from the time I spent with Pappy that night. In addition to his personal recollections, he presented me with a very detailed personal history he had written of the Squadron.

His unpublished history, which he entitled *Red Light—Green Light, Geranimo!* took years to assemble. He made only a few copies of his work, and I was thrilled that he entrusted me with his only copy so that I could take it with me and duplicate it. We talked for ninety minutes. Pappy remained very much the colonel as he sat ramrod straight in his chair and spoke of his beloved squadron.

The author with Phillip "Pappy" Rawlins.

He told me that he had begun his military career in the late 1930's as an infantry officer and had attended flight school in 1941, after which he attended C-47 transition school. It was there he had been spotted by Henry Osmer and held over as an instructor. Osmer had then offered Pappy the job of operations officer of the 77th Squadron when he (Osmer) was told to form the squadron as part of the new 435th Troop Carrier Group in late 1942. Both men took the squadron from a paperwork organization to a highly trained troop carrier unit that they led into combat from D-Day until it was disbanded in 1945. Obviously when Colonel Osmer was promoted to Deputy of the 435th Troop Carrier Group, there was no more qualified candidate for Squadron Commander of the 77th than Pappy Rawlins. There was a glow in his eye as he told me how happy he was for Hank Osmer when he was moved up to Group Command; but one of the few times in our interview when I saw a smile on his face was when he said how proud he was to have been recommended, and appointed, Commanding Officer of the 77th Troop Carrier Squadron.

Later that night I had dinner with a wonderful group of people: Abe and Selma Friedman, Joe and Halmar Flynn, Ray and Shirley Geddes, and Don and Sue Kane. It was a very enjoyable meal, during which, suprisingly, a great deal of the conversation did *not* revolve around WWII and the shared experiences of the men at the table. We talked about home towns, world politics, travel, children, and friendship. I felt honored to be with these people, and as they talked I hoped that all of them could be with us in Normandy when we honored their comrades with Jesse's plaques.

Once again I left a reunion of my uncle's comrades and sat in a taxi thinking about what was happening with my odyssey. Unlike the departure from San Antonio in 1998, when I assumed that the odyssey was ending, I was now thinking about what was coming next: another trip to Normandy.

CHAPTER 7
Normandy 2001

"What did you think?"
"Freedom! Freedom! Here comes freedom!"

Conversation between Margaret Young
and a French woman at the Bisset farm,
LaMarouette, Founecrop, Normandy
France
September 6, 2001

"I am 73, and I remember that time.
I am French today because of
what these Americans did."

Michel Gaudry
Dulenay farm,
Clainville, Normandy
France
September 6, 2001

Over the next several months there was much use of e-mail and telephones to coordinate our Normandy trip. With great trepidation I contacted Michel Gaudry and asked if he would help on the French side of the Atlantic—quite a request of a man whom I had met only once. I need not have worried, as Michel willingly said he would do all he could to help. I was also in touch with Philippe, who would assist Michel as he could from his home in Cher. What helped considerably, here in the States, but most importantly with contacting Michel and Philippe, was that in the short interval since my last trip to France in 1998, almost all of the participants had obtained access to e-mail. The twelve-to-fifteen-day turn-around time for letters to and from France was now down, in many instances, to hours.

Excitement was high among those who had been at the 435th reunion. At one point we had twenty-four people planning to make the trip. The list of those who wanted to attend but eventually had to drop out was heartbreaking. The reason that many of the main characters in the story had to remain at home was particularly disturbing. In the time period between the 435th Tucson reunion in September 2000 and September 2001, illness of the veteran or his spouse caused Don Kane, Jesse Harrison, Pappy Rawlins, and Jack Urbank to be unable to go. Ray Geddes also had to drop out.

Two of my cousins, Katherine Smith and Margaret Young, had gotten caught up in the story of our Uncle Joe and decided to join us. Katherine and her husband Ken had wanted to make the trip in 1998 but had other commitments. They signed on early for the trip and would play an important role in our adventure. Margaret and her husband Wilson completed the family members who would travel with us. Bud Busiere, true to his word at the reunion, was the only D-Day veteran able to make the trip. Art and Patti Morin had planned to go from the first, and would carry Jesse's plaques across the Atlantic. The last member of the group who would make the trip was John Merkt. John had also lost an uncle on D-Day. S/Sgt. Robert Walsh was the radio operator on the third plane that the 435th lost in Normandy, piloted by the operations officer for the 75th TCS, Captain Seymour Malakoff.

Denise and I departed from the United States on Labor Day, 2001. We arrived in Paris the next day and met our intrepid group at the Hotel des Ducs de Bourgogne. As all of the parties had arrived at different times and none had met each other previously—except, of course, my cousins—we were not sure how we would finally get assembled. It turned out not to be difficult. Through a series of messages and phone calls we all assembled in Margaret and Wilson's room. Wilson served wine and French bread as the group went around the room and introduced themselves.

Bud and Louise Busiere were the only "Greatest Generation" members with us. They had traveled from Collinsville, Ohio, and this was the latest of several trips they had made to France. While they had visited the American Cemetery in Normandy and other WWII sites, they had never known where to look for the crash sites of Bud's comrades from the 77th squadron. Bud was particularly thinking of his best friend from the 77th, Melvin Isserson, who had been the flight engineer on my uncle's plane.

John Merkt was the same general age as the rest of us in the "next generation," born from the period of 1939 to 1949. He told us he was a banker from Louisville, Kentucky, and like most of us in the room had grown up hearing stories about his uncle who had been killed on D-Day, with no further details available. He had contacted me through researching what had happened to his uncle and a phone call to Mark Bando. When he heard we were going to Normandy and could possibly visit the location of his uncle's crash, he had jumped at the opportunity and adjusted his work schedule to make the trip. John and I had met just before leaving for Paris. His son Matt lives in Arlington, Virginia, not far from my home in Alexandria; and John had stayed with Matt for several days before flying to Paris out of Dulles Airport.

Art Morin explained to the group how he and Patti had become involved after answering my postcard to him the previous winter—again brought about through Mark Bando's seemingly endless contacts.

My cousin Katherine, who as a child was the only one of our generation to have actually known my Uncle Joe, explained how she and her husband Ken had been following my research for years and had wanted to make the trip in 1998. They had retired to a new home in South Carolina in 1999 and considered this trip an important part of their plan to make retirement an adventure.

Katherine's sister Margaret told the group how she and I had often sat with my grandmother (we are only two months apart in age) as she told us stories of our uncle and her many efforts to find out what had happened to him.

After the introductions were completed, we left the hotel as a group and walked several blocks to a restaurant named LeChein que Fumé, where we continued to become acquainted over dinner. Afterward, several of us walked to nearby Notre Dame Cathedral and then returned to the hotel. It had been a long day from home to Paris, and the next morning promised to begin another exciting chapter in our adventure.

Dinner in Paris, September 4, 2001.
L-R: Wilson and Margaret Young, Denise McLaughlin (hidden), Katherine and Ken Smith, John Merkt, Bud and Louise Busiere, author, Art and Patti Morin.

September 5 began with a short trip to the St. Lazare train station and then a two and one-half hour journey from Paris to Normandy in very comfortable and modern first-class railroad accommodations. We arrived in Carentan—where the men of G/501 had participated in liberating and then defending the city from the 13th to the 17th of June 1944—and were met by a smiling and cheerful Michel Gaudry.

Denise and I were thrilled to meet our friend from the 1998 visit, and it was only moments after our arrival that Michel was making jokes about the size of our bus (four times the size needed, but the only one available on that day) and the terrible tribulations that he was having to endure because of our visit. His smile and humor were, once again, infectious, and in only minutes he had charmed our entire group.

We boarded our oversized bus and traveled to St. Mere-Eglise, where we met Philippe and checked into the Hotel du 6 Juin—greeted once again by owner Sebastian Daher. It was wonderful to see Philippe and disappointing to hear that Bill and Genevieve would not be with us for this visit. Genevieve was ill and could not make the trip to Normandy. Philippe did, however, call Bill, and we spoke on the phone updating each other on events since our last visit. We had lunch in a small restaurant in St. Mere-Eglise and spent much of the afternoon touring the shops and museum before an early dinner in the same restaurant adjacent to the St. Mere-Eglise town square where we had spent our first evening in Normandy in 1998.

After dinner several of us, including Michel, Philippe, Wilson Young, Ken Smith, Art Morin, and myself, left St. Mere-Eglise and drove to the two crash sites. We had decided that actually placing the plaques on the walls the next day could be a problem, as rain was expected, and we did not know how long it would take to secure the anchors for the mounting screws. Further, the daylight lasts until almost 10:00 P.M. in Normandy during September, and there would be ample time; we hoped to have both plaques secured to their walls before darkness. Our first stop was at the farm where Jim Hamblin's plane had been lost. Here we met the owners, Regis and Patricia Bisset. An attractive couple in their 30's, they seemed most anxious to assist with placing the plaques and getting to know us. Their English was on a par with our minimal French, and Philippe and Michel were kept busy translating the ongoing conversations between the Bissets and our group.

Regis was well supplied with both tools and skills to assist in our project. From our group Ken and Art worked well with Regis, despite the fact that sometimes they simply had to point and nod, since Michel and Philippe were unable to translate the nuances of language regarding drill bits and stone-cutting.

Although we had gathered at Regis' home, the first plaque was placed at Mr. Dulenay's farm. We arrived at the site and met Mr. Dulenay, along with a cheerful older man who worked for him and was immediately dubbed by the group as "The Captain" due to his saluting everyone present on a regular basis.

A general site to mount the plaque was chosen on the wall of the house, just a few feet from the road and immediately adjacent to the gate that provided entrance to the field where the plane had crashed. My two cousins-in-law began to show their talents at this point as Ken, a skilled carpenter, became the ad hoc foreman of the project, working with Art and Regis to determine how best to place the plaque on the stones and mortar that made up the wall of Mr. Dulenay's house. Mr. Dulenay made his contribution to our effort by

Claude Dulenay, Ken Smith, and Michel Gaudry (translating) discuss placement of the plaque on the wall of Mr. Dulenay's home.

loaning us a ladder to allow Ken and the others to reach the selected location. Wilson Young became the resident video cameraman and began to record the event. He would seldom put down the camera over the next two days, and the results of his effort are several hours of absolutely priceless recordings for those of us who were there, and especially for the others who could not make the trip.

Art and I very carefully unpacked the first plaque on the road. It was a moving moment for Art as he looked at the names, including Art Morin, Sr., who was listed as a survivor. I told Art that his dad would be proud of him for being a part of this effort. Art nodded his head, but did not answer. We smiled at each other, and he held the plaque up for several of the group to take pictures.

After photographing the plaque, our group moved to the wall where Ken and Regis had determined the plaque would most likely fit. The wall consisted totally of stone and mortar, and finding a perfect location where all of the securing bolts would enter into the stone was a challenge. Finally a good location was found, and Art's portable drill went to work on the stones. A rotating team of Ken, Regis, and Art worked for twenty minutes before all four holes were completed. Then the plaque was placed against the wall and four screws worked into the stone.

Art Morin, Jr., Ken Smith, author, displaying the plaque at the Dulenay farm.

I was standing across the narrow road, watching all of this take place when Ken did a most wonderful thing; he looked at me and held out the screwdriver that he had used to start the bolts into their holes and said, "I guess you've earned the right to do this." I walked across the road and put the final turns on each bolt. I had tears in my eyes when I finished. All of this was on video, thanks to Wilson; and when we were done we took turns posing for pictures in front of the plaque with Mr. Dulenay. The first plaque was now fixed to its permanent home, and we almost cavalierly packed the tools and other equipment,

Ken Smith (on ladder), watching the author make the final turns to secure the bolts on the plaque at the Dulenay farm.

telling Mr. Dulenay that we would return in the morning to "dedicate" the plaque; then we got into our cars and drove back to Regis' farm.

The first plaque is attached to the Dulenay farmhouse. L-R: Ken Smith, Claude Dulenay, Art Morin, author, Michel Gaudry. September 5, 2001.

Placing the second plaque took much less time than the first, as the construction crew knew exactly which drill and bit would do the job, and the ground next to the wall on Regis' home was easier to work from, not requiring the use of a ladder. Just before the late loss of daylight in that portion of the world, and after our good-byes to Regis and Patricia, we returned to the hotel.

Those who had not been able to fit into the cars were waiting for us at the hotel when we returned. We immediately ran Wilson's video of our efforts on the small screen attached to the camera so that everyone could see how we had attached the plaques to the wall.

As the group gathered around the tiny screen, I motioned Art aside, and we went to my room and placed an overseas call to Jesse Harrison. It was dinner time in Connecticut, and Jesse was watching the evening news when his phone rang. "Jesse," I said without any introduction, "the plaques are up!" At first I thought that the old pilot had not heard or understood what I had said; then I heard him begin to try to get out some words. He was beginning to cry, and he said, "Finally, after so many years. I can't tell you how wonderful this news is to me." Then he yelled the news to Sheila. He returned to the phone and began repeating how happy he was at hearing our news. I passed the phone to Art. Jesse told us that he would call Pappy Rawlins and Joe Flynn to get the news out to the 77th. Art told Jesse that we had videotaped our work and would also record the dedications the next day. Jesse was still thanking us as we said good-bye and returned to the others in the hotel lobby.

While Art and I had been talking to Jesse, the others had been talking with Philippe about his books. He and Eric had published a paperback about the Magneville crash and the memorial stone that had been dedicated in 1995. He is also completing work on a hardcover book that details all of the thirty-eight planes that were lost while dropping American paratroopers on D-Day. Earlier that evening the entire group had signed a copy of Mark Bando's book, *101st Airborne (The Screaming Eagles at Normandy)* [see Bibliography], which we presented to Philippe as a gift for all that he had done to create the situation that had brought our group to Normandy.

After the presentation to Philippe, we listened as Michel explained his plan for the next day. He and Philippe had, as usual, several surprises for us; and there was a schedule that had to be organized so that events could be coordinated. Finally, our plans were set and we all retired to our rooms for a good night's sleep after a long day, hoping that the weather forecast for rain in the morning would prove false.

I arose on the morning of September 6, 2001, fifty-six years and three months since my uncle had died only a few miles from our hotel, and began to go over the few notes that I had prepared for our dedication of the plaques. I had asked the 77th and G/501 veterans who could not make the trip if they would like me to read their comments on this day, and several had replied. I had some notes of my own, and both Katherine and Bud would speak at the Schaefers' crash site. I put all the notes, my cameras, and film into my backpack, and Denise and I joined the others for breakfast at 8:00 A.M. We were all glad to see that while the sun certainly was not shining, there was no rain falling, and our bus was parked outside the hotel, ready to take us out on a day that would be filled with tears as well as laughter, surprises, and newfound friendship.

Michel had procured a smaller bus that fit our eleven travelers nicely. We took the same route from the hotel to Mr. Dulenay's farm that we had taken in Philippe's car in 1998. All went well until we got to the back roads past Picauville—which can better be described as *lanes* rather than *roads*. Twice during the last portion of our trip we met automobiles coming in the opposite direction, and it was necessary for the car to stop and back down the road it had just traveled, in one case quite a distance. Apparently this does not cause the consternation that it would in the United States; both drivers waved happily to us, and we waved back, as our journey continued.

We arrived at the farm at approximately 9:00 A.M. as the clouds became more threatening and a slight mist hung in the air. Mr. Dulenay and "The Captain" were waiting for us as we filed off the bus and began to gather around the plaque. We began our activities by presenting Mr. Dulenay with a framed picture of my uncle, along with the same words describing Joe that we had presented to Mr. Lebruman in 1998. In this case the picture showed my uncle standing next to the aircraft that had come down in the field next to the road on which we stood.

The next order of business was to complete Jesse Harrison's plan to dedicate the plaques to his colleagues from the 77th Squadron and the men of G/501. As I stood in front of the plaque, and began to speak to the group, I was surprised to see Philippe emerge from the rear of his car and come up next to me with a bouquet of flowers, in the middle of which was an American flag. He placed the bouquet beneath the plaque and then stepped to the side of the group. This was so typical of this wonderful guy! Denise and I had spoken the night before of finding flowers, but had not been able

Claude Dulenay with photograph of Joseph Sullivan.

to locate a floral shop in St. Mere-Eglise. That Philippe would think of the importance of the flowers, and go to the expense—complete with an American flag—was very touching to the entire group. I thanked Philippe for his wonderful gesture, and continued my remarks, briefly outlining the twenty years of research and events that had brought the fifteen individuals, French and American, to this small farm in Normandy on September 6, 2001.

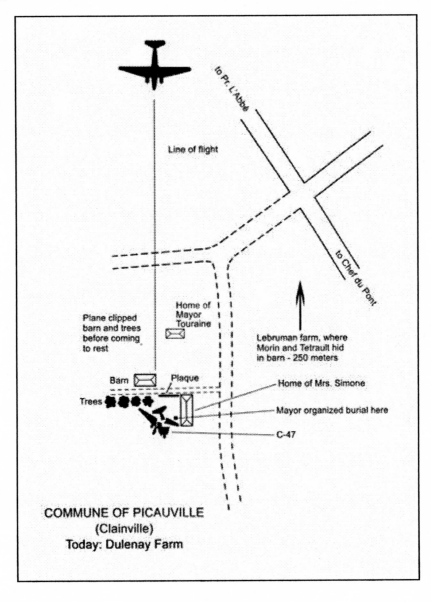

Plaque at the Dulenay farm. Flowers and American flag supplied by Philippe Nekrassoff. [M. Young]

We started our ceremony with Margaret reading aloud the words on the plaque. Her strong voice lost its rhythm only once, when she read the name of our uncle:

AT THIS LOCATION
NINETEEN AMERICAN SERVICEMEN
GAVE THEIR LIVES FOR FREEDOM
0120 hours   June 6, 1944

Air Crew: 77th Squadron
435th Troop Carrier Group

Captain John Schaefers	Pilot
2nd Lieutenant Thomas Ashworth	Co-Pilot
1st Lieutenant Joseph J. Sullivan	Navigator
T/Sgt Melvin Isserson	Engineer
S/Sgt David Mackenzie	Radio Operator

G Company
501st Parachute Infantry Regiment
101st Airborne Division
Sgt John A. Schadt
Cpl Eugene W. Morrison
Cpl William A. Sobieralski
Pfc Tony A. Burnett
Pfc Harry A. Brown
Pfc Anthony Salemi
Pfc Milo W. Ludy
Pvt Ollie W. DeHaven
Pvt James Reynolds
Pvt Michael A. Mastandria
Pvt Michael L. Pushcare
Pvt Corwin J. Randt
Pvt Erland W, Chellin
Pvt Felix J. Lopachin
SURVIVORS:
S/Sgt Charles F. Word
Pfc Lucien A. Tetrault
Pvt Arthur E. Morin

Next, Katherine spoke for our family, as she wanted to remember our grandmother on this occasion.

Katherine Smith - "Katherine Seelbach-Sullivan, I believe that you know your grandchildren, Margaret, Jerry and I, along with a wife and husbands, have come to this hallowed ground to pay tribute and bring some closure to the saga of your son Joseph, over whose disappearance and death you wept so many tears. This mission will hopefully bring some peace to the family. We pledge to keep Uncle Joe's memory alive through our children, grandchildren, nephews, and nieces. In Jesus' name we pray...Amen."

Next, Bud, our only D-Day veteran, spoke about how blessed he felt representing his comrades of the 77th Squadron, especially those who had wanted to make the trip and were unable to do so, and particularly his good friend Melvin Isserson from New York City, who had died at this site. He also explained to those present how the aircraft on which he had been flying could not have been more than a quarter of a mile to the east of the aircraft that crashed where we had gathered, but that with the timing, only seconds before the jump, and his responsibilities in releasing equipment bundles, he did not even realize that the 77th had lost two aircraft, and only found out about the losses when his aircraft returned to Welford Park.

When Bud finished, all of us could almost hear the endless stream of C-47's passing over the farm on that night, and imagine the horrendous sound of John Schaefers' plane as it came flaming out of the sky to tear off the top of the trees in the field and crash, inverted, only yards from the house in which Mrs. Simone and her family must have been stricken with fear.

I concluded our ceremony by reading the comments of several individuals who had very much wanted to participate in the events, but could not be there. First I read the words of Jesse Harrison:

"I wish to thank the people who live here and have so graciously permitted the installation of these plaques on their buildings. I am honored to have helped to make this day possible, just sorry that it has taken 57 years to honor our fallen comrades, my personal friends. These men gave their lives that we might live in peace; may we never forget their sacrifice. May God bless all who are here today and those who have made this day possible. Jesse Harrison, pilot, 77th Troop Carrier Squadron, June 6, 1944."

Next I read the words of Mark Zunk, an attorney from Indianapolis, Indiana, and the nephew of Private First Class Harry A. Brown, a twenty-one-year-old last-minute replacement in G/501:

"I recall my twenty-first birthday. I was in college and had midterm exams scheduled. Because of my studies I couldn't go celebrate in any of the ways brand new 21-year-olds do. Then I remembered my uncle, Harry Brown. When he turned 21 he was in a foreign land, training to go into battle and risk his life for his country. He never saw another birthday after that. I had the freedom and the opportunity to be a college kid because of the sacrifice of my Uncle Harry and a few million other guys just like him. I'll treasure that gift, and I'll make sure that a little boy, my son, who carries the name of his Uncle Harry, appreciates that gift as well."

Joe Flynn had written to me that he didn't want any formal words read on his behalf, but he would like to have it mentioned that he and Joe and John Schaefers had slept in adjoining bunks for many months at Welford Park, where he had grown to respect each of them as friends and fine officers. I mentioned that Joe's friendship to my uncle had been proved many times over as he corresponded with my grandmother after the war, and that when our paths had crossed he had gone out of his way to ensure that I could gather all the information possible on my uncle's last year of life.

Finally, I presented each member of our group with a clear plastic bag containing an individual metal relic that had been found on the crash site by a historian who had covered the site with a metal detector in the 1980's. The relics had been a gift to me from Mark Bando.

At this point the mist had stopped falling, and as a group, we walked into the field where the plane had actually crashed. When we started toward the gate leading into the field, I suddenly saw Michel standing in front of me. He was crying, and he told me that what we had just done had reminded him of being a young boy during the German occupation, and how it was the Americans who had returned France's freedom. We embraced, and walked into the field together as Mr. Dulenay opened the gate for us.

I walked with Michel into the field where my uncle had died and began to explain to the group, as Philippe had done for me three years earlier, what had happened in 1944. I pointed to the trees on the northeast side of the field and described how those trees were once again the height they had been fifty-seven years earlier, and that they had lost their top twenty feet when John Schaefers' plane had torn through them. The fence that separated the field in which the plane had crashed from the next field had been there in 1944 and remained in 1998. It was now

Dulenay Farm:
Picture taken from location of the main wreckage of the aircraft.
Margaret and Wilson Young are standing where the temporary graves
were located.

gone, and I showed them where copilot Thomas Ashworth's body had been found after being thrown from the wreckage. Finally I pointed out that the vegetable garden against the wall of the house was where Mayor Touraine and the local residents had buried the bodies that they had removed from the wreckage on June 7th, when the fire had finally burned out. These temporary graves did not, of course, include the remains of my uncle, which remained within the charred wreckage.

A short period of silence followed my description as each of us simultaneously began to process in our minds what had happened on this very spot, the lives that had been lost, and the sorrow that nineteen families had endured when the news had finally reached them of the loss of their loved one. I don't know who mentioned that we needed to record the presence of the group on this location, but literally every camera in the group was rotated amongst Philippe, Michel, and several others as various group photographs were taken in the center of the field. When the picture-

American visitors at the Dulenay farm, September 6, 2001.
L-R: Wilson and Margaret Young, Louise and Bud Busiere, John Menkt,
Denise and Jerry McLaughlin, Patti and Art Morin, Katherine and Ken Smith.

taking was completed we took turns profusely thanking Mr. Dulenay and finally boarded our bus to proceed to the Bisset's farm for the dedication of the second plaque.

On the ride between the two farms, someone on the bus asked if the rest of us had noticed Mr. Dulenay during the ceremony. Several of the group replied immediately, saying that his cheeks had been covered with tears as he held my uncle's picture while standing on the edge of our group during our ceremony. At that moment I felt considerable regret, as I realized that while he had shed tears along with the rest of us, he could not have understood a single word of what had been said, as no translation to French had been made.

Little did we know that while the first dedication had been emotional because of the family connection for the Sullivan and Morin descendants, the second dedication would affect all of us because of the reception we would receive from other guests we would meet on the Bisset farm. Our bus followed Philippe's car into the courtyard, where we were met by Regis and Patricia as well as fifteen neighbors who had been invited by the Bissets to take part in the plans they had for our visit. The guests included Patricia's mother and a group of men and women who had been children living in the general area of the house on June 6, 1944. All of these people had been invited to participate in the dedication of the plaque and to provide us with firsthand descriptions of what they had witnessed that night.

Michel introduced us to the group of French guests and then began to tell us the role that each of them had played in the story on June 6, 1944. Two of the women visitors had actually been asleep in what was now the Bisset's home but in 1944 had belonged to their parents. One of the men had been sleeping in an outbuilding adjacent to the courtyard. Two other men had lived on a nearby farm with their parents, and had—like Charles Lebruman—arrived at the farm to investigate the crash despite whatever dangers might have been involved.

The discussion that ensued had a measure of frustration to it in the challenge faced by Michel as the only truly bilingual person among the approximately thirty persons present. The story that evolved, as the speakers became more and more animated, was one of a night of considerable chaos, thundering noise and confusion, along with much suffering. The night had begun for these young people—all had apparently been teenagers or younger—with the sounds of aircraft overhead, not at all unusual at first. Then the noise of the aircraft had become more powerful than they had ever heard before, as the armada of troop carrier aircraft flying at very low altitude reached its zenith.

Next there had been activity from German anti-aircraft units and, finally, paratroopers from one of the serials preceding the 435th landed on or near the farm. One of the Frenchmen in the group showed us the location, only a few feet away from the plaque we were about to dedicate, where an American had used the wall at the entrance to the

The stone pillar (left of the fence) at the entrance to the Bisset farm that a 101st paratrooper used for cover in a firefight with German troops prior to the crash of Hamblin's aircraft.

136

farm's courtyard for cover as he engaged in a firefight with German soldiers. While the fighting was going on in and around the courtyard in which we now stood, the children, and several adults, were hiding in the farm buildings doing their best to avoid being injured by stray gunfire.

During what they thought was as chaotic a situation as possible, things got even worse when Jim Hamblin's C-47, engulfed in flame, came out of the sky, damaging the roof of the barn, and coming to rest in the apple orchard behind the house. Despite our inability to speak French, we were quite taken aback by the animation the story tellers exhibited as they agreed—and we heard from Michel's description—of the absolutely frightening sound the plane made as it fell from the sky and crashed just yards from the house.

The description that followed was even more chilling, as the group lost its animation and became quite somber. Michel translated the horror they still felt at remembering the agonizing screams they had heard from within the burning wreckage. They also told us that several hours later, when the

Michel Gaudry translating to the group the recounting of events that occurred on the Bisset farm June 6, 1944.

shooting had stopped and they began to move about the farm grounds, they had found parts of bodies surrounding the house and on the roof of the barn. Michel's description of this grisly scene was followed by a short silence until Margaret asked the woman who had been most vocal in her description,

"What did you think?" Michel translated her response: "Freedom! Freedom! Here comes freedom!"

At this point, the mist began to turn to raindrops, and we decided to start the dedication of the second plaque, the entire group exiting the barnyard and lining up on the road. I did not want to make the same mistake we had made with Mr. Dulenay and leave the French citizens wondering—or insulted—that we did not translate our remarks from English to French. We would have to use the now exhausted Michel to translate both my remarks and the written comments from the veterans who were unable to be present. Michel smiled, as always, and readily agreed to interpret for the benefit of the Bissets and their guests.

The local residents of Hamblin crash site describe events to their American visitors.

As he had at Mr. Dulenay's farm, Philippe placed a bouquet with an American flag beneath the plaque, which the Bissets had covered with a white shroud. I made comments similar to those I had made at the dedication of the first plaque and then explained, through Michel, that I would read comments from the pilot who had procured the plaques, and from two men who would have been names on the plaques but for random acts of selection that are so often the difference between life and death. Once again I read Jesse's comments thanking the Bissets for allowing the plaque to be placed on their wall. The script proved difficult for Michel to translate literally without written words, so I gave him the comments of Don Kane and Ray Geddes to read in his own words. He read, in French, to the group:

Don Kane - "After all these years a plaque marks the crash site that took the lives of the Third Squad, Third Platoon, G Company of the 501st Parachute Infantry Regiment on D-Day during the invasion of Normandy. Through a twist of fate, at the last moment, I was moved from this plane to another in the formation. As a result I am the only survivor. You who died at this site were as close to me as family. We were together through Toccoa, jump school, Tennessee maneuvers, and training in England. We slept in the same hut, went on pass together, got drunk together, and shared letters from home. I am old now, and don't travel well; but in my heart I am here with you, and rejoice that you are being properly remembered. I have often wondered what it would have been like had you all landed safely and we had fought together as a unit. For me it would have been a comfort to be in combat with those I knew and trusted at my side. Some will read this plaque and exclaim 'How sad;' for me it is more than that. I knew you."

Ray Geddes - "All the paratrooper names on the two plaques were Company G men, as was I. At least 22 of them I knew personally, most of them from Camp Toccoa, Georgia. One, John C. Berlin, was a tent-mate during the 1943 Tennessee maneuvers. If Berlin would have acceded to my request to switch the officers to which we were assigned (we were both radio operators), my name would be on the *Wall of the Missing* above Omaha Beach instead of his. These plaques are being dedicated through the efforts of many people. Some of us participants on D-Day 1944, both French civilians and U.S. soldiers, are still living. Future travelers and historians will now be able to pinpoint the area where World War II ended for two planeloads of young, healthy American men."

When Michel finished reading the veterans' comments, John Merkt stepped forward and read the words and names on the plaque:

AT THIS LOCATION
TWENTY-ONE AMERICAN SERVICEMEN
GAVE THEIR LIVES FOR FREEDOM

0120 hours   June 6, 1944

Air Crew: 77th Squadron
435th Troop Carrier Group

First Lieutenant James J. Hamblin	Pilot
Second Lieutenant Joseph P. Kowalski	Co-Pilot
Staff Sergeant Milton S. Jones	Engineer
Sergeant Clarence A. Reverski	Radio Operator

G Company
501st Parachute Infantry Regiment
101st Airborne Division

2nd Lt Everett G. Crouch
Sgt Matthew J. Yaquinto
Cpl James M. Young
Cpl Melvin D. Edwards
T/5 John C. Berlin
Pfc Frank N. Goodall
Pfc Charles L. Smith
Pfc Walter A. Simmons
Pvt Earl F. Williams
Pvt George N. Vathis
Pvt Edward Dziedzic
Pvt Leonard L. Brown
Pvt Donald M. Plourde
Pvt Edward L. Jones
Pvt Manuel R. Vasquez
Pvt Joseph C. Siriane
Pvt Jack Marlow

When John finished, Bud took his place on the road and stated (he had not mentioned this previously) that he had been the flight engineer that had accepted from the factory the airplane that crashed at this site, and that he had flown on that plane from the United States to England, and then through a year of training in England. A short time before D-Day his crew had been given another aircraft, which had caused him considerable annoyance as he considered that aircraft to be "his" airplane.

Art Morin asked to speak when Bud finished, and he asked Michel if he would translate some special thoughts that he had for the French men and women gathered with us. In a totally impromptu and moving speech, Art told the group that he was the son, and only child, of one of the American

After the dedication of the plaque on the Bisset farm, and impromptu remarks by Art Morin, the French and American groups mingled on the road, taking pictures and shaking hands.

paratroopers who had landed near this house on D-Day. He described how his father, a brave and injured 19-year-old American soldier, had been helped by a French family that night, and that had it not been for the courage that the French civilians had demonstrated by helping his father, he and his children might never have been born. There wasn't a dry eye among the thirty of us, French and American, when Art finished.

After Art's words there was a general mingling of our two groups and much picture-taking, with everyone taking turns standing next to the plaque. The group slowly moved back through the courtyard and, as had been the case at the Dulenay farm, to the location where the plane had come to rest:

in this instance, the apple orchard. Regis explained through Michel that the orchard had been allowed to deteriorate over the years, probably as a result of the fire from the plane crash. He was planting new trees and hoped to have the orchard flourishing again in several years.

Plaque at the Bisset farm, with flowers and flag provided by Philippe Nekrassoff.

As we talked, the Bisset chicken brood ran amongst us. Once again, as he had done in 1998, Philippe explained to the Americans the details he had learned of this crash site, and described how he had found several dog tags and other metal objects when he searched the grounds with a metal detector in the early 1990's. He also showed us a picture taken in 1947 of local residents standing before the wreckage. We then heard voices calling from the direction of the main building and were told by Regis that we were being summoned to lunch.

This was a surprise for us Americans, but obviously well anticipated by our new French friends, who more or less herded us toward the courtyard. We were ushered into a very large room in a building attached to the Bisset living quarters. A table ran the length of the room, where a large fireplace with a burning fire was a welcome source of warmth after the cold drizzle we had been standing in all morning.

Regis now formally took on the role of host and welcomed us to his and Patricia's home; he asked us to take seats at the table, on which were pitchers of sparkling apple cider, as well as orange juice and water. As we were getting seated, Patricia and her mother passed among us with platters of homemade bread and elaborately prepared hors d'oeuvres. This was only the beginning of the planned meal and festivities. We talked to each other, and attempted to speak to the French guests, one of whom passed around a picture of her sister in her wedding dress, made from the white silk of a paratrooper's reserve

Hamblin crash site, circa 1947.

parachute that had arrived in France on June 6, 1944.

Regis had disappeared, and now returned with bottles of wine in each hand, while Patricia and several helpers placed platters of beef and pork on the table, along with bowls of pasta salad and rice. The meal went on for more than half an hour when, once again, the Bissets reappeared in the doorway with cheese, more bread, and champagne. By this time we Americans were feeling overwhelmed by the hospitality, and somehow found we were conversing with our French counterparts despite the lack of a common language. The champagne inspired several toasts of a patriotic and international flavor, and then the final course was presented to the group by Patricia, with a special explanation. She had prepared a rice pudding, with the most important ingredient being milk obtained only a few hours earlier from a somewhat famous local cow by the name of *Margarite*. The now noisy crowd gave a cheer for Margarite, and the delicious rice pudding was consumed posthaste.

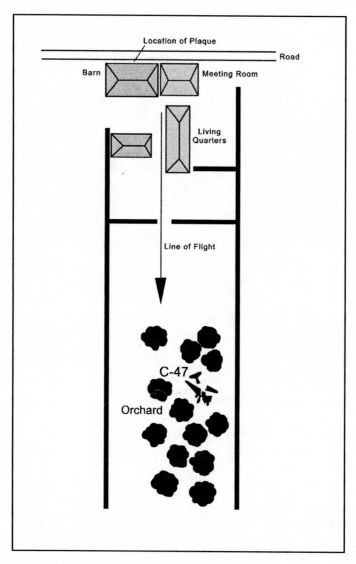

Commune of Picauville
(Founecrop)
Today: Bisset Farm

With the dessert we were served coffee in tiny, delicate cups.

As the dessert and coffee were finished, we felt that it was time to go; but Regis then entered the door from the house with a final liquid to be served. He carried a large crystal decanter with a narrow neck and a glass stopper. The locals immediately began to cheer, and Ken Smith (who had traveled previously in Normandy) said to me, "Oh, oh, it's calvados!" This local brand of homemade liquor is produced from apples and, as it turned out, would best be measured in octane rather than proof. There was a ritual for pouring the calvados through sugar cubes before consuming it that several in the crowd savored. Others of us simply reverted to the American tradition, and drank "shots" of the powerful liquor from our glasses. The large crowd quickly consumed what was in the bottle, and now it was *really* time to leave.

As we gathered in the courtyard, before getting on the bus, Michel asked us to take a moment so that he could explain to us some local Norman lore.

French and American guests at the Bisset farm.

He told us that while the people of Normandy are friendly to strangers, they tend to be cautious when welcoming guests into their homes. He said that when Normans truly welcome you to their home, the hospitality is unending. The Bissets and their neighbors and friends had certainly opened

145

their doors, literally and figuratively, to our group. Ken Smith wrote in his diary of the trip that night, "After fifty-seven years and many changes in their lives and governments, these people stood as a rock-solid simple testament to the true love and gratitude felt by just regular people for the extraordinary commitment taken by strangers on their behalf. Young men from a far away country, and another way of life, risked giving their lives for these French people. They had not been forgotten."

The final ten minutes in the Bisset courtyard were taken up with all of us Americans being taught the proper way to depart a French gathering of this sort by placing a kiss on both cheeks of those who were departing and remaining. Art Morin was making his second round of kissing the Bissets

L-R: Mrs. Lebruman, Art Morin, Jr., Charles Lebruman, Gilberte Richard.

and the French guests when Patti pulled him into the bus.

By any measure, we had experienced a full day. But more was to come. Michel and Philippe had arranged a visit to the Lebruman farm so that Art could meet the man who had hidden his father and Lucien Tetrault on the morning of June 6th.

We arrived at the farm, and on this occasion were met by Mrs. Lebruman, as well as her daughter Gilberte, whom we had met on our visit in 1998. It was clear as soon as Mr. Lebruman appeared that, as Mrs. Lebruman had informed us, the ravages of Alzheimer's had taken hold of this brave man. He had to be helped with each step, and his awareness of the situation would clearly come and go on a minute-by-minute basis. It was a sad sight. Art began to explain to Mr. Lebruman that he was the son of the man the family still referred to as *Arthur*, but had not seen since 1944. The impact of who Art was must have gotten through to Mr. Lebruman, because he suddenly began to cry and wipe the tears from his eyes.

Gilberte told us she believed that her father had made the connection with our earlier visit and the fact that Art was *Arthur's* son. Mr. and Mrs. Lebruman and Gilberte then led us back to the barn where Art Morin, Sr. had been hidden, and Art went through the door and up the ladder that his father had climbed as a young soldier fifty-seven years earlier. When he emerged his eyes were red.

There wasn't much that the rest of us could say. We walked back to the driveway of the Lebruman home, and there was much handshaking and "thank you" translations from the group, and a very tearful good-bye between Mr. Lebruman, Gilberte, and Art.

The bus returned us to St. Mere-Eglise, where it was an early night for everyone. Despite the full day, I lay awake. Finally I walked out to the patio in front of the hotel. As I tried to digest the events of the last twenty-four hours, I reflected on the comments that my cousin Katherine had made about our grandmother at the Dulaney farm, the hospitality of the Bissets, and of the moving visit to the Lebruman's home. Finally, I thought of the two plaques that would keep the memory of my uncle and thirty-nine others alive. It had been a good day!

The next morning we gathered in the front room of the *Hotel du 6 Juin*, and Sebastian served us his special breakfast of juice, hot chocolate, and French bread. The first item on our list of stops that day would be the main reason that John Merkt had made the trip with us. We would visit the site where Captain Seymour Malakoff's aircraft from the 75th Squadron of the 435th TCG had crashed, with the loss of his entire crew, including radio operator S/Sgt Robert Walsh, John's uncle.

Michel had arrived at his usual early hour, followed by the bus at 8:30

A.M. We immediately boarded and set off for the Malakoff crash site. Under Michel's direction we pulled to the side of a road that was much different from the two locations we had visited the day before. There were no houses to be seen in either direction, and the only way to enter the field in which Captain Malakoff's plane had crashed was to climb through a narrow barbed-wire fence. Eventually we got the entire crowd through the opening and Philippe again explained the circumstances of the crash. Philippe seemed ill at ease and was constantly looking around the field as he talked. Finally, his smile returned and he called a welcome to a man walking across the field. Philippe introduced

Robert "Donald" Walsh, radio operator 75th TCS. KIA, June 6, 1944. Uncle of John Merkt.

This photograph of the wreck of Captain Malakoff's aircraft was taken circa June 8 by Lt James Haslam, the assistant regimental S-3 for the 501st. Haslam had jumped with a Pathfinder group, been captured on June 7th, and managed to escape. He had picked up a German camera during his adventures, with which he took several pictures at the crash site as he searched for the 501 headquarters location. [Mark Bando]

the man as William Herbert. [39]

William had lived in the area his entire life, and as a young boy had visited the crash site during D-Day afternoon and had taken several souvenirs from the wreckage. He told us that he was honored to meet a family member of one of the men from the plane, and he presented John with a radio microphone that he had kept for fifty-seven years, obviously a prized possession. John, completely taken aback, told Wiliam that his uncle had been the radio operator on the aircraft. The microphone in John's hand might well have been the one his uncle had used on a daily basis. Michel pointed to heaven and exclaimed, "Mon Dieu!" As William continued his story, he pointed out that the actual depression in the ground caused by the plane was still very much evident, indicating that the plane must have come down in a nearly vertical attitude to cause such a gaping hole in the earth.

It was clear that John needed some private time on the site. We left him standing near the depression in the ground and walked back to the narrow entrance we had used to enter the field. As we climbed through the wire, we met Madame Clence Frigot. She told us that her late husband had inherited the surrounding fields from his father, and that he also had visited the site of the crash on several occasions in the aftermath of D-Day. John had returned by that time, and

John Merkt (R) and William Herbert.

he also spent time with Madame Frigot, learning more details of the crash as she had heard them from her husband. While John was saying his good-bye to William and Madame Frigot, Ken remarked to me that although only forty-two of the troop carrier planes that had flown over France on D-Day had been lost, there were obviously hundreds of stories attached to the loss of each plane that did not return. Very true words.

Michel had a full day planned for us after the visit to the Malakoff crash site. We drove through Carentan and stopped where a roadside marker indicated the 101st had fought a battle that became known in local folklore, as the "Cabbage Patch" battle.

Bud Busiere wearing his 'mission hat' in 1944

Bud Busiere, wearing his "mission hat" at the bridge where it is believed Luther Knowlton met a 4th Division tank coming from Utah Beach. Knowlton had Bud's hat with him at that historic meeting.

We continued on, eventually arriving on the road that Don Kane, Ray Geddes, and G Company had been walking down on the way to Pouppeville when they met the German patrol coming out of the town. Michel had the bus stop at the building that had been German headquarters in the town—where Ray Geddes had tested the German rifle on the ironwork—and then proceeded on past the town where a small, but to us, important event was noted. We stopped at what we believed to be the bridge where Lieutenant Luther Knowlton and Sergeant Gerald Ficociallo had met the Fourth Division tank advancing from Utah Beach. At this point Bud stepped from the bus and placed on his head the top hat that he had loaned to Knowlton before he jumped in Normandy. We took Bud's picture standing on the road, the hat having returned to the location of the linkup fifty-seven years after D-Day.

Leaving Pouppeville, the bus took us to the American Cemetery at Omaha Beach. Returning after three years gave Denise and me an even more solemn perspective on what this small piece of United States territory means to so many American families as we thought of the final scene in the movie "Saving Private Ryan," which was filmed in the cemetery. Once again we walked through this beautiful and haunting memorial. As in 1998, the cemetery had many visitors.

This time we decided to walk down to the beach on the long stairway to the dunes below. It is quite a feeling to stand on what was the landing site that became known as "Bloody Omaha" and look up the bluffs above the beach. We stood there with the wind blowing and small children squealing as they played in the sand on this chilly but sunny day. It was difficult to believe that so many had died exactly where we stood as the situation had deteriorated and General Bradley had considered pulling the troops off of this beach in what would have been a major Allied reversal on D-Day. American bravery by, in the words of Steven Ambrose, the American high school classes of 1942 and 1943, had carried the day, and the U.S. Army had advanced over the bluffs and into the Norman countryside.

We walked back up to the cemetery, where we visited the graves of the men from my uncle's crew, and I took a picture of Everett Crouch's grave for Don Kane. As we walked toward our bus, one of the group pointed out that there was music playing, and we all paused to listen. We had not heard the music on our last visit, nor before we went to the beach; but, surely, you could hear the strains of the "Washington Post March." Ken said that earlier he had heard "God Bless America." It certainly was a poignant moment.

Joe Sullivan's family on Omaha Beach.
L-R: Denise and Jerry McLaughlin, Wilson and Margaret Young,
Katherine and Ken Smith.

When we returned to the bus, Michel was about to tell us of the next stops he had planned, but I interrupted him and took several minutes to thank him for all he had done and present him with two books on the subject of D-Day that I knew he had wanted but had been unable to obtain. I also gave him the 77th Troop Carrier Squadron hat that Joe Flynn had given me in 1998. Michel was most happy with his gifts, and the trip continued as he directed the bus down the coast. We stopped at the Utah Beach memorial where, in 1998, Bill Phillips had shown us the road on which he walked off the beach. We then proceeded on to Pointe du Hoc, and finally to the Airborne Museum in St. Mere-Eglise. Thus ended another long and interesting day.

That night as the group sat at dinner, we concluded that there was one more requirement to accomplish before we left. We would have to make a personal and special "thank you" to the Bissets for all they had done for us at their home. After we finished dinner we returned to the hotel and I had everyone sign another copy of Mark Bando's book, as we had done for Philippe two days earlier. We also marked the pages that referenced the crash of Jim Hamblin's plane in the Bisset orchard.

A final visit with the Bissets. L-R: Author, Art Morin,
Patricia and Regis Bisset, John Merkt, Ken Smith.

As the only car that we had available belonged to Philippe, we could not all pay a visit to the Bissets (probably for the best—thirteen unexpected visitors might be too much even for Regis and Patricia). The team we sent consisted of Ken Smith, Philippe, Art Morin, John Merkt, and myself. We did surprise the Bissets, and explained that we wanted to thank them one final time, and present them with the book, which all eleven visitors had signed. They were most happy with the book, calling for another round of pictures, followed inevitably by the requirement of toasts—for which Regis brought out his calvados. We escaped the Bisset home after almost an hour of visiting and returned to the *Hotel du 6 Juin*, once again, a tired and fulfilled group.

Our final day in France began early, as we gathered for the last time in Sebastian's "living room" with the usual juice, bread, and cocoa while we waited for our bus to arrive. We said our good-byes to our host, and then departed for the Carentan Station, followed by Philippe and Michel in their cars.

Carentan, September 8, 2001.
L-R: Michel Gaudry, author, Philippe Nekrassoff.
(Michel is wearing his 77th TCS hat.)

From Carentan we began our trip to Paris, where the group split up for the last time, some remaining in Paris to tour the city, Katherine and Ken to visit several other locations.

Denise and I left that afternoon to visit friends in Dublin. I told her about the two previous occasions when I had left a group of people connected with the story of my uncle and wondered if the odyssey was over. This time, I told my wife, the story was truly finished.

An Author's Musings

But was the story finished?

After we put up the plaques in 2001, the story of the men from the 77th Troop Carrier Squadron and G/501 continued to unfold. Ray Geddes put me in touch with Art Couchman, the nephew of medic Eddie Hohl, and I learned of Laurence Legere's efforts over the years to find the family of the man who had given his life to save Legere. Art told me how Eddie's sister had had a vision similar to my grandmother's on the same day, June 6, 1944—the day her brother and my uncle had died. Ray also introduced me to Cliff Marks, son of Lieutenant Nathan Marks, who was killed at Pouppeville, and Cliff shared material from his father's letters to his mother during the months spent at Camp Mackall and in England.

Perhaps the biggest news that emerged was the June 6, 2003, award of the Distinguished Flying Cross (DFC) to Jesse Harrison for his courageous and amazing flying and on-the-mark navigation in the early morning hours of June 6, 1944. This series of events began when Jesse had arranged for Henry Osmer to meet him and Ray Geddes at the 2002 reunion of the 501st PIR in Florida. During that reunion Osmer mentioned to the group that Jesse had received the DFC for his efforts on D-Day. Later, in private, Jesse corrected his ex-squadron commander, telling him that it was another pilot from the 77th, Captain Theron Anglemyer, who had received the DFC that night in Normandy; Jesse had been decorated in Holland the following September. Osmer was taken aback—sure that he had recommended Jesse for the decoration after hearing what Jesse had done during the mission debriefing. When he returned home, Hank Osmer began making telephone calls; and on June 6, 2003, Jesse received his Distinguished Flying Cross from Congressman John B. Larson in his local town hall in Rock Hill, Connecticut: fifty-nine years after he earned it.

As I began to assemble this book, I was contacted by members of other families that had suffered a personal loss when the plane carrying my uncle to his death came to rest on Mrs. Simone's farm. Earlier, I had heard from Mark Zunk, the nephew of Pfc Harry Brown. Next, the niece of John Schaefers contacted me, as did Brian Williamson, vice president of the Museum of the Soldier in Portland, Indiana. Brian was representing the family of Pfc Milo Ludy, a Toccoa man and Colonel Ewell's jeep driver.

Ludy's widow had presented some of Milo's letters and uniforms to the museum.

T/4 Edwin Hohl
(KIA June 6, 1944).
[Arthur Couchman]

Pfc. Milo Ludy
(KIA June 6, 1944).
Courtesy of the family of Milo Ludy
and the
Museum of the Soldier
Portland, IN

The names from the plaque in Clainville were now becoming real people to me. I learned that John Schaefers was an artist as well as a pilot, and that Milo Ludy wanted the war to end as quickly as possible so that he and his wife could start a family. Harry Brown had been an All-City football player at George Washington High School in Indianapolis, class of 1941, and while home on leave after the Tennessee Maneuvers in 1943 was mistaken for being in the "Canadian Army" because of the unique airborne uniform. Harry celebrated his twenty-first birthday while at Lambourne, but he never got to vote or realize his dream of playing college football.

Forty-three men had left England on the two planes that were lost to the 77th Squadron in Normandy. Three survived the night, and, in fact, the entire war. Forty men died. Forty families of men from the 77th or G/501 were notified within the next several weeks that their loved ones were missing or killed. My uncle, Charles Breen, had taken his family, including daughters

Katherine (age 6) and Margaret (7 months), to visit his mother-in-law the day that the Sullivan family received word that Joe was missing in action. Charles recorded the arrival of the news in his family memoirs:

"Katherine and the kids and I were visiting Mamma [Joe's mother] on Sunday. We were getting ready to leave when the doorbell rang. Vin [Joe'e brother] went to the door and didn't come back for a little while. When he did, his face was pale as he said, "Mamma, there's someone who says he has to see you." She went to the door and came back holding a telegram in her hand, her face distorted with shock and grief. She kept saying softly, over and over, 'No...No.' We tried to comfort her and were able to take the telegram from her grasp. It said that Joe was missing in action on D-Day. We tried to encourage her by saying he probably was missing in the confusion of the day and would turn up safely. But she must have had an inner sense of knowing. I have never before seen, and hope never again to see, someone in such a complete state of shock."

Art Couchman wrote to me of how the Hohl family received the news of the medic's death. Eddie's niece Lois was at home with Eddie's mother when it happened: "It was a couple of days after D-Day. Lois saw a car pull up and two soldiers (I assume they were officers) came to the door. Lois started screaming, and the rest was all downhill."

The families of John Schaefers, Milo Ludy, Harry Brown, and the thirty-five other families no doubt had suffered notifications equally as shocking. Everyone in the United States in 1944 who had a relative in harm's way must have lived with the fear of an impersonal telegram or a car with military officials arriving at their doorstep.

As Ken Smith said to me at the Malakoff crash site, the story for each family involved in this small piece of history is minuscule in the epoch of World War II, but enormous to the individual families involved.

Thus, the story of my uncle, and his comrades, ends at this point. Those who survived faced eleven more months of war. How did the survivors fare as the war progressed, and afterwards? The next two chapters recount perils, victories, and losses experienced by the men of the 77th Troop Carrier Squadron and G Company, 501st Parachute Infantry Regiment.

There is also an appendix that includes additional material pertinent to the story. And finally, there is an update on what happened to each man after he returned from the most traumatic years of his life. To a man, these veterans have led a long and fruitful existence since WWII. Their memories of those years have provided us with the story of this small piece of history, in which each of them played a part.

CHAPTER 8
The 77th Squadron
After D-Day

"Ours was a family affair, and remains so today."

Phillip C. "Pappy" Rawlins,
Red Light, Green Light, Geronimo,
A History of the 77th Troop Carrier Squadron in WWII.

Jerome J. McLaughlin

After the parachute drop on the night of June 5–6, the 77th Squadron prepared for its second D-Day mission: towing 82nd Airborne Division gliders to Normandy on the evening of June 6. The squadron again sent twelve aircraft and an equal number of gliders off the runway at Welford Park. Colonel Osmer remained behind for this mission, which was led by Pappy Rawlins. Eight 77th crews who had not flown the parachute drop the night before were assigned to the glider tow. The four remaining slots in the twelve-ship formation were filled by Pappy Rawlins and the three flight leaders who had survived the parachute mission: Captains Mueller, Kelly, and Coffey. Mission scheduling called for the 77th aircraft, leading the 435th, to leave Welford Park at 9:45 P.M. and to arrive over the Landing Zone (LZ) at dusk. Almost from the beginning, problems occurred. First, Frank Coffey's tow line parted, and he and his glider returned to Welford Park as the other aircraft departed for France. Next, Lieutenant Ortho Lusk returned to Welford with an engine problem. His glider also landed safely at Welford. [Both gliders were successfully delivered to Normandy by Coffey and Lusk on June 7 attached to a serial flown by the 437th TCG.]

The remaining 77th tow planes and gliders, along with the rest of the 435th Group, continued on a direct route to Normandy that would take only half the flight time of the more complex route flown by the parachute mission the previous night.

Pappy Rawlins described the approach to France in his history of the squadron, "As we approached the continent we knew what Sir Francis Scott Key meant by "bombs bursting in air." With the immediate arrival of darkness, all the shell-fire aimed at us, which was considerable, was magnified. It appeared that the entire coast of France was opening up at us. Although the fireball was frightening, the 40mm flak was inaccurate."

As the 435th approached the Landing Zone the EUREKA-REBECCA equipment indicated that the LZ had been changed by pathfinders on the ground from south of St. Mere-Eglise to northwest of the town. The entire serial changed course and the gliders were released into the new LZ, an area about which none of the glider pilots had been briefed. Just as the gliders were being released, the squadron was hit by an intense barrage of accurate antiaircraft fire. Although eight 77th planes were hit, all were able to remain in the air. The glider crews were not so fortunate. Despite the plan for day-light glider landings, the motorless pilots found that there was, in fact, no daylight left to help them land in an unknown landing zone. The lead glider, piloted by the 77th Glider Operations Officer, Lieutenant Joseph Herriage, ran into a stone wall that was hidden by darkness in the field that he had quickly selected for his landing. Herriage, his co-pilot F/O Howard Davis, and all the glider infantry soldiers aboard their Horsa glider were killed. [Davis survived for several days in a field hospital before he succumbed to his injuries.]

Operational flying to France was placed on hold after the D-Day glider mission until June 25th, when secure landing strips were established on the continent. During the June 7–25 period the 77th performed training to flight-check new power crews and glider pilots who had arrived just prior to D-Day. On June 25th Colonel Osmer led five 77th aircraft to France on the first of what would be hundreds of resupply flights to the continent.

Flights to and from France continued until July 18, when Colonel McNees took the 75th, 76th, and 78th Squadrons of the 435th to Italy for the airborne invasion of southern France. Colonel Osmer remained at Welford with the 77th and several squadrons from other groups to form a provisional group that continued flights to France and began rehearsals for a proposed airborne drop outside of Paris, code-named Operation TRANS-FIGURE. On August 18 Osmer received the operational order to prepare to implement TRANSFIGURE the following day. Once again the entire night before the mission was spent preparing aircraft and men for

Henry Osmer after landing the first 77th aircraft in France on June 25, 1944. The planes quickly had their cargo unloaded and were reconfigured to carry wounded back to Welford Park.

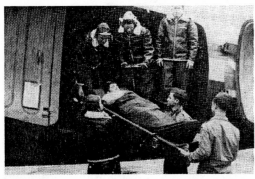

Wounded GI's being taken from a 77th plane at Welford Park.

the drop, only to have the mission canceled when it was learned that U.S. ground forces had advanced to the area of the drop and the mission was scrubbed.

Colonel McNees and the rest of the 435th returned to Welford on August 24 from the successful "Champagne Campaign," as the operation for the drop in southern France was nicknamed, and Osmer's provisional group was disbanded. McNees was happy to be told by Osmer that the previous day (August 23) the 435th had been honored with an Air Medal for their performance on D-Day. The six months of training that the group had so diligently performed between January and June 1944 had paid off!

Flights to the continent with ammunition, gasoline (in five-gallon cans), and other much needed supplies continued, interspersed with training flights for paratroop and glider operations, as did the medical flights bringing wounded back from France.

435 TCG men loading 5-gal. gasoline cans into a C-47.

On September 1, 1944, another airborne operation order was received; and again it was canceled the next day, when General Patton advanced so quickly that he overran the drop zone of what was to have been called Operation LINNET. This was followed by another preparation and stand-down on September 11–12. Finally, on September 14, the fourth order since Normandy for a parachute drop operation was received; this operation, code-named MARKET-GARDEN, was to become the 435th's third combat operation. It was documented in later years by Cornelius Ryan's book and the movie entitled *A Bridge Too Far*. The 77th Squadron flew combat missions on four consecutive days for MARKET-GARDEN, September 17–20, 1944.

On September 17, the 77th TCS sent eighteen aircraft on a five-hour round-trip to Eindhoven, Holland. All of the aircraft returned safely to Welford Park despite twelve of the eighteen being damaged by antiaircraft fire. They dropped a total of 283 paratroopers from the 502nd PIR in Drop Zone C, located northwest of Eindhoven. The squadron history notes that one paratrooper refused to jump and "was brought home and turned over to the Airborne Liaison Officer."

There was a very tense moment for the squadron as they approached Drop Zone C. Suddenly a large mass of C-47's from the 436th Troop Carrier Group cut across the path of the 77th as the 436th aircraft attempted to correct a navigational error and move to Drop Zone B. Colonel Osmer was able to avoid the crossing aircraft by leading the 77th in a climb to approximately 1,000 feet just as the 77th reached the drop zone. As a result of the life-saving climb, the 502nd troopers jumped at an excessive height, but without problem, since there was no enemy activity in the drop zone area.

The second mission to Holland, on September 18, 1944, transported fifty-four glider infantrymen from the 327th GIR and eighteen tons of their equipment on sixteen gliders. Eight aircraft were damaged by antiaircraft fire on this mission, but there were no 77th casualties.

On September 19 the luck of the 77th turned sour. As depicted previously, Jesse Harrison and his crew had to parachute to safety from their burning aircraft as the 77th carried sixteen gliders from various 101st artillery units to Landing Zone W.[40] Two 77th glider pilots, Flight Officers Lawrence Kuhole and F. M. Mason, were cited for distinguished flying by landing their damaged gliders after they had been wounded on the approach to the LZ. Another 77th glider pilot was missing in action after the mission, but later returned to duty. Lieutenant Dave Mueller lost an engine to ground fire after he released his glider and had to make an emergency landing near Ghent, Belgium. He and his crew were amazed at the number of damaged C-47's on the field when they landed, and the equally large number that followed them to the emergency field. So many aircraft ended up at Ghent on the 19th that it took days for parts to be sent from England and the planes to be repaired. Mueller's crew chief, Sergeant Arland Murphy, finally took parts off several other planes, and the crew was able to return to Welford Park on September 21.

The 77th's final mission to Holland, on September 20, was a resupply flight in which no gliders were used, and equipment bundles were pushed from the cabin doors of the C-47's.

After MARKET-GARDEN, the 77th continued to send ten to fifteen aircraft per day to France on resupply and medical missions. While Jesse Harrison was in Southampton being treated for his burns, another tragic event hit the 77th. The aircraft that Jesse had flown across the Atlantic and on the Normandy mission, the *Urgin Virgin*, was lost in a crash that claimed four more 77th airmen. The Virgin was lost on October 17, 1944, when nine aircraft flew a resupply mission to France under the command of Captain John Kelly, and returned without the usual cargo of wounded aboard. They were returning to England when they received word that the weather at Welford Park was quickly deteriorating. Kelly felt that they could reach the base before conditions closed the field, and he brought the formation down to minimum altitude and in a single line so that the planes flew one behind the other in a "trail" formation. Soon conditions worsened, and Kelly ordered the pilots to reverse their course and attempt to return to France.

Lieutenant Joe Flynn, flying at an altitude of less than 100 feet, came upon a British fighter base and quickly swung his plane in for a landing. He ordered his radio operator to send out a constant signal for the other planes to use in locating the field; his actions enabled two additional planes to land at the British field.

Other planes from the formation elected to climb above the clouds; this group eventually landed as far away as Ireland and Scotland. Still others had luck similar to that of Flynn, and flying at treetop level, were able to find airfields in England.

Lieutenant Andrew Jordan, flying the *Urgin Virgin*, ran out of luck. He elected to remain below the clouds and flew into the side of a hill, killing all on board, including Charles Darby and a last-minute addition to the crew,

Corporal David McMahan, who had replaced Crew Chief Emilio Giacomin in order to make the minimum number of hours required to get his flight pay for the month of September.

During October and November 1944, the 77th functioned more or less as an airline, transporting supplies and wounded back and forth across the English Channel on a regular basis. The event of note was the assignment of the 77th's original commander, Colonel Osmer, to become Executive Officer of the 435th TCG, and the elevation of Operations Officer Major Phillip "Pappy" Rawlins to the 77th Squadron Commander job. The Squadron also began practicing operations with the European Theater's newest airborne unit, the 17th Airborne Division.

The 435th Officers Club bar, where Abe Friedman told the author that his birth had been celebrated in 1944 by Joe Sullivan's buying multiple rounds of drinks.

December 1944 was a difficult month for the 77th. The weather was terrible, allowing only 104 round-trip flights to the continent. On the days when flying was possible, the crews and aircraft that did not fly to the continent began practicing "double tows," wherein each C-47 pulled two gliders. This would be the method used to land glider infantry in the upcoming Operation VARSITY with the 17th Airborne Division.

During the week before Christmas 1944, the 435th once again had three squadrons on a special mission; and, again, the 77th remained at Welford Park. The men knew of the problems ensuing from the German Ardennes offensive and sat at Welford, grounded by weather. On December 23 the weather cleared over Belgium, and the first combat supply mission in support of the 101st Airborne Division at Bastogne was mounted. The 77th was the only 435th squadron at Welford Park, and Pappy Rawlins had seventeen aircraft from the 77th ready to fly the emergency mission.

He managed to find three additional aircraft and crews and personally led the twenty aircraft on the resupply flight. They left Welford at 12:50 P.M., carrying twenty-three tons of ammunition and food. The drop occurred at exactly 3:45 P.M., and the squadron returned from the five-hour mission at 5:55 P.M. Six aircraft sustained damage from antiaircraft fire, but were repaired overnight and ready to go the next morning.

The next day, December 24, Colonel Osmer returned to Welford Park with the remainder of the 435th group and led the entire group on another resupply mission. The 77th successfully dropped nine tons of ammunition and gasoline, with slight damage to eight aircraft by antiaircraft fire.

The 77th returned from the Christmas Eve mission to immediately re-pair and re-load the aircraft for an anticipated Christmas Day drop. Dense fog, however, covered the Welford area during the night. The squadron diary reports the fog was so thick that men who attended midnight Mass had trouble finding their way back to the barracks. Even worse, a thin coat of ice covered the entire area. These conditions canceled all flying activity, and the men of the 77th spent Christmas Day on the base, where there was considerable talk about the men of the 101st, with whom they had worked so often in the past, and the terrible situation in which the 101st was "celebrating" Christmas.

The weather improved on 26 December, and the 77th flew fourteen aircraft to Bastogne in a fifty-six-plane 435th serial, dropping seventeen tons of artillery shells, ammunition, and gasoline. Once again, they paid a deadly price for their efforts. The Germans had brought additional antiair-craft resources to bear, and ten of the 77th aircraft on the mission were hit by antiaircraft fire. The copilot of one plane, Lieutenant Charles R. Trout, was severely wounded in the arm; his pilot, Lieutenant Harry H. Clausen, had to make a harrowing solo landing at an advanced airstrip in France to get medical aid for Trout while the crew chief and radio operator worked to keep him from bleeding to death.

The next day Clausen attempted to fly the damaged aircraft back to Welford Park without a copilot or navigator. He and the remainder of the crew were killed when he became lost and crashed into the English Channel. [41]

The 77th TCS's C-109 on its hardstand at Welford Park. The C-109's were B-24 bombers reconfigured as fuel tankers to deliver gasoline to Gen. Patton's Third Army. According to Joe Flynn, one of the few troop carrier pilots with heavy bomber flying experience, all of the C-109's assigned to the 435th TCG were wrecked by C-47 pilots who lacked experience in such large aircraft.

On December 27, the 77th flew their final mission to Bastogne, arriving at the same time as General Patton's advanced elements entered the 101st perimeter, thus ending the siege. Ten planes from the 77th dropped sixteen tons of supplies in perfect flying conditions and safely returned to Welford Park with only one plane receiving minor damage.

January 1945 marked the squadron's fourteenth month overseas. The men remembered the terrible flying conditions in which they had arrived, and saw even worse weather conditions than in December 1944, severely limiting both training for the upcoming Operation VARSITY and transport flights to the continent.

On January 17, 1945, an awards ceremony for the entire 53rd Troop Carrier Wing took place at Welford Park. Four officers from the 77th received awards, including Jesse Harrison, who received the Silver Star for his actions on September 19. His copilot, Philip Sebeck, was awarded the Distinguished Flying Cross, as were Flight Officers Kuhale and Mason.

Henry Osmer sent a command car to Southampton to bring Jesse Harrison to the ceremony. A reception was held at the Officer's Club, and when Jesse was unable to feed himself because of his heavily bandaged hands, the Deputy Group Commander demonstrated his strong feelings for "his boys" of the 77th by personally feeding Jesse his meal.

January was the last full month that the squadron spent in England, as it had been decided that the troop carrier groups needed to be closer to the fighting to reduce the length of their missions.

On February 13, one year to the week after their arrival at Welford Park, advanced elements of the 77th left the station in trucks and jeeps bound for Bretigny Airfield, twenty miles south of Paris, France. While the four squadrons had been quartered together at Welford Park, in permanent structures and a common mess area, the move to Bretigny meant being spread around the new airfield and, for the enlisted men, living in "field" conditions; e.g., in tents, while the officers were quartered in requisitioned chateaus. There was a common mess tent for 77th personnel, including officers and enlisted men. The one benefit to this change was that Pappy Rawlins approved the hiring of French cooks, who, all agreed, significantly improved the 77th's meals.

The weather in France was far superior to that in England, and more cargo flights to advanced supply depots were scheduled, as well as additional training with the double tow gliders and the 17th Airborne Division. Still more flying was done back to Welford Park, where lumber was put on C-47's and gliders and flown to Bretigny to build frames and floors for the enlisted men's tents.

With the 435th TCS settled in France and the weather improving, the troop carrier war effort reached its WWII zenith. The new technique of using a double tow also required a large increase in the number of glider pilots assigned to each squadron, for which many stateside power pilots became involuntary recruits levied from training commands.

Operation VARSITY, the final and largest Allied airborne assault of World War II, took place in an assault across the Rhine River on March 24, 1945. The 77th Squadron put eighteen C-47's and thirty-six gliders into the air, carrying 17th Airborne Division troopers from the 194th Glider

Infantry Regiment. Their destination was Landing Zone S near Wesel, Germany. Casualties were high for the seventy-two glider pilots of the 77th Squadron; eight were killed and four wounded seriously enough to require hospitalization. Two 77th aircraft made emergency landings at forward fields because of flak damage. Both returned to Bretigny the next day. The VARSITY mission also put the 77th Squadron in the history books when the glider pilots from the 77th became famous as infantrymen in the "Battle of Burp Gun Corner."

Gene Fosburg (right) with his friend, Ed Clark, and a member of the Women's Army Corps at the Bretigny railroad station in early 1945.

Pappy Rawlins [from his unpublished history of the 77th Troop Carrier Squadron] - "The work of the glider pilots did not end with their landing on enemy soil after crossing the Rhine. Apropos of their previous training, when the 77th glider pilots landed in LZ *S*, they became a glider pilot infantry platoon of the 435th Glider Pilot Company [each squadron in the 435th mounting one platoon], with a definite tactical mission. This was the first time in military history that an all-officer infantry company was formed...they were supplied with weapons by the 17th Airborne Division, and assigned to hold a cross-roads. As the platoon of 77th glider pilots set up their defensive positions at the designated intersection, they were accompanied by an Associated Press reporter by the name of Howard Cowan. In the engagement that followed, named "Burp Gun Corner" by Cowan, a company of German infantry, supported by armor, launched a night attack against the intersection and were repulsed by the intrepid pilots with help from the heavy weapons platoon of the 194th GIR. One of the attacking

German tanks was put out of action by a pilot firing a bazooka for the first time in his life. The next day, as the pilots marched back across the Rhine, they asked that Cowan refer to them in his story with a new designation they had made for themselves, the *77th Glider and Anti-Tank Squadron.*"

Operation VARSITY was the last combat action of the war for the 77th Squadron. They continued to fly supplies to the advancing armies crossing Germany during April, and on May 7, 1945, the war in Europe ended with the German surrender. There was considerable flying during the next month to transport prisoners of war back to France and displaced persons closer to their homes in eastern Europe. On June 23 orders arrived sending the 77th back to the United States, to Hunter Field, near Savannah, Georgia. As was the case on the trip to Europe, the air echelon would fly via the southern route, and the ground echelon would travel by ship—the U.S. Army Troop Transport *Edmund B. Alexander*, out of LeHarve, France. The squadron was scheduled to reassemble at Baer Field, Ft. Wayne, Indiana, on or about August 15, 1945, to be re-equipped with C-46 aircraft and redeployed to the Pacific for the invasion of Japan.

The plans for the 77th Squadron to deploy to Japan never came to fruition, as V-J Day and the end of World War II occurred on August 15. As fast as the men of the 77th returned from their leave to Baer Field, they were offered immediate discharge from the service. Others were able to obtain discharges from local bases near their homes, and never returned from their leave. Because of these events, after their takeoff from Bretigny on June 27, 1945, the 77th Troop Carrier Squadron never again appeared as a single unit. [42]

Where They Were When the War Ended

Bud Busiere - "I was at Orley Field in Paris when the war ended in Europe. We had flown some big shots, who had something to do with the peace negotiations, to SHAEF Headquarters, which was located nearby. When the news was announced, a P-47 (fighter) Group put on a show, buzzing the field; it was tremendously exciting."

Joe Flynn - "On May 7, 1944, I had flown deep across Germany, to Czechoslovakia, with a cargo of fuel and ammunition. On the return trip, somewhere in eastern France, I heard on the Armed Forces Radio that the Germans had surrendered. We were bringing back American airmen who had been in German prison camps and had been liberated by our advancing armies. This trip they were mostly B-24 crewmen, and I remember that one, a navigator, was sitting in front with me, in the right seat, when we heard the surrender news. He immediately, with great pleasure, passed on the news to all the passengers."

Jesse Harrison - "Sheila and I had been married for about five weeks. We were traveling west on Route 40 on our way to Jefferson Barracks, in my home town of St. Louis. When the news broke we were in Columbus, Ohio. Everyone was in the streets celebrating; it was impossible to walk, much less drive, so we pulled into a motel, registered, and then joined the party. We were treated like royalty by all the folks in Columbus that day. I called ahead and told them I would be late in reporting. When they said there was not a problem with my arriving late, we stayed an extra day in Columbus."

Paul Krause - "I certainly do remember the day the Germans surrendered. We almost got shot down! Our crew was flying home after dark when we saw the lights of Paris for the first time: the blackout was over. We flew toward the city to get a first-hand view of the celebration, and as we got close we saw tracers all over the sky. Everyone with a gun was shooting into the sky just like they do in Texas on New Year's Eve. Mueller quickly turned away, and we headed back to Bretigny."

Pappy Rawlins - "When the VE-Day announcement was made I had flown a resupply flight to Germany and was returning with emaciated survivors from a concentration camp. That evening, with Joe Flynn flying copilot, I took our C-109 (a B-24 converted for use as a gasoline tanker) and flew over Paris. We flew lower than usual and between a "V" of search lights at the Arc de Triomphe. It was a sight to behold!"

George Winard - "I was in Paris on a three-day pass on VE Day. It was an unforgetable sight to watch the euphoria and unrestrained joy of all the people of the city. There were GI's and servicemen from all around the world in Paris at that time. At first I watched all of them celebrate from an outdoor cafe on the Champs de Elysee. Later I participated."

The officers of the 77th lead aircraft for the dropping G/501 on D-Day. L-R: Navigator Abe Friedman, Squadron commander (pilot) Henry Osmer , and co-pilot Robert Clark. Photo taken at the 40th D-Day anniversary celebration and reunion of the 77th TCS. (Friedman)

CHAPTER 9
G/501 After D-Day

"I'm not a hero,
but I certainly am a survivor.
I did what I had to do."

Don Kane, 1999

After jumping from the planes of the 77th squadron on D-Day morning, the men of G Company were to endure thirty-five days in Normandy that would reduce their ranks by more than eighty percent. They would begin a story of sacrifice, loss, and, finally, victory that would last for eleven months.

According to George Koskimaki, General Taylor's radio operator, the Division command element and the 3rd Battalion of the 501st began to assemble almost immediately after the drop. Koskimaki believes that two hours after the jump, at 3:30 A.M., General Taylor had forty-five of his staff and approximately an equal number of 3rd Battalion infantrymen in his group. More than likely, most of the infantry came from G Company.

The first combat for the G Company troopers was on the outskirts of the village of Pouppeville, on the morning of June 6 as depicted in Chapter 6.

Site of G/501 first action on 6 June. Captain Kraeger, Virgil Danforth, and Don Kane were on the right side of road. The Germans approached the turn on the left, the same side as Ray Geddes and medic Eddy Hohl.

Paratroopers, drawn by the sound of the roadside firefight during which Major Legere was wounded and Medic Eddy Hohl killed, increased the size of the attacking force as they moved toward Pouppeville. It had reached 150 men by the time that the actual attack on the town commenced. During the thirty-minute fight to secure the town, G Company endured more casualties, including the deaths of Lieutenant Nathan Marks, Private James Hubbard, and several other enlisted men. The German commander of the Pouppeville garrison formally surrendered to the Americans at 12:30 P.M. General Taylor's goal of linking up with the 4th Division succeeded at approximately 2:00 P.M., as Lieutenant Luthur Knowlton and his platoon sergeant, Gerald Ficociallo, met a 4th Infantry Division unit consisting of several tanks and accompanying infantrymen from the 8th Infantry Regiment coming off of Utah Beach. [43]

*Ray and Shirley Geddes standing on the road leading to
Pouppeville, on which Ray had engaged in his first firefight
on June 6, 1944. Laurence Legere was wounded, and medic
Eddy Hohl killed in the road at the bottom of the picture.*

The Fourth Division passed through Pouppeville as the men of G
Company continued to "clean up" the town, searching for additional
Germans who might have been hiding, collecting weapons, and
turning prisoners over to the divisional provost marshal. Many of the
G Company men were disappointed in the caliber of the German soldiers
that they fought in Pouppeville, most of whom were not even German, but
conscripts from countries occupied by the Nazis. It would not be long until
the men of G Company would meet first-line German soldiers—in the form
of their counterparts—German paratroopers of the Sixth Fallschirmjager
(Airborne) Regiment.

After the fighting was finished in Pouppeville, General Taylor moved
on to set up the divisional headquarters in the town of Hiesville. The 3rd
Battalion followed later in the afternoon. It was a sleepless night for the
men of G Company. While their first day of combat had exhausted them,
few could sleep; instead, they pondered what peril might occur if they did
not remain awake.

German Headquarters in Pouppeville in 1944, center of the battle for the town. German prisoners were placed in the barn behind the automobile. Lt. Marks and other U.S. KIA's were buried on the left where the hedge stands today.

The 3rd Battalion was held in division reserve on June 7. During that day many of the G Company men remember a change of attitude on their part toward their comrades in the glider regiments as they witnessed the chaotic arrival of several glider serials, and the fatal results of many of the "landings." They also saw the results of other tragic glider crashes from serials that had arrived on June 6th. The casualties for glider soldiers during landings among the hedgerows caused G Company men to conclude that, compared to glider riding, parachuting was the less dangerous way to enter combat.

Many of the men also noticed, for the first time, the glider pilots. They remember that some of the glider pilots seemed to be "lost souls" after they landed, while others joined in the combat action with the airborne soldiers. Most of the pilots eventually followed the instructions that they had been given before departure; e.g., locate the Divisional Headquarters in order to obtain transportation to England. When the pilots did reach Headquarters, most were not released but were pressed into service guarding prisoners or assisting medical personnel.

On the morning of June 8th, the 3rd Battalion was released for combat. G Company ate their breakfast of C-rations as they prepared to attack the town of St. Come-du-Mont. The attack was to be preceded at 4:45 A.M. by an artillery barrage, which the men remember as only "three or four rounds followed by the order to advance." The 3rd Battalion of the 501st had been

Ray Geddes and his family at location where he was wounded on June 8, 1944, at "Dead Man's Corner."

attached to the 506th PIR for this engagement. Lieutenant Colonel Ewell was assigned to lead the attack on the town from the south. As he had only 160 men, less than two full companies, a battalion of glider infantrymen was also placed under his command. G Company was on the left of the 3rd Battalion line with the glidermen to their left.

Almost immediately the Company began taking casualties, the most significant of which was Captain Kraeger, who received his second wound of the campaign. He was wounded in the arm, seriously enough that he had to leave the Company, reluctantly, for medical assistance. He was evacuated and did not rejoin the Company until they returned to England. Lieutenant

Barker, who had been jumpmaster on Jesse Harrison's aircraft, took over the Company. Sergeant William Burns was killed when he was shot through the head while leading his men in the attack.

The fight for St. Come-du-Mont lasted most of the day as the Germans made a determined effort to hold the town by dedicating the reenforced 1058th Infantry Regiment to its defense. Six German counterattacks were launched from the town during the course of the day in an effort to stop the 101st advance, each attack being stronger than the last. Ray Geddes, who had been drafted to operate Lieutenant Colonel Ewell's radio, was wounded in the eye by shrapnel during this period while working with Ewell to call in artillery on one of the German attacks. [44]

Late in the afternoon, Ewell rose another notch in the eyes of his men by personally leading a hastily assembled group of 3rd Battalion troopers in a classic infantry charge into the flank of the final German attack of the day. Ewell's heroic efforts ended the German counterof-fensive to defend the town; and the area in which the fighting occurred, later known as "Dead Man's Corner," was secured. The 506th broke into St. Come-du-Mont from the north, and the Germans withdrew across the Douve River to fight another day.

Entrance to German aid station at Dead Man's Corner, where Ray Geddes was first treated, by a medical team of German paratroopers.

On June 9 G Company and the rest of the 3rd Battalion were moved to Vierville, where the entire 501st was finally reconstituted as a regiment. They remained in divisional reserve on June 10 and 11. On June 12 they led the attack on the town of Carentan. Casualties were high as they advanced over a narrow footbridge and engaged in house-to-house fighting within the city itself. When the fighting for Carentan was finally done, G Company and the entire 501st were ordered to dig in along the south side of the city, along with the 506th, to repel an expected German counterattack. What the men mostly remember of their time in these defensive positions is an artillery barrage launched by the Germans. Many G Company veterans who served with the Company throughout the entire war still remember that barrage as the worst they would ever endure, to include the hell of Bastogne the following December. Several German attempts were made to recapture Carentan, the most significant of which was made on June 13, by the 17th SS Panzer-Genadier Division. It was successfully repulsed in the 501st area with timely help from tanks of the Second Armored Division.

The battle for Carentan was the last major engagement for G Company in Normandy. After more than a week in their defensive positions at Carentan they were moved several times into non-combat areas, including Cherbourg, until they were evacuated over Utah Beach on July 10. Of the 119 enlisted men and eight officers who jumped on June 6, only twenty-four were present to walk off the beach, Lieutenant Knowlton and twenty-three NCOs and enlisted men. Twenty-six of those not with the Company had been wounded. Several, such as Captain Kraeger, Art Morin, and Lew Tetrault, would return to the Company in England. Ray Geddes and many others had such debilitating wounds that their service with the 501st was ended. The most tragic statistic was that sixty-nine of the 127 men who left Welford Park on the night of June 5th—fifty-four percent of the company—had been killed in action, and thirty-one of the sixty-nine had been killed before they could even leave their aircraft. G Company had been in Normandy for forty-two days and had suffered eighty-five percent casualties. When the Company left their positions to be relieved by arriving infantry, Jack Urbank turned over an area that he had been defending with only seven men to an entire platoon of replacements.

The trip back to England took place on a Navy LST. The troops arrived in Southampton in the dark and were greeted by a new weapon that could reach them even across the English Channel. A V-1 terror weapon, the first crude unmanned missile developed by the Germans, crossed the path of the LST. The men remember it today as sounding like an outboard motor. Suddenly the motor stopped, and shortly afterwards a tremendous explosion was heard. From the Southampton docks the Company was put on a train with the other survivors of the 3rd Battalion. Later they transferred to trucks and returned to Lambourne.

Don Kane remembers that when G Company was dropped off in their company area, the men started to realize how few of them had survived. During the time in France, with all the confusion of the jump, combat, and men going on different assignments, there had been less than full realization of the level of losses the Company had suffered. Kane started to enter his squad's barracks and stopped at the door. He realized for the first time that he was the only survivor, the rest of the squad having been killed with the loss of Lieutenant Hamblin's plane. He walked to the company orderly room and asked to be reassigned; he would not stay in those barracks alone.

Shortly after the return to Lambourne, the veterans of Normandy were given a one-week leave in Edinburgh, Scotland. Transportation was supplied by a local troop carrier squadron. (There is no record showing whether the aircraft were from Welford Park and the 435th.) The G Company survivors filled only two planes, as compared with the seven aircraft necessary to hold all of the men on the trip to Normandy.

The most vivid memory of the trip for many of the men is the "chicken" contests played by the pilots on the way to Scotland as they competed against each other to see how low they could get over the ocean. Spray flew from the propellers of both planes as they got within several feet of the waves; then the pilots challenged each other on how close they could come to mountain tops. G Company arrived safely in Edinburgh despite the antics of the C-47 pilots, and enjoyed a week of drinking and the pursuit of local women. The men found the Scottish barrooms more like American taverns than the sedate British pubs, and they enjoyed the noise and boisterous behavior of their Scottish hosts.

When the survivors returned to Lambourne, they learned that replacements had arrived from the United States to fill the empty bunks of the men lost in Normandy. Most of the new men had left New York on the Queen Mary the day after the Company had jumped into Normandy. Leadership changed as many of the veterans were promoted to Corporal or Sergeant and new officers arrived. Luther Knowlton remained a platoon leader, and both Captain Kraeger and Lieutenant Norman Barker returned to the Company from the hospital. Lieutenant Kenneth Holmes, a combat veteran of Normandy, was transferred from I Company to replace Lieutenant Marks.

A boxing tournament was held on July 21, at which Jack Urbank noticed Jesse Harrison sitting with a group of fellow officers from the 77th Squadron. The men talked briefly, glad to see that both had survived Normandy; but it was not possible for them to have the indepth conversation both would have liked.

The company left Lambourne during late July, when Colonel Johnson was able to obtain space and tents to assemble the entire regiment at his headquarters location at Hampstead-Marshall. Daily arduous training began again, and lasted into September. Finally the Company was up to full strength and ready for another mission.

There were several false alarms. On August 31 the Company was actually assembled for a mission, only to have it canceled. Finally, on September 16, Captain Kraeger told the men to get ready for what would become their second combat jump. This mission would last for seventy-two days and be the most frustrating of the war for the men of G Company, because of its length, the conditions under which it was fought, and the loss of the two men they had most depended upon for leadership since the company's inception: Colonel Howard Johnson and Captain Vernon Kraeger.

The 501st assignment was to jump near Eerde, Holland, in support of General Bernard Montgomery's attempt to rush through Holland and invade Germany from the north in the operation code-named MARKET-GARDEN. The newly formed British and American First Allied Airborne Army, including the American 82nd and 101st Divisions, the British First Airborne Division, and the Polish Parachute Brigade, would lead the operation. The airborne forces were to hold the road through German-held territory in Holland, between Einhoven and Arnhem, while Montgomery drove his Second Army, led by the XXXth Corps, through the airborne-held "carpet" to Arnhem and then into Germany itself.

On their second combat operation, G Company did not fly with their long-time colleagues from the 435th TCG, but with another group located at Chilbolton. On a perfect autumn day, the flight from England took several hours. At Drop Zone A, Captain Kraeger and the men of G Company landed with the rest of the 2nd and 3rd Battalions of the 501st near the town of Eerde.

Since the confusion of the night jumps in Sicily in 1943, and Normandy the previous summer, airborne doctrine had been changed. The MARKET-GARDEN jump was conducted in daylight rather than as a night operation. Daylight airborne operations had been tested in southern France, after Normandy, and remained in effect for the rest of the war. Many of the men described the jump in Holland as a classic, almost parade-ground, deployment. G Company landed on soft, plowed farmland and assembled within forty-five minutes. Several men, including Don Kane, reported that children were in the DZs helping them collapse their parachutes as if the landing were part of a game. While many of the troop carrier squadrons transporting the 101st on 16 September suffered losses from antiaircraft fire, the 3rd Battalion had no repeat of Normandy; not a man was lost to antiaircraft fire prior to the jump. [45]

G Company assembled with the rest of the 3rd Battalion on the edge of the DZ and marched through the town of Eerde, remembered by the men as immaculate and filled with cheering residents. Several miles south of Eerde the battalion took up position to deny the highway between Eerde and St. Oedenrode to the Germans as Montgomery's forces supposedly would advance north to Arnhem. Because the entire 101st was stretched so thin over their section of "Hell's Highway," the next several days were filled with all the Division's regiments being maneuvered by General Taylor both to stop German attempts to cut the highway and preemptive strikes to stop the Germans from launching attacks. On September 19th the entire 3rd Battalion was moved back into Eerde. They maintained a defensive line around the town for the next three days, until September 21.

It was during the occupation of Eerde that G company received perhaps its greatest blow of the war. Captain Vernon Kraeger, the man who had led the Company since Toccoa, was killed in an almost casual manner by a stray piece of shrapnel. Jack Urbank remembers the day very well; it was his 22nd birthday. Urbank was particularly close to his captain, a man who was a decade his senior and a professional soldier. According to Urbank, during the afternoon of September 21 there were random exchanges of artillery and mortar fire between the Germans and G Company. One shell landed near Kraeger and several other men, including Kraeger's runner, Warren Purcell, and the Company communications sergeant, Don Castona. The only man hit was Kraeger, who received what appeared to be a minor head wound. A medic inspected the injury, told the Captain that it was only a scratch, and applied a Band-Aid. Several minutes later Kraeger collapsed. The men rushed him to a nearby aid station, where they were told that he was dead.

The effect on the Company was profound. Kraeger was the only company commander for whom most of them had ever served. He was aggressive, courageous, and a true leader. The Company could not imagine another man leading them in combat. None of the surviving members of the Company remember who assumed command immediately upon Kraeger's death. (The long-time executive officer, Lieutenant Norman Barker, had previously been evacuated with a leg wound.) Eventually, another 3rd Battalion officer, Lieutenant George Stanley from H Company, replaced Kraeger. Stanley was an excellent officer with a good combat record. He quickly gained the respect of the men in the Company, and led them until the end of the war.[46]

On the night of Captain Kraeger's death, the 3rd Battalion was part of a quickly planned attack on the town of Schijndel, located to the west of Eerde. The attack was launched at 11:30 P.M., with G Company following behind H and I Companies as the battalion assaulted the town moving west from Eerde while the 1st Battalion approached from the north. The purpose of the operation was to disrupt German preparations for an attack against Eerde and the highway. The Germans holding Schijndel employed a rapid-fire antiaircraft weapon on the road that 3rd Battalion was using to enter the town, forcing them into the ditches on the side of the road.

Despite the Germans' superior firepower, and a small force of their infantry that somehow got behind G Company, the two 501 battalions seized Schijndel before dawn.[47] Once again, Julian Ewell endeared himself to the men of his battalion, as he participated in the house-to-house fighting in the town alongside the men of G company, using only his sidearm as a weapon.

G Company lost several men, killed and wounded, to sniper fire in Schijndel, and in action with the Germans attacking from the Company's rear. Finally, with the arrival of daylight, word came for the battalion to return to their original positions in Eerde. No explanation for seizing and then abandoning Schijndel was ever passed down the chain of command to the men; and as the battalion withdrew to Eerde the men of G Company, still stunned by the loss of Captain Kraeger, were bitter over the additional sacrifice and effort that had gone—so far as they knew—for naught.

(Tactically, the action had accomplished its mission. German offensive preparations had been disrupted, and many prisoners and much equipment had been seized. Colonel Johnson had apparently planned on holding the town, but ordered the withdrawal of the battalion to its original positions only after attacks against the 2nd Battalion required that he consolidate his defenses around Eerde to protect the main highway.)

The Germans did not give up after the night battle at Schijndel. A major attack took place, on September 24, when they reassembled their forces and attempted to take Eerde by attacking across a railroad line to the north of the town. The area of the attack has become known as the "Sand Dunes." This action was particularly difficult, and G Company was nearly overrun by German armor when they were sent to reinforce the 1st Battalion troops defending that area. When the fighting was over and the Germans had withdrawn, more than 100 enemy weapons were collected from the German dead in front of the line that G Company had defended, some as close as twenty-five yards from the front of the company's positions. [48]

After the intense fighting on September 24, G Company and the entire 501st remained in more or less static conditions around the town of Veghel, to the north of Eerde. The situation was almost a repeat of Normandy, where the men had been told they would be pulled out of the lines and replaced by infantry after the initial combat had been completed. Instead, the arrival of British armor and artillery units to provide support usually attached to standard (non-airborne) infantry units boded poorly for a pullout back to England.

On October 2nd the 501st was relieved by the 327th GIR, and marched to Veghel, where they received a hot meal followed by most welcome hot showers. Then they were given the bad news. They would not be going back to England to prepare for another mission; they were to ride trucks to the north, toward Nijmegan, in an area between the Rhine and Waal Rivers, where they would dig in and support the British XXXth Corps. They arrived at their destination on October 4. The area was, and still is, referred to by the men of the 101st as "The Island" due to its location between the two rivers. Here the men dug what eventually became elaborate underground bunkers and lived miserably for the next two months under the command of General Montgomery. They ate British food, smoked British cigarettes, and cursed the weather and wet ground.

The area occupied by G Company was behind a mud flat that kept the Rhine River and the Germans several hundred yards away. The 501st was located between the other two parachute regiments of the division, with the 506th to the left and the 502nd on the right. Frequent patrolling and artillery exchanges were the main forms of combat between the two sides. The mud flat in front of G Company contained a nearly destroyed brick factory that was used as a listening post at night to provide warning of any night attack or German patrols. The nightly trips to the brick factory, the highly stressful hours spent in total darkness and silence, and then the dangerous return trip prior to sunrise each morning were not popular with the men.

The Company had been on The Island for only four days when they received their second major blow of the campaign in regard to the loss of a leader. On October 8, only two weeks after the loss of Captain Kraeger, they lost their colorful regimental commander, Howard "Jumpy" Johnson, to the same fate—a stray artillery round. His last words, as he was being administered to by the 501st medical staff, were, "Take care of my boys." Perhaps because of their physical location near the regimental headquarters, G Company provided most of the men for the honor guard at Johnson's funeral. Don Kane and Jack Urbank were among the squad who fired tracer rounds into the sky as Johnson was laid to rest in a temporary grave near his headquarters. General Taylor replaced Johnson as regimental commander with Julian Ewell, the 28-year-old commander of the 3rd Battalion. Major George Griswald, from Ewell's staff, moved up to command the battalion.

The miserable living conditions, constant patrolling, and occasional firefights with German patrols went on for almost two months. Finally, Montgomery released the division from his command; and on November 25, after seventy-one days in Holland, the 101st left The Island and turned their positions over to Canadian troops. Prior to leaving, Ewell held a memorial service for his predecessor and the 679 other 101st Airborne Division troopers who had died in Holland.

As the men of G Company left The Island in a truck convoy, they passed through the first town they had seen in Holland, Eerde. They recalled how clean and tidy the town had been when they had first entered it. As the company left Holland, the town was a shambles. After surviving four years of WWII without damage, it had taken "liberation" to bring ruin to the town's inhabitants.

Along with the rest of the division, G Company was trucked from Holland to Camp Mourmelon le Grand, near Reims, France. What had seemed a lifetime of events to the Company had taken place in only six months, since June of the same year. Worn uniforms were turned in to the Quartermaster, and weapons were turned in to the armorers for reconditioning and cleaning. The men were issued passes, in small groups, to Reims and to Paris, eighty miles to the south. They learned to drink French 75's, a mix of champagne and cognac. There was considerable talk among the men as to how long they would be out of combat and what the next mission would entail. The Toccoa men, veterans of both the Normandy and Holland campaigns, hoped that with the arrival of the newly activated 17th Airborne Division from Ft. Bragg the 101st would have a good rest before returning to combat. All of this conjecture ended with the unexpected German attack in Belgium on December 16. G Company was awakened at 3:00 A.M. on the morning of December 18 by the Company Charge of Quarters, Don Castona, and told they were returning to combat. The men were incredulous. They were told to pack any belongings they would be leaving behind, to obtain their weapons and what ammunition was available from the armorers, and to stand by to move out to meet a powerful German attack in the Ardennes area of Belgium.

The Company's third and most arduous campaign was about to begin. Laurence Critchell would later write, "What had been learned in Normandy and put to work in Holland had fused the organization into a single weapon of war. With Bastogne, the regiment came of age." [49]

G Company had always prided itself on how well prepared it was when entering combat, each trooper having been thoroughly briefed on the mission and fully equipped to do the job. This campaign began with one in ten men not even carrying a weapon as they boarded open tractor-trailer trucks that would carry them to the fighting. Most of the men did not have winter clothing. They had no idea what was going on in Belgium. Some veterans were on leave and would not return to fill out the Company rolls until several days later. Many of those who were present were replacements who had never seen combat. Everyone knew that General Taylor was in the United States and that the Division Artillery Commander, Brigadier General Anthony McAuliffe, was the Acting Division Commander. In the vernacular of the day, the men mumbled, "SNAFU!!"

The 501st was the first regiment of the division to board the Air Corps trucks that took the division to Belgium. They left Mourmelon at 2:00 P.M. on December 18 for the 130-mile trip. The men had no idea where they were going, only that there had been a German breakthrough and they were headed toward the sound of the guns. The truck column carrying the division eventually extended for ten miles, with the 327th GIR riding the final vehicles. The convoy carried the men for more than eight hours, through the cold winter day and into the night. At 10:30 P.M. the trucks stopped and the men were told to dismount and dig in for the night.

Before dawn on the morning of the 19th, G Company was formed up with the rest of the battalion and began to march toward the town of Bastogne. The men were amazed at the numbers of U.S. soldiers and equipment they met *going in the opposite direction.* They could not believe that they were advancing to combat with the Germans while thousands of other American soldiers were, at the same time, retreating on the same road. What is more, the men who were retreating wore full winter field gear and carried weapons. Hundreds of trucks and armored vehicles were also part of the retreat. Today they remember that many of their comrades who had arrived in Belgium without weapons or winter uniforms attempted to obtain them from the retreating soldiers. Few were successful.

G Company marched into Bastogne and found that the entire division had been assigned sectors, by regiment, to defend the town in a 360-degree circle—an ominous foreboding of what was to come. The 501st, being in the forefront, was deployed northeast of the town, where the most imminent German threat appeared. Eventually the 506th was placed on the 501st left flank, with a railroad line dividing their areas of responsibility. The 327th took over the territory on the 501st's right flank.

Colonel Ewell deployed his 1st and 2nd Battalions to the northernmost and central sections of his assigned area of the defensive perimeter. The 3rd Battalion including G Company was delayed by the massive traffic jam of retreating forces going south through Bastogne. When Griswald finally moved his battalion through the town, Ewell placed the troops in the southernmost portion of the 501st defensive perimeter, specifically into the area around the two tiny hamlets of Mont and Neffe. When G Company passed through Mont they heard German armor in the woods ahead of them and dug in to withstand an expected attack. Shelling from German guns inside of Neffe began almost immediately. Lieutenant Stanley had his men dig in around Mont and sent a patrol led by Second Lieutenant James McKearny and Sergeant Don Castona into Neffe in order to ascertain German strength. McKearny and Castona returned with their men under cover of darkness with the news that the Germans held the town in strength. The 3rd Battalion dug in and waited for sunrise.

December 20th was a calm day in front of G Company as the men improved their defensive positions and kept careful watch on the fields that separated them from the Germans in Neffe. The quiet, however, ended during the early evening, when the famed Panzer Lehr Division launched a combined infantry and armor attack against the entire 3rd Battalion line. The artillery fire preceding the attack was so intense that all the telephone lines from the Battalion to Regimental Headquarters were cut. The infantry attack was well conducted, and was almost successful in several areas.

The men of G Company killed and wounded hundreds of German soldiers of the 901st Panzergrenadier Regiment as they crossed the fields between Neffe and Mont and tried to climb fences that separated the pastures. American tank destroyers supporting the battalion were able to successfully neutralize the German armor supporting the attack from nearby woods. Before the attacked ended, at 11:00 P.M., Griswald had to commit all of his reserves as the Germans pressed their attack to split the American lines. The line held.

All day on December 21, the men of G Company stared out across the fields in front of them and looked at the hundreds of German corpses hanging on the fences. The 901st Panzergrenadiers had been eliminated as a functioning unit, and there was no further German activity in front of the battalion that day. It was also on the 21st that the men of G Company began to hear the noise of combat from various areas on the compass. By the morning of the 22nd they were sure they were surrounded.

During the next seven days the Germans would continue to attempt to locate a weak spot in General McAuliffe's defense around Bastogne. Each time the Germans would try a new area to test the glidermen and paratroopers of the 101st and their new-found friends from the 10th Armored Division. Each time the Americans successfully repelled the attacks.

December 22nd turned out to be one of the most famous days in 101st Airborne history. It was on this date that the Germans sent a small party of men, under a flag of truce, through the lines of the 327th GIR with a demand for the Division's surrender, to which General McAuliffe uttered his now famous one-word reply, "NUTS!" During this period, with the exception of the four-hour truce called by the Germans on the 22nd, the 3rd Battalion was kept on the alert by various German probes attempting to find a weak spot in the American lines.

The morning of December 23rd changed the world for the 22,000 Americans surrounded at Bastogne. The sun came out, and with the sun came the overwhelming might of American air superiority. For the defenders of Bastogne the return of the Air Corps meant two things: suppression of German movement, particularly armor, and the arrival of supplies via air drops from the same troop carrier units that carried the 101st into combat in Normandy and Holland. The first aircraft to appear over Bastogne were P-47 fighter/bombers that mercilessly attacked the German forces surrounding the town. Many times the airmen simply followed tracks left in the snow to find German tanks and destroy them where they hid in wooded areas. The first C-47's appeared on the scene at mid-morning, dropping pathfinder units. Later, at 11:50 A.M., the first resupply flight arrived, dropping 144 tons of food, medical supplies, and ammunition. Each regiment was ordered to send vehicles to the drop area to bring supplies up to the front lines.

While morale soared, stomachs were filled, and guns and cannon loaded with fresh ammunition, the situation in Bastogne remained serious. The Germans still surrounded the town. However, the arrival of air support, and the strong northern drive of George Patton's Third Army, ensured that the German situation would soon change. G Company saw little of the previously aggressive Germans after December 23rd. On Christmas Eve, and early Christmas morning, the Division was on the receiving end of enemy bombing attacks. The two bombing attacks were made on the town of Bastogne itself, and even several miles away in Mont the men of G Company were amazed at the concussion caused by bombs as compared with that caused by artillery.

Finally, on December 26th, the American 4th Armored and 83rd Infantry Divisions entered Bastogne from the south, and the siege was lifted.

The arrival of fresh troops and armor led the men of G Company to believe that the worst was over, and that they would return to Mourmelon while the newly arrived infantry would take the fight to the Germans. Unfortunately, that was not to be the case.

Although the 327th GIR and the 502nd PIR had taken severe casualties while defending against strong German attacks on the west and north sides of Bastogne, the 501st had endured comparatively few casualties during the siege. However, the list of killed and wounded in the entire battalion would soar during the American offensive that followed the relief of Bastogne.

The lifting of the seige signified that the Americans would go onto the offensive. The most serious action for G Company was an attack against heavily-dug-in Germans in a forest known as *Bois Jacques*. The 2nd and 3rd Battalions of the 501st, along with elements of the 506, attacked into the forest on January 3. Casualties were heavy for the 3rd Battalion, which attacked across a 500-yard front. The men fought an epic battle the entire day, and finally had to withdraw to their original positions due to the intense German shelling and the lack of armor support on the 501st's right flank. Several more days of fighting were required to finally capture the *Bois Jacques*.

On January 9th the 501st remained in the forefront of the American advance, and was attacking the town of Recogne, when they suffered another significant loss of leadership. Julian Ewell was riding to the front in his jeep when he was wounded, along with his driver and bodyguard, by German artillery. The two enlisted men managed to get Ewell to an aid station, from which he was evacuated with a serious shrapnel wound. He was replaced by his executive officer, Robert Ballard. The attack on Recogne stalled late in the day, and that night severe shelling by the Germans caused more than 150 casualties in the 3rd Battalion alone.

Finally, after a month of combat, the 101st was relieved. On January 21, the men again mounted open trucks. They hoped that they were returning to Mourmelon, but that was not to be. They traveled instead for two days until they reached the Alsace-Lorraine area between Germany and France, which was considered a very low-key, but still front-line, area. The Division remained in Alsace-Lorraine for more than a month, and finally returned to Mourmelon, where they were awarded a Presidential Unit Citation for

Bastogne—the first time that coveted award had ever been given to an entire division.

For the first time since returning from Normandy, the men of G Company had an extended rest from combat. Leave was granted, and with large amounts of back pay in their pockets the men traveled to Paris, London, and the Riviera. After several weeks of this wonderful activity, the 501st was separated from the rest of the Division. The men would remain on "standby" in Mourmelon while the other three regiments were transported to the Rhur region of Germany, where it was feared that a "Redoubt" of hard-core Nazis was preparing to make a last stand. The 501st had a different mission. They were to stand by and jump on prisoner-of-war or concentration camps if the approach of the Allied armies might lead the Germans to begin the massacre of prisoners. Fortunately there was no cause to use the 501st, and the war in Europe ended on May 7, 1945.

After V-E Day the entire 101st was sent to occupy the area of Hitler's Bavarian retreat, Berchtesgaden. It was a time of rest and reward for the men of G Company. The 501st traveled from Mourmelon to Berchtesgaden by truck, along the famous German Autobahn. On one occasion the trucks stopped and the men investigated an area cut out of the adjacent woods. They

G-501 marching on V-E Day.

found a camouflaged aircraft storage area, with strange aircraft that had no propellers parked under the trees. Later they learned that the aircraft were Messerschmidt 262's, the world's first jet fighters. The Germans had been so desperate to hide from the prowling Allied air forces that they had been forced to keep the planes under cover in the woods and use the Autobahn as a makeshift runway. When G Company arrived at Berchtesgaden they were housed in modern military barracks that until recently had held the SS troops who had protected Hitler's home.

They found superb horses in a nearby military cavalry stable. G Company began to ride the horses instead of using vehicles on daily road patrols—a decision that separated the country boys from the city slickers in the company. Many of the men visited Hitler's mansion and had their pictures taken standing in what had been the Fuhrer's picture window, looking out across the Alps. There were not many Toccoa men left in the Company by this time—perhaps fifteen—and these few truly knew what sacrifice had been made in the journey from Georgia, in 1943, to Berchtesgaden in 1945. None of them could have imagined themselves posing in Hitler's living room only thirty-two months after beginning basic training.

A point system was instituted at the end of the war to determine who among the several million Americans in Europe would go home first. With the August surrender of the Japanese, the system went into full speed. Toccoa men such as Jack Urbank, Art Morin, Don Castona, Warren Purcell, Wilber Ingalls, Fred Orlowsky, and Don Kane more than met the requirement for release from the service based on length of service, overseas time, combat duty, and decorations. As the points were tallied, all of these men left the Company, one at a time. Most of the men arrived in their hometowns in December 1945, exactly three years after most of them had volunteered for airborne service when they joined the Army. As with their comrades in the 77th TCS, the end of service for the veterans of G Company, 501st Parachute Infantry Regiment was not done formally; and in many cases there was not even time for good-byes. Paraphrasing a famous general of WWII, these soldiers just seemed to fade away.

On August 20, 1945, the 501st Parachute Infantry Regiment was disbanded. [50]

Where They Were When the War Ended

Don Castona - "Sometime around VE-Day I was in Paris on leave. It was raining and we went into a bar to get out of the rain. There was quite a party going on when we got inside. A woman was dancing on the bar. Somehow she ended up with a pistol. She was waving it around and scaring the hell out of everybody. Someone tried to get the gun away from her, and it went off. I got hit in the neck and the bullet came out under my left arm. I had gone through the entire war with only one small scratch, and then I almost died in that bar after the war was all over."

Ray Geddes - "I was on duty as an MP in Baltimore. The town went wild with the news that the Germans had surrendered. The girls were kissing anyone in uniform. A car crowded with people stopped at the corner and passed us a bottle. I hate to admit it, but contrary to what they say in the movies, we accepted a drink while on duty."

Wilber Ingalls - "I marched in the parade at Mourmelon on the day that the war ended. There weren't many of us left from the Toccoa days, maybe four or five. Those of us that were left marched with tears in our eyes that day."

Don Kane - "On VE day, May 7, 1945, I was on a pass to the Riviera. When the news broke, the French took to the streets waving banners and singing. A group of us went to the Red Cross, found an American flag, and had our own parade."

Fred Orlowsky – "I had just gotten out of the hospital [after having been wounded at Bastogne] and was at a replacement depot in Germany, trying to get back to the 501st. The word spread like wildfire that the Germans had surrendered. All I can remember is that there was a lot of drinking that day, and I ended up with the worst hangover of my life."

Warren Purcell - "I was on leave the day the war ended. I returned to Mourmelon and they told us to get into dress uniforms for a parade. Fortunately, I was very good friends with the G Company clerk, and he took my name off the roster for the parade."

Jack Urbank - "I was stationed at Auxell le Petit, near Rheims, where

General Eisenhower had his headquarters. We were having a marathon vollyball game when we heard the war was over."

L-R: in both photos: Jack Urbank and Fred Orlowsky. Photo on left taken in 1944, after Normandy. Photo at right taken in 2001 when the two men were reunited after 57 years.

Another View of Victory

by
Michel Gaudry

If you were French in World War II, the important date for you is not the day the war ended for the Germans but the day you were liberated. For me, a 16-year-old boy living in Dieppe, the most important moment was on the first of September in 1944 when the Canadian army came to our town. Our friends were yelling that the English had arrived, and my father put his French flag in the window. Then we were told the Germans were still in town, and we were terrified and hid the flag. Finally we saw the soldiers and learned they were Canadian.

I went up to a Canadian soldier on the first tank to arrive and said to him in my best English, "Welcome, it is good to see you here." The soldier took my hand and in a pure Norman dialect he said to me, "Ou sont les boches!!!" I learned that many of the Canadian soldiers came from families that had emigrated from the Normandy area.

Later we went to the town hall where they were shaving the heads of several young ladies. A soldier asked me why it was being done, and I told him it was because they had been "friends" with the Germans. The soldier didn't understand; he told me that the Canadian soldiers like girls, too.

After the women were punished there was dancing in the streets. There were too many men carrying the Croix de Lorraine, the symbol of the French underground; many of them were lying. (I worked with a local architect, and we had spent much time drawing the local German beach defenses so they could be sent to England.) I met a black Canadian soldier who liked me, and he gave me a German P-38 pistol. When I started pointing it around, he decided that I was too young to have the gun and took it back.

Several days later the Canadians left and the Americans arrived. It was wonderful— there was jazz music, Glenn Miller, chewing gum, cigarettes, chocolate, and the delicious soft sound of their boots on the ground. I will always remember how loud the German boots were on the street, and the American boots were so soft.

End Notes

1. Devlin, Gerard M. *Paratrooper*. St. Martins Press, New York, 1979; p 371.

2. Knowlton brought the hat back from Normandy and returned it to Busiere. Bud still has his mission hat, and wears it every New Year's Eve.

3. Blair, Clay. *Ridgeway's Paratroopers*. Dial Press, Doubleday and Company, Garden City, 1985; p 221.

4. It was not until 2000 that it was revealed, through Art Morin, Jr., that his father had also been wounded from the explosion in the cockpit, having taken shrapnel to his lower mouth and chin.

5. See newspaper description in Appendix.

6. As a sign of his confidence in the 435th, Taylor had McNees personally drop his HQ group the following September in Holland.

7. Gene's friend from the galley, Ed Clark, still calls to deliver birthday greetings every November 4.

8. All of Joe Sullivan's quotes are from letters he sent home to his family in Woodhaven, Queens, in New York City.

9. Amy Whorf-McGuiggan, Master's Degree thesis.

10. See Appendix for Darby's story.

11. Burgett, Donald E. *Currahee! A Screaming Eagle at Normandy*. Presidio Press, 1999, p 59.

12. Blair, Clay. *Ridgeway's Paratroopers*. The Dial Press, Doubleday and Company, 1985, p 203.

13. *Ibid.*

14. Critchell, Laurence. *Four Stars of Hell*. The Declan X. McMullen Company, 1947, p 8.

15. The goat remained with the company for some time. Lieutenant Nathan Marks wrote

home to his wife on September 21, 1943, "Our goat is still with us; how the hell he manages to keep up is a mystery to me. Sooner or later some trooper is going to get really hungry and the goat will be no more." What eventually happened to Geronimo remains a mystery.

16. Critchell, op cit.

17. Critchell, Ibid. p 17.

18. Description supplied by 501 historian Mark Bando.

19. "The troops we fought with in Charlotte were there for jungle warfare training. The guy who started the fight was Ken Belles from first platoon of G Company." (Don Castona)

20. Devlin, *Ibid*, p 366.

21. Critchell, *Ibid.*, p 34.

22. Critchell, *Ibid.*, p 37.

23. Blair, *Ibid.* p 218-219.

24. Koskimaki, George E. *D-Day with the Screaming Eagles.* 101st Airborne Division Association, *1970; p* 60.

25. Each man was given an airsickness pill before takeoff that caused drowsiness. Many men slept for the entire trip to France.

26. Morrison survived. He crawled into the ditch on the edge of the field, covered himself with a parachute, and stuck a morphine syrette into his leg. He remained in the ditch until discovered on June 7 by a parachute recovery detail. There is some discussion regarding the fate of another member of Jack Urbank's mortar squad who jumped from Harrison's plane. Urbank believes that Clarence Klopp was killed by the heavy machine gun fire during his descent, or immediately after landing. However, Klopp's headstone located in the American Cemetery in Normandy indicates that he was KIA on June 11.

27. The reader will note that a half-century has resulted in different stories from both men. They still argue over who wanted to attack the machine gun, and who did not.

28. Don Burgett has since published three additional books: *The Road to Arnhem, Seven Roads to Hell*, and *Beyond the Rhine,* about his participation in Market-Garden, Bastonge, and the final months of the war.

29. In 1996 Mark Bando found Lucien Tetrault living in Florida and called me with Tetrault's address. I sent a letter with a Xerox copy of the pages from Mark's book that mentioned Tetrault's name and the crash of Joe's plane. "Lew" Tetrault called me when he got the letter and we talked for some time. He was very happy to have the material, he said, because his children thought his stories about the war were all made up. He told me a version of his stay at the Lebruman farm that was more complete and differed in several ways from Charles Lebruman's version. He also described to me events in the plane when it was hit by the antiaircraft fire. His description matched what I had read in the original reports, but included more details. The first hit, according to his description, was a major explosion that happened on the cockpit side of the bulkhead separating the paratroopers from the flight crew. This explosion, he told me, was so large that he did not believe any of the flight crew could have survived. Several of the paratroopers were also injured from the cockpit explosion, apparently by shrapnel coming through the bulkhead. He said that almost simultaneously another explosion occurred in the tail of the plane. Realizing that the plane was doomed, the jumpmaster, Sergeant Word, yelled "Let's go," and Tetrault immediately followed Word out the door, landing on the Lebruman farm. With regard to his stay with the Lebrumans, he said that Charles did visit the crash site in the hours immediately after the crash, and that when he returned he had several pairs of dog tags that he had taken from bodies of some of the paratroopers. Tetrault was angry with Charles because, when they both visited the site the next day, Tetrault realized that the burned bodies would be very difficult to identify without the dog tags. He also said that he and Morin only stayed with the Lebrumans for several days, rather than a week. He told me that on June 9 or 10 they were hiding in the barn when some 82nd Airborne men came through the farm, and he and Morin decided to leave with them. Within an hour the group ran into German infantry, and in the firefight that followed Tetrault was wounded and became separated from the rest of the paratroopers. He told me that he hid in the woods for four days, without food, until a young French boy found him, fed him, and then helped him to a nearby American field hospital. The rest of Tetrault's WWII career, as he tells it, remained difficult and frustrating. He was hospitalized in England for his wound in Normandy, and missed the next campaign, in Holland. He finally returned to G Company in time to travel with them to Bastogne, where he was wounded again in the company's opening moments of combat in that battle. He believes he was placed in the last ambulance to leave Bastogne before the town was surrounded. He never returned to G Company. (See Appendix for the statement Charles Lebruman made to Lieutenant Hoover regarding his activities on June 6.)

30. The statement read: "Pictured on the reverse side - Lieutenant Joseph Sullivan, United States Army Air Corps. Picture taken at the time of his commissioning as an officer in September 1943. Lieutenant Sullivan was a musician—he played the saxophone—and had been in training as a stockbroker when called into the Army in 1941. His first assignment was as a musician in the band of the 22nd Infantry Regiment. He was accepted into officer training in 1942, and then attended one year of navigation school to obtain his commission. He was navigating a flight of three

aircraft carrying a portion of the bodyguard for General Maxwell Taylor to its drop zone when his plane was shot down near Picauville, shortly after 1:00 A.M. on 6 June 1944. Lieutenant Sullivan was survived by his mother, an older brother, and two sisters. He is buried in a military cemetery on the edge of New York City, two miles from the home in which he was raised. His name appears on a memorial plaque at a major intersection near his home, with the names of others from the community killed in World Wars I and II. "

31. Pederson successfully landed his glider in the center of the landing zone.

32. See Appendix.

33. Hohl received a posthumous Silver Star for his sacrifice.

34. Don Kane, later that night, described to me the following: "I was on the right side of the road, walking behind Kraeger when we met the Germans. My recollection of the encounter was that Kraeger initiated the attack. As soon as he jumped out of the ditch and started firing at the Germans, all of us close to him jumped up and followed in a charge. The Germans never made it out of the ditch where they had taken cover." Fred Orlowsky, during a telephone call later in the year, also described the action on the road into Pouppeville as follows: "I will never forget that Colonel Ewell was walking right down the middle of the road. We saw some 506 guys in a ditch as we walked by and he remembered how they were always yelling their battle cry 'Currahee' while in training. He said to them, 'Hey boys, give us a loud Currahee.'" Later Orlowsky was next to Lieutenant Marks when he was killed by a sniper. "It wasn't like the movies, he just got hit and fell down." Orlowsky told me that after the battle he heard Captain Kraeger say that if he had used standard doctrine in attacking the town and used mortars, instead of having his temper get the better of him and leading a charge into the enemy, there probably would have been fewer casualties. There is published documentation that Kraeger was livid at the loss of so many of his men in the two aircraft that were shot down. His rage may well have influenced his actions when the first Germans appeared on the scene.

35. The Urbanks graduated from Hudson High School, Hudson, Ohio, with the class of 1940. Jack went to work at a local fruit farm upon graduation, and entered the Army in December 1942, the same month as Don Kane and Ray Geddes. Immediately after his induction he volunteered for the parachute infantry.

36. Warren wore his uniform to the formal dinner at the 501 reunion in 2001.

37. For further information on what happened to Major Legere, see Appendix.

38. It wasn't until writing this chapter that I learned that Jesse had had the plaques made through a friend in the trophy business, and that he had paid for them himself.

39. We learned that his name was "William" rather than the French "Guillaume" because his father, a French WWI veteran, had made friends with an American named William, and named his son after his American friend.

40. These artillery units were made up primarily of parachute-trained troops. The inability of the units to find and operate their guns in Normandy had led to the decision to deliver the men and equipment together, on gliders, for MARKET-GARDEN.

41. Lieutenant Adrian R. Dempster wrote the official report on this incident. After the war Pappy Rawlins wrote, "There was considerable discussion among the pilots regarding this incident. The consensus was that the flight [from A-83 to Welford Park] should not have been made. With the hydraulic system shot out, it would have been necessary to fly with the gear down, and possibly with the flaps down, which considerably reduced the airspeed and caused the engines to exceed the normal fuel consumption. Weather conditions were marginal at Welford...[this incident] certainly caused the air crews to be considerably more careful."

42. The 77th Squadron has been reactivated several times since WWII. Today the men and women of the 77th Squadron are a reserve air refueling unit operating from Seymour-Johnson AFB in Goldsboro, North Carolina.

43. For many years it had been written in history books that Knowlton and Ficociallo were the first men to effect a linkup between the airborne and infantry who came over the beach. Today it is generally understood that the first contact was effected three hours earlier by Lieutenant Eugene Brierre, who had jumped with General Taylor and was dispatched by Taylor to contact the seaborne forces.

44. Geddes was treated by a captured German doctor in the house located at "Dead Man's Corner," which had been turned into an aid station. He was evacuated to England, and lost the sight of one eye as a result of his wound. He served the remainder of the war in stateside assignments as an instructor and military policeman.

45. There is a story among the surviving G Company veterans that Captain Kraeger's plane was hit by antiaircraft fire, and that a shell passed between the captain's feet and exited through the roof of the plane without hindering the flight of the aircraft in any way.

46. See Appendix for Kraeger biographical information.

47. Don Kane received high, if not official, praise for his actions that night from Sergeant Melton "Tex" McMorries, a G Company machine gunner who would become well-known for his exploits in Holland and Bastogne: "One of the ammo bearers left 500 rounds of MG ammo in the open field [which was being] swept with

MG fire....Donald Kane, a squad leader, jumped up and ran for it, saying, 'I'll get it.' Suppose he figured the ammo bearer could not muster the nerve, and he would die. Somehow, Kane made it." [Bando, Ibid; p 48]

48. Bando, *Ibid*, p 51.

49. Critchell, *Ibid*.

50. The 501st has been reactivated on several occasions since the end of WWII, but never as a full regiment. Today the 501st exists as an infantry battalion stationed in Alaska.

Bibliography

Bando, Mark. *The 101st Airborne at Normandy.* Motor Books International Publishers and Wholesalers, 1994.

Bando, Mark. *101st Airborne from Holland to Hitler's Eagle Nest.* Motor Books International Publishers and Wholesalers, 1995.

Bando, Mark. *101st Airborne The Screaming Eagles at Normandy.* MBI Publishing Company, 2001.

Blair, Clay. *Ridgway's Paratroopers.* The Dial Press, Doubleday and Company, 1985.

Breuer, William B. *Geronimo!.* St. Martin's Press, 1989.

Burgett, Donald E. *Currahee! A Screaming Eagle at Normandy.* Presidio Press, 1999.

Critchell, Laurence. *Four Stars of Hell.* The Declan X. McMullen Company, 1947.

Devlin, Gerard. *Paratrooper*! St. Martin's Press, 1979.

Devlin, Gerard. *Silent Wings*, St. Martin's Press, 1985.

Gilmore, Lawrence J. and Lewis, Howard J. *History 435th Troop Carrier Group.* Keys Printing Company, 1946.

Koskimaki, George E. *D-Day with the Screaming Eagles.* 101st Airborne Division Association, 1970.

Koskimaki, George E. *Hell's Highway.* George E. Koskimaki (Publisher), 1989.

Koskimaki, George E. *The Battered Bastards of Bastogne.* Quebecor Printing, 1994.

Rawlins, Phillip C. *Red Light, Green Light, Geronimo* (an unpublished history of the 77th Troop Carrier Squadron, 435th Troop Carrier Group, in World War II), 1993.

Wolfe, Martin. *Green Light*! University of Pennsylvania Press, 1989.

Picauville se souvient..., Association Picauville et ses souveniers de guerre et Editic, 1994.

Appendix

Chain of Command

U.S. Army Air Force Troop Carrier Squadrons and Groups

Most of the narrative in this book concerns the 77th Troop Carrier Squadron. A squadron was the basic operational element that carried out the troop carrier mission; i.e., delivery of airborne (paratroop and glider) forces into combat zones. The original table of organization for the 77th squadron called for the squadron to have twelve operational aircraft when tasked with a combat mission. The aircraft flew in four elements of three aircraft each, designated *A, B, C*, and *D*. Only the element leaders had navigators on board.

The 77th was one of four squadrons that made up the 435th Troop Carrier Group. A Group was composed of four operational squadrons and a command/administrative element known as the Headquarters Squadron. (The four operational squadrons in the 435th Troop Carrier Group were the 75th, 76th, 77th, and 78th Squadrons.)

The commander of the 435th Troop Carrier Group, Colonel Frank McNees, was responsible to the commander of the 53rd Troop Carrier Wing, who, in turn, reported to the commander of the 9th Air Force Troop Carrier Command. See below for the 77th Troop Carrier Squadron chain of command on D-Day.

Chain of Command

77th Troop Carrier Squadron June 6, 1944

9th Troop Carrier Command, Major General Paul L. Williams

    53rd Troop Carrier Wing, Brigadier General Maurice M. Beach

        435th Troop Carrier Group, Colonel Frank McNees

            77th Troop Carrier Squadron, Lt. Col. Henry Osmer

                B Element - Aircraft #1, Capt. John Schaefers

                    Aircraft #2, Lt. James Hamblin

                    Aircraft #3, Lt. Jesse Harrison

U.S. Army Airborne Infantry Companies and Battalions

Most of this narrative concerns G Company, a portion of the 3rd Battalion of the 501st Parachute Infantry Regiment. The company is the basic operational element that carries out operational infantry missions. The table of organization for an airborne infantry company in 1944 called for a "headquarters" element consisting of the company commander, executive officer (second in command), and up to ten enlisted men, along with three 40-man platoons of riflemen. An airborne infantry battalion consisted of a headquarters company and three infantry companies. Each infantry company was designated by a letter; i.e., *A, B*, and *C* for the three companies in the 1st Battalion; *D, E*, and *F* for the 2nd Battalion; and *G, H*, and *I* for the 3rd Battalion. A regiment consisted of a headquarters element and three battalions. G Company of the 501st Parachute Infantry Regiment, was by designation of the letter "G," assigned to 501st's 3rd Battalion.

Company commanders, reported to the battalion commander who, in turn, reported to the regimental commander. See below for the G/501 chain of command on D-Day.

Chain of Command

G Company, 501st Parachute Infantry Regiment June 6, 1944

VII Corps, Lieutenant General J. Lawton Collins
(4th Infantry, 82nd and 101st Airborne Divisions)

   101st Airborne Division, Major General Maxwell Taylor

     501st PIR, Colonel Howard Johnson

       3rd Battalion 501st, Lieutenant Colonel Julian Ewell

         G Company, Captain Vernon Kraeger

           3rd Platoon, Lieutenant Everett Crouch

           Aircraft #1 Jumpmaster, S/Sgt. Charles Word

           Aircraft #2 Jumpmaster, Lt. Everett Crouch

           Aircraft #3 Jumpmaster, Lt. Norman Barker

WWII Unit Chronologies

77th Troop Carrier Squadron/ 435th Troop Carrier Group

G Company/501st Parachute Infantry Regiment

1942

November	-	501st Parachute Infantry Regiment formed, Camp Taccoa, Georgia

1943

January	-	501st began basic training at Camp Taccoa
February	-	435th Troop Carrier Group formed, Bowman Field, Kentucky
April	-	501st moved to Jump School at Ft. Benning, Georgia
May	-	435th moved to Sedalia, Missouri, for Group training
	-	501st moved to Camp Mackall, North Carolina for advanced training
July	-	435th moved to Pope Field, North Carolina, began training with 501st
	-	77th Squadron and G/501 completed first jump together
August	-	435th participated in Ft. Benning jump school training
September	-	Tennessee maneuvers - both units participated
October	-	435th air and ground echelons began movement to England
November	-	435th air and ground echelons reunited at Langer, England

1944

January	-	501st traveled by ship to England, assigned 101st Airborne Division; quarters established at Lambourne

February	- 435th permanent station (#474) established at Welford Park
March	- Demonstration jump for Prime Minister Winston Churchill
May	- Operation Eagle D-Day rehearsal drop; both units participated
June	- D-Day - 77th Squadron dropped G/501
July	- 501st relieved in Normandy, returned to Lambourne
August	- 435th awarded Distinguished Unit Citation and Air Medal for D-Day
September	- Operation MARKET-GARDEN—both units participated
November	- 501st relieved in Holland, moved to Mourmelon, France
December	- Bastonge, Battle of the Bulge - both units participated

1945

January	- 501st transferred to Alsace-Lorraine
February	- 435th moved from Welford Park to Bretigny, France (Station A-48)
March	- 435th participated in Operation VARSITY
	- 501st returned to Mourmelon
	- 101st Airborne Division received Presidential Unit Citation for Bastogne
May	- German surrender
	- 501st moved to Bavaria
July	- 435th returned to United States for redeployment to Japan
August	- Japanese surrender, end of WWII
	- 501st disbanded in Bavaria
September	- 435th disbanded, Kellogg Field, Michigan

Charles Lebruman Statement
(copy)

(This statement was made circa 1948, regarding the crash of Captain Schaefers'plane, and Mr. Lebruman's provision of aid to Private First Class Tetrault and Private Morin.)

My name is Charles Lebruman, and at the time of the events I was 23 years old and lived with my parents at the location called *Montessy County* of Picauville.

In the night of 5–6 June 1944, the German DCA attacked part of the evening. As we could not sleep because of the deafening noise caused by the passing airplanes, we paid close attention to what was happening around us.

While looking at the sky, we saw very clearly an airplane flying at an approximate altitude of 250 meters, which had one of its motors on fire. These events took place around 2300 hours and 23:30. The sky was clear, but as I remember, it was not a starry night.

As we were looking, captivated by the sight of the plane, we saw distinctly a silhouette of a man jumping off the crippled machine. While continuing to observe, we saw the same man land on some branches immobilized at 2.5 meters from the ground, and his parachute covered the top of the tree. He was able to separate himself from his gear, which he abandoned on the site. Hereafter, he left his equipment at a barn next to the farm.

After a short lapse of time while the cited events took place, we heard explosions, one of which was major. We immediately thought of the plane that had just landed with difficulty.

My brother-in-law and I decided to go to the site of the crash. The sky was red on the side of Clainville and we went in that direction. At our arrival, we could not get close to the accident. We were 80 meters away because of the constant explosions. Moreover, the heat from the fire was such that we couldn't get any closer. We then left and decided to go back to the site the next morning at dawn. We returned then to the site with three to four persons. At our arrival, the sad scene was as follows: the plane was completely burned. The cabin was completely dismantled next to Madame Simone's house, which was spared from the fire, God only knows why.

The body of the machine was burning still, but the fire was contained by itself.

I picked up what was on the ground spread around the soldier's gear, which was mostly burned. All of the occupants in the plane were completely pulverized. I collected personally as I walked through the site eight to nine dog tags, as well as rings. I gave to Mr. Rachine all these objects. Marcel Rachine lived at the time in the village of Picauville.

The mayor, Mr. Touraine, asked many of us to help bury the bodies at the foot of the hedges bordering the field. We attempted to gather the maximum of personal belongings for each soldier for future identification of these men.

In what concerns me, I offered shelter for ten to twelve days to two soldiers who told me that they were able to jump off the plane before it crashed.

One of them, was Lucien, who spoke French. The other paratrooper was injured in the leg and stayed in the hayloft most of the time while his companion went through the countryside looking for his compatriots.

To provide them with food, I would get bread from the bakery of Chef du Pont, which was managed by Mr. Queniet.

When I took the food in the barn, I had to use a ladder to reach them. We had an agreed upon sign: Lucien gave me his grasshopper, which I activated when I was going to go up the ladder so that they would know it was me coming.

After twelve days in our company, during a nerve-wracking time because of the presence of the Germans who were looking for the paratroopers, these two soldiers finally joined their ranks after the region had been liberated.

Since that day, we never saw them back again.

This declaration wa made at Montessy

Translation, Statement of Mrs. Lebruman
(copy)

I, the undersigned, Mrs. Lebruman, Augustine, living at the village of Montessy at Picauville, declare:

At about 11 o'clock in the evening, on the 5th of June 1944 (solar time), an American transport airplane crashed at about 300 meters from my house.

We took care of paratrooper Tetrault, John A, and also of his friend, Morin Arthur E, who had a sprained ankle and who stayed several days at home.

In reference to Tetrault's sayings, three crew members only succeded [*sic*] in bailing out of the plane.

My son visited the scene of the crash: he gathered eight or nine identification tags and also one ring.

He gave all those items to Tetrault.

I cannot say how many soldiers died in this accident.

If my memory does not fail, John Tetrault went and visited the plane in the morning of the 6th of June but did not tell me anything special.

S/ Lebruman Augustine,

Translated by:
/S/
Letang Jean
Interpreter.

Call on "Poopville" (Pouppeville)

(The following document was prepared by Clifford Marks, of Seattle, Washington.)

[Cliff Marks is the son of Lieutenant Nathan Marks, G Company, 501st PIR. Lieutenant Marks was killed by a sniper on the morning of 6 June 1944 while participating in an attack on the town of Pouppeville.]

That's the name of S.L.A. Marshall's chapter in his book, *Night Drop*. This is a summary of the events surrounding the death of my father, Lieutenant Nathan Marks, in that town in Normandy on June 6, 1944. I have gathered this information from several sources, including:

George Koskimaki, *D-Day With the Screaming Eagles*

S.L.A. Marshall, *Night Drop*

Mark Bando, *The 101st Airborne at Normandy*

Leonard Rapport and Arthur Northwood, Jr., *Rendezvous With Destiny: A History of the 101st Airborne Division*

Stephen Ambrose, *D-Day*

Interviews with Fred Orlowsky, Walter Turk, and Ray Geddes

A serial of forty-five planes took off from Welford Airfield in England late on 5 June 1944. The serial comprised the 3rd Battalion, 501st Paratroop Infantry Regiment, 101st Airborne Division, along with medical and communications personnel of the Division Headquarters parachute echelon. Lieutenant Colonel Julian Ewell commanded the 3rd Battalion of the 501st PIR; Brigadier General Maxwell Taylor was the commander of the 101st. Eisenhower, the supreme commander, paid a visit to the airfield just before departure. Eisenhower shook the hand of Taylor as the troopers boarded the planes. The planes fell into single file and followed the lead craft. As each plane passed his position, Eisenhowr saluted. Walter Turk said that Eisenhower "stuck his head in the door of our plane as we waited to taxi out into the runway. He wished us luck."

The 3rd Battalion of the 501st PIR was a reserve battalion assigned to drop as protective cover and to provide security for the 101st Airborne Division's Head-quarters personnel on Drop Zone "C" near Hiesville. The 677 troopers dropped from the forty-five planes between 0120 and 0126. Of the forty-five plane serial, three were shot down (two of G Company and one of H Company). The rest of the serial landed reasonably close to the designated assembly area near Hiesville.

Walter Turk lost his memory on the way down. The last thing he remembered until morning was his jumpmaster announcing, "Five minutes to go." Turk told me that this was Lieutenant Marks. As he jumped, connector links apparently slammed him in the back of the helmet and knocked him silly. David Mythaler and Fred Orlowsky found him disoriented and tied a rope around him like a leash and led him around until dawn. Turk said he "talked long and loud out of my head. We were surrounded by Germans. I guess they fired at the sound of my voice. I feel I owe my life to Fred and the other trooper."

Turk's first memory was when his buddies were asking, "Do you know where you are?" He told me one of the first things he remembers was my father asking him if he was okay not long before my father was killed. Ray Geddes says the exact time he landed was 0125 because that is what his watch indicated after being broken as he hit the ground. He says that he was getting ready to pull the pin on a grenade and throw it at a couple of American troopers "when (thank God) I saw the shape of their helmets in the moonlight. I'll never forget that one. It was close."

Until dawn Ewell's men stayed just south of St. Marie-du-Mont. Maxwell Taylor landed near Holdy. In the assembly area General Taylor called his officers together and decided to wait until there was light enough to find a landmark. Headquarters personnel also included Brigadier General Anthony McAuliffe (later of "Nuts" fame at Bastogne). Taylor and accompanying men soon met up with Ewell's group.

At first light General Taylor saw the church spire of St. Marie-du-Mont and determined that they were assembled near two of the vital exits leading up from Utah Beach: Causeways 1 and 2. The 506th Parachute Infantry Regiment was assigned to capture these causeways leading inland from Utah Beach, but none of the men from that regiment were seen in the vicinity. Taylor's group was top-heavy with staff and officers. The group included two generals, three colonels, a major, several captains, and some lieutenants. So even though the 3rd Battalion was supposed to be in Division Reserve, General Taylor decided to use Ewell's men to go to the causeways.

Because of the limited number of personnel (only about eighty-five men), it was decided to only go for the lower causeway, Exit 1, which led through Pouppeville. There were so many officers and so few enlisted men in the group that even lieutenants were assigned as scouts and riflemen. Colonel Ewell was given command of this force with Taylor saying, "Never in the history of warfare have so few been led by so many."

There were at least two instances of contact with French civilians in the early morning hours. Captain Vernon Kraeger* told Corporal Virgil Danforth and Major Larry Legere to scout out their position and pick up information. They went to a farmhouse and met a farmer and his wife. Although they spoke no English, the farmer confirmed the location on a map. The wife sliced a little bread and poured a little *rouge ordinaire,* which they shared with the Americans. The other contact involved General Taylor himself. Taylor, who spoke French, visited a farmhouse; the farmer and his wife were not surprised to see him. They said the next town was Pouppeville and gave directions. The farmer gave the Americans a bullet, which he asked be used on the Germans, and wished them good luck.

On the way to Pouppeville the men spotted a German platoon walking right at them near the approach to Exit 1. Both groups took cover in roadside ditches. Captain Kraeger, commander of Company G, jumped into the road and walked toward the enemy. He was angry because two planes of his company had been shot down and only three of the 36 had survived.

Fred Orlowsky recalled: "We were going down a dirt road. We had flanker guards out....There was shooting up ahead. Corporal Danforth and Captain Vernon Kraeger...were shooting Germans in a ditch at the side of the road." Danforth shot eleven Germans in one group in the ditch on his side of the road. They were all shot in the head; the only part sticking up above the ground, according to Danforth. Danforth won the Distinguished Service Cross for his efforts at Pouppeville. By the time the group reached Pouppeville at about 0900 the patrol had grown to 150 men.

The group drew fire from the outlying buildings. Ray Geddes remembers walking down the left side of the road. Major Legere moved up the road and was shot in the leg by a sniper. The medic, Edwin Hohl, with Red Cross armband on both sleeves, responded; and, as he was kneeling beside Legere, was shot by the unseen sniper and killed instantly with a bullet in the chest. Geddes was ten feet from Hohl when he was killed, and the same sniper shot unsuccessfully at Geddes. Luther Gulick was also killed at about this time.

The scouts on the flanks discovered where the firing was coming from and stilled it with several bursts. The column began to move again. Ewell coordinated the attack through the town. The Germans defended the village and the men of the 3rd Battalion pursued them. When the Americans drew near, the Germans jumped to the next house beyond, firing as they ran. The infantrymen went through Pouppeville using tactics for which they had been trained. Orlowsky said that some were sent in one direction and some in another to try and surround a large house where most of the firing was coming from. Kraeger was wounded in the arm but refused to leave.

Private James Hibbard started through a garden gate and was shot down by a sniper. Corporal Joe Garcia heard a group of Frenchmen inside another garden and stepped inside to investigate. A German waiting beyond the fence put eight bullets into him.

Danforth said that the Germans began to withdraw into their headquarters as the Americans came into town. The defense in the town was not very organized so they cleaned it out pretty quickly, but when they hit the headquarters building it was a different story: "They had two snipers in a tree that we couldn't see and they killed Lieutenant Nathan Marks and Private First Class Bob Richards and one other from my squad."

Fred Orlowsky said, "I saw Lieutenant Nathan Marks get shot in the forehead while peering around the corner of a small building toward the larger house where the Germans were holed up." In a similar manner Colonel Ewell thrust his head around the corner of a house as his group attacked the headquarters with rifle and grenades. A sniper glanced a slug off his helmet, leaving him with a large dent for a souvenir. Danforth was also hit by a bullet that split in two after hitting his helmet, with one fragment going into his skull, causing him headaches that lasted long after this encounter.

By 1100 hours Ewell reached the German command post. A German soldier rushed out wanting to surrender his force. A group of thirty-eight enemy soldiers trooped from the building with arms raised. Some of the soldiers were Russian Georgian troops fighting for the Germans. The enemy had twenty-five dead and wounded, while the Americans lost six killed and twelve wounded in the three-hour fight. The local populace soon were peering from the windows and moments later were in the streets offering refreshment to the soldiers.

After the Americans took the village, the paratroopers linked up with the men of the 4th Division, 8th Infantry Regiment, some in tanks, who approached up the narrow road from Utah Beach. This was the first meeting of the paratroopers and the seaborne invasion force.

War correspondent Robert Reuben prepared his first dispatch. The message was attached to the leg of a pigeon that arrived in Dover, England early in the afternoon with the first eye-witness account of the fighting in France. The message read, "Paratroopers take Pouppeville. "

Later that afternoon the American dead, including Lieutenant Marks, were buried temporarily in the courtyard of the building used by the Germans as their headquarters. From my father's Deceased Personnel File there is a letter from a Private John Gower:

SUBJECT: Burial of Dead.

On June 6, 1944, at 1600 I had occasion to bury six American soldiers in a little orchard in Pouppeville in France. These men were killed in action. They were buried in a common grave and their personal effects (which were collected by me) were turned in to a medical officer at Company A, 265 Medical Battalion.

The orchard is in a courtyard of a large house that was being used as the headquarters for the Germans stationed in the village. It is a large house on the left side of the road coming up from the beach. At each man's head was placed a cross with their name and serial number. A list of their names was turned in and radioed to their outfit. I do not remember all of their names, and I lost the list when I was evacuated.

This is as nearly accurate as I can make it:

1) First Lieutenant Nathan Marks;
2) T/5 Edmund S Hohl, Med. Det.;
3) Corporal Garcia;
4) Hibbard;
5) Richards;
6) [*but pencilled in*] Henry L. Gullick.

Missing Aircrew Reports

Transmittal for Original Missing Aircrew Report for Captain Schaefers' Aircraft, dated September 22, 1944

(Begins on next page)

~~CONFIDENTIAL~~ (1) msc

HEADQUARTERS
EUROPEAN THEATER OF OPERATIONS
UNITED STATES ARMY

JWP/wej

AG 360.33

APO 871
22 September 1944

SUBJECT: Missing Air Crew Report.

TO   : Commanding General, Army Air Forces, Washington, D.C.
         Attention: Statistical Control Division

    1. Forwarded herewith Missing Air Crew Report of the Ninth Air Force.

    2. Records of this headquarters indicate the present status of the crew members of aircraft number 43-30734 to be as shown below:

Pilot	Captain	John M. Schaefers,	O-737654	KIA 6 Jun 44
Co-pilot	2nd Lt.	Thomas Asworth, Jr,	O-668541	KIA 6 Jun 44
Navigator	1st Lt.	Joseph J. Sullivan,	O-811795	MIA 6 Jun 44
Aer. Eng.	T/Sgt.	Melvin Isaacson,	32781102	MIA 6 Jun 44
Radio Oper.	S/Sgt.	David Mac Kenzie,	36506067	KIA 6 Jun 44

    3. Information received from the 101st Airborne Division indicates that all passengers aboard subject aircraft are present or accounted for.

    4. Correspondence has been initiated by this headquarters to obtain additional information concerning the loss of subject aircraft. Action will be forwarded to your headquarters upon completion.

        For the Theater Commander:

H. M. RUND,
Lt. Col, AGD,
Asst. Adjutant General.

1 Incl:
Missing Air Crew Report, 435 T.C. Gp
C-47A, 43-30734, 6 June 1944.

MC-27447

- 1 -

AC-10-12521

(Memo No 35-6, Hq. Ninth Air Force, 15 Feb 44, cont'd)

8414

C O N F I D E N T I A L

WAR DEPARTMENT
HEADQUARTERS ARMY AIR FORCES
WASHINGTON

DECLASSIFIED
E.O. ....

785072

MISSING AIR CREW REPORT

IMPORTANT: This report will be compiled in triplicate by each
Army Air Forces organization within 48 hours of the
time an airplane is officially reported missing.

1. ORGANIZATION: Location USAAF Sta A/B___ Command or Air Force IX TCC
   Group 435 Squadron 77 Detachment None

2. SPECIFY: Point of Departure Sta A/B___ Course 92° T.M.C.
   Intended Destination Sta 444___ Type of mission Parachute Drop

3. WEATHER CONDITIONS AND VISIBILITY AT TIME OF CRASH OR WHEN LAST
   REPORTED Mist, Low Ceiling

4. GIVE: (a) DATE 6 June 1944 Time 0120 __ and Locality of Etreville, France
   of last known whereabouts of missing airplane.
   (b) Specify whether (x) Last sighted; ( ) Last contacted by Radio;
   ( ) Forced down; ( ) Seen to crash; or ( ) Information not available.

5. AIRPLANE WAS LOST, OR IS BELIEVED TO HAVE BEEN LOST, AS RESULT OF:
   (Check only one) ( ) Enemy Airplane; (X) Enemy Anti-Aircraft;
   ( ) Other circumstances as follows:

6. AIRPLANE: Type, Model and Series C-47A ; A.A.F. Serial No 43-1073A

7. ENGINES: Type, Model and Series R-1830-92 ; A.A.F. Serial No (a) 43-99070
   (b) 43-99704 (c) (d)

8. INSTALLED WEAPONS (Furnish below Name, Type and Serial No)
   (a) None (b) (c) (d)
   (e) (f) (g) (h)

9. THE PERSONS LISTED BELOW WERE REPORTED AS: (a) Battle Casualty X
   or (b) Non Battle Casualty

10. NUMBER OF PERSONS ABOARD AIRPLANE: Crew 5 Passengers 17 Total 22
    (Starting with pilot, furnish the following particulars: If more than
    10 persons were aboard airplane, list similar particulars on separate
    sheet and attach original to this form.)

Crew Position	Name in Full (Last Name First)	Rank	Serial
1. Pilot	CRAWFORD, JOHN H	Captain	O-7376A
2. Co-Pilot	ANTONICH, THOMAS (NMI)	2d Lt	O-809A
3. Navigator	MCMILLAN, JAMES J	1st Lt	O-811795
4. Aerial Engineer	Freeman, Melvin (NMI)	S/Sgt	378110
5. Radio Operator	Mackenzie, David (NMI)	S/Sgt	380807
6. Passenger	Lord, Charles F	S/Sgt	107706
7. Passenger	Schmidt, John A	Sgt	128890
8. Passenger	Petrak, John A	Pfc	11105

APPENDIX NO 1A
-1-
C O N F I D E N T I A L

C O N F I D E N T I A L

(Appendix No 1A, Memo No 35-6, Hq. Ninth Air Force, 15 Feb 44, Contd.)

9. Passenger ___ Lo Pachia, Felix F ___ Pvt ___ 36029131 KIA

10. Passenger ___ Chellis, Roland M ___ Pvt ___ 36630479 KIA

See attached sheet.

11. IDENTIFY BELOW THOSE PERSONS WHO ARE BELIEVED TO HAVE LAST KNOWLEDGE OF AIRPLANE AND CHECK APPROPRIATE COLUMN TO INDICATE BASIS FOR SAME.

Name in Full (Last Name First)	Rank	Serial Number	Contacted by Radio	Last Sighted	Saw Crash	Saw Forced Landing
1. HARRISON, JESSE M	1st Lt	0-575591		X		
2. MAHER, PHILIP J	2d Lt	0-745396		X		
3. DiLuzio, Rocco	T/Sgt	3531507			X	

12. IF PERSONNEL ARE BELIEVED TO HAVE SURVIVED, ANSWER YES TO ONE OF THE FOLLOWING STATEMENTS: (a) Parachutes were used _____ ; (b) Persons were seen walking away from scene of crash _____ or (c) any other reason (Specify) _____ Unknown

13. ATTACH AERIAL PHOTOGRAPH, MAP, CHART, OR SKETCH, SHOWING APPROXIMATE LOCATION WHERE AIRPLANE WAS LAST SEEN.

14. ATTACH EYEWITNESS DESCRIPTION OF CRASH, FORCED LANDING, OR OTHER CIRCUMSTANCES PERTAINING TO MISSING AIRPLANE.

15. ATTACH A DESCRIPTION OF THE EXTENT OF SEARCH, IF ANY, AND GIVE NAME, RANK AND SERIAL NUMBER OF OFFICER IN CHARGE HERE ___ No Search ___ .

Date of Report ___ 8 June 1944 ___

(Signature of Preparing Officer)
JACK MIMS,
2d Lt, Air Corps,
Unit Personnel O.

IDENTIFYING MARKS ON PLANE OTHER THAN SERIAL NO.

THE LETTERS "IB" ON NOSE JUST BEHIND PILOT'S WINDOW.
THE LETTER "T" ON TAIL FIN.

OCT 5 1944

RECEIVED

APPENDIX NO 1A
-2-
C O N F I D E N T I A L

MISSING AIR CREW REPORT cont'd.   C O N F I D E N T I A L

PARAGRAPH 10: (Cont'd) - NUMBER PERSONS ABOARD AIRPLANE:

ALL PASSENGERS WERE MEMBERS OF 501 PARA. INF. REG., 101 AIRBORNE DIV.

11.	Passenger	Brown, Harry S.	Pfc	15382931
12.	Passenger	Baldat, Anthony	Pfc	13143375
13.	Passenger	Lady, Milo W.	Pfc	35571350
14.	Passenger	DeHaven, Ollie W	Pvt	35200856
15.	Passenger	Reynolds, James	Pvt	14142691
16.	Passenger	Mastandrea, Michael A	Pvt	32686086
17.	Passenger	Pushaus, Michael L.	Pvt	33558809
18.	Passenger	Sandt, Corwin J.	Pvt	36821661
19.	Passenger	Morrison, Gene W	Cpl	19193153
20.	Passenger	Morin, Arthur R.	Pvt	31311366
21.	Passenger	Schierelski, William A	Cpl	32197602
22.	Passenger	Burnett, Tony A	Pfc	19126110

-3-

(These pages were copied from damaged original.)
(Memo No 35-6, Hq, Ninth Air Force, 15 Feb 44, contd)

WAR DEPARTMENT
HEADQUARTERS ARMY AIR FORCES
WASHINGTON ·

MISSING AIR CREW REPORT

Important: This report will be compiled in triplicate by each Army Air
Forces organization within 48 hours of the time an airplane is officially reported
missing.

1. ORGANIZATION: Location <u>USAAF Sta 474</u> Command or Air Force <u>IX</u>
    <u>TCC</u> Group <u>435</u> Squadron <u>77</u> Detachment <u>None</u>

2. SPECIFY: Point of Departure <u>Sta 474</u> Course <u>82 T.C.</u>

3. WEATHER CONDITIONS AND VISIBILITY AT TIME OF CRASH OR
    WHEN LAST REPORTED <u>Mist, Low Ceiling</u>

4. GIVE: (A) DATE <u>6 June 1944</u> Time <u>0120B</u> and Location <u>Etienville,</u>
    <u>France</u> of last known whereabouts of missing airplane.
    (b) Specify whether (X) Last sighted; ( ) Last contacted by Radio;
    ( ) Forced down; ( ) Seen to crash; or ( ) Information not available.

5. AIRPLANE WAS LOST, OR IS BELIEVED TO HAVE BEEN LOST, AS
    RESULT OF:
    (Check only one) ( ) Enemy Airplane; (X) Enemy Anti-Aircraft;
    ( ) Other circumstances as follows: _____
    _____

6. AIRPLANE: Type, Model and Series <u>C-47A</u> ; A.A.F. Serial No <u>43-30734</u>

7. ENGINES: Type, Model and Series W-R1830-92 ; A.A.F. Serial No (a) <u>43-</u>
    <u>99070</u> (b) <u>43-99724</u> (c)_____ (d) _____

8. INSTALLED WEAPONS (Furnish below Make, Type and Serial No)
    (a) None (b) _____ (c) _____ (d) _____
    (e) _____ (f) _____ (g) _____ (h) _____

9. THE PERSONS LISTED BELOW WERE REPORTED AS: (a) Battle
    Casualty __X_____ or (b) Non Battle Casualty _____

Jerome J. McLaughlin

10. NUMBER OF PERSONS ABOARD AIRPLANE: Crew 5
    Passengers 17 Total 22
    (Starting with pilot, furnish the following particulars: If more than 10 persons
    were aboard airplane, list similar particulars on separate sheet and attach
    original to this form.)

Crew Position	Name in Full (Last Name First)	Rank	Serial Number
1. Pilot	SCHAEFERS, JOHN H.	Captain	O-737654
2. Copilot	ASHWORTH, THOMAS (NMI)	2d Lt	0-668541
3. Navigator	SULLIVAN, JOSEPH J.	1st Lt	0-811795
4. Aerial Engineer	Isserson, Melvin (nmi)	T/Sgt	32781102
5. Radio Operator	Mackenzie, David (nmi)	S/Sgt	36506067
6. Passenger	Word, Charles F.	S/Sgt	14079063
7. Passenger	Schadt, John A.	Sgt	12209989
8. Passenger	Tetrault, John A. Lucien	Pfc	11103562
9. Passenger	Lo Pachin, Felix J.	Pvt	36029191
10. Passenger	Chellin, Erland W.	Pvt	36630479

APPENDIX NO 1A

–1–

A20

(Appendix No 1A, Memo No 35-6, Hq, Ninth Air Force, 15 Feb 44, contd.)

11. IDENTIFY BELOW THOSE PERSONS WHO ARE BELIEVED TO HAVE
    LAST KNOWLEDGE OF AIRPLANE AND CHECK APPROPRIATE
    COLUMN TO INDICATE BASIS FOR SAME.

Name in Full (Last Name First)	Rank	Serial Number	Contacted by Radio	Last Sighted	Saw Crash	Saw Forced Landing
1. HARRISON, JESSE M.	1st Lt	0-675587		X		
2. SEBEK, PHILIP J.	2d Lt	0-745196		X		
3. DiLuzio, Rocco	T/Sgt	15315879			X	

12.   IF PERSONNEL ARE BELIEVED TO HAVE SURVIVED, ANSWER
YES TO ONE OF THE FOLLOWING STATEMENTS: (a) Parachutes were used
____ ; (b) Persons were seen walking away from scene of crash _____
_____ or (c) Any other reason (Specify) Unknown

13. ATTACH AERIAL PHOTOGRAPH, MAP, CHART, OR SKETCH,
    SHOWING APPROXIMATE LOCATION WHERE AIRPLANE WAS
    LAST SEEN.

14. ATTACH EYEWITNESS DESCRIPTION OF CRASH, FORCED
    LANDING, OR OTHER CIRCUMSTANCES PERTAINING TO MISSING
    AIRPLANE.

15. ATTACH A DESCRIPTION OF THE EXTENT OF SEARCH, IF ANY,
    AND NAME, RANK AND SERIAL NUMBER OF OFFICER IN CHARGE
    HERE _____No Search_____.

                Date of Report _____8 June 1944_____

                _____
                (Signature of preparing Officer)
                JACK MIMS,
                2d Lt, Air Corps,
                Unit Personnel O.

Jerome J. McLaughlin

IDENTIFYING MARKS ON PLANE OTHER THAN SERIAL NO.

THE LETTERS "IB" ON NOSE JUST BEHIND PILOT'S WINDOW.
THE LETTER "P" ON TAIL FIN.

PARAGRAPH 10: (cont'd) – NUMBER PERSONS ABOARD AIRPLANE:

ALL PASSENGERS WERE MEMBERS OF 501 PARA. INF. REG. 101
AIRBORNE DIV.

11. Passenger	Brown, Harry B.	Pfc	15382931
12. Passenger	Salemi, Anthony	Pfc	13143375
13. Passenger	Ludy, Milo W.	Pfc	35571350
14. Passenger	DeHaven, Ollie W.	Pvt	35200856
15. Passenger	Reynolds, James	Pvt	14142691
16. Passenger	Mastandrea, Michael A.	Pvt	32886086
17. Passenger	Pushcare, Michael L.	Pvt	33558899
18. Passenger	Randt, Corwin J.	Pvt	36821681
19. Passenger	Morrison, Gene W.	Cpl	19193353
20. Passenger	Morin, Arthur E.	Pvt	31311366
21. Passenger	Sobieralski, William A.	Cpl	39197602
22. Passenger	Burnett, Tony A.	Pfc	19126110

-3-

Official Statements of G/501 Personnel Regarding the Loss of Captain Schaefers' Aircraft

STATEMENT ON MISSING AIRCRAFT NO 43-3073h

I, S/Sgt Charles F. Word, ASN 14 079 003 was jumpmaster of plane number 43-3073h on the night of 6 June 1944. On approach to the drop zone the plane was hit by anti aircraft fire and I was ordered by the crew chief to jump. The crew Chief was in cotact with the pilot by phone, when he gave the order to jump, I yelled "lets go" and jumped.

To the best of my knowledge crew chief did not have on a prachute and as far as I know none of the crew got out of the plane. I landed near Picouville, France.

Charles F. Word
CHARLES F. WORD
S/Sgt Co "G"

Statement on Missing Plane Number 43-3073h

I, Arthur E. Morin, ASN 31 311 366 was a passenger in plane number 43-3073h the night of 6 June 1944. I was jumping number fifteen in a seventeen man stick.

The plane was hit twice by anti-aircraft fire, the first time in the radio compartment and resulted in two casualties of para- chute echelon. The ship was on fire as a result of first hit as well as the two men near radio compartment door.

The second hit was near tail of plane and on baggage compart- ment door. Right after the first hit on plane the jumpmaster, S/Sgt Word, hollered, "Let's go" and I bailed out landing near Picouville, France. In order to get out it was necessary for me to climb up to- wards the door over other members of stick who were laying on floor of plane and dive out the door.

The crew chief did not have a chute on and to the best of my knowledge none of crew members got out of the plane.

Immediately after I landed the plane crashed in flames approxi- mately 250 yards from me and exploded.

Arthur E. Morin
Arthur E. Morin,
Pvt 31 311 366

Official Statements of 77th Personnel Regarding the Loss of Captain John Schaefers' Aircraft

REPORT OF PILOT ON C-47A, No. 43-30720.

We were flying on the right wing of the third flight of the second wave. Captain Schaefer's was flying lead ship of the third flight of the second wave.

When we were in a few minutes of our DZ Captain Schaefer's left wing burst into flames. I'm not sure whether the underneath of the ship was on fire or not.

We were flying about 1800 feet at 140 mph. My Co-Pilot gave me the time of 0119 that Captain Schaefer's plane caught fire, he continued on course then peeled off and went down under me. I did not see him crash.

It is possible that his paratroopers had time to jump.

JESSE M. HARRISON,
1st Lt, Air Corps,
O-815592
77th T.C. Sq.
435th T.C. Gp.

REPORT OF CO-PILOT ON C-47A, No. 43-30720.

We were flying on the right wing of the third flight of the second wave. Captain Schaefers was flying lead ship of the third flight of the second wave. We crossed landfall at approximately 1800 feet. Captain Schaefer's ship was alright at that time.

At 0118 we gave the paratroopers warning that we were approaching the DZ. At 0119 I saw the left wing of Captain Schaefer's ship burst into flames. He continued to fly on course losing approximately 300 feet, it seemed that he was flying with the automatic pilot.

As his stick of paratroopers had been standing for one minute it is possible that they did jump. I did not see anyone jump as the flames were so bright.

I did not see the plane crash.

PHILIP J. SEREK,
2d Lt, Air Corps,
O-745196
77th T.C. Sq,
435th T.C. Gp.

REPORT OF CREW CHIEF ON C47 A - No. 42-24095

8 June 1944

Our ship was flying on the left wing of the first flight of the second wave. Captain Schaefers was flying lead ship of the third flight in the second wave. I was standing at the rear door about four minutes from the DZ getting ready to release the door load, when I saw the left wing of Captain Schaefers ship catch on fire.

He continued on course at 1000 ft. for approximately 200 yards, then went into a gentle glide to the left. I watched the plane until it hit the ground; it did not explode but continued to burn.

I did not see anyone leave the ship as the door was on the side opposite me.

ROCCO DI LUZZIO,
T/Sgt., Air Corps.
Crew Chief

Jerome J. McLaughlin

Ludy Obituary

Provided by the family of Milo Ludy and the Museum of the Soldier, Portland, IN. Originally printed in Commercial Review newspaper, Portland, IN, July 24, 1944. Birth date should have been 1922.

YOUTH KILLED IN FRANCE ON D-DAY

Pfc. Milo Ludy, 22, Loses
Life On First Day Of
Invasion

Mrs.. June Ludy of Portland received a telegram Friday night from the War Department informing her that her husband, Pfc. Milo Ludy, 22, was killed in action in France, on June 6, D-day. He had been reported as missing in action in a telegram received by his wife on June 28.

Young Ludy, a member of the Paratroop Infantry, had arrived overseas in January 1944 after entering the service in December 1942.

He received his basic training at Camp Toccoa, Ga., and was stationed at Ft. Benning, Ga., and Camp McCall, N. C., before being sent overseas. He last visited in Portland in December, 1942.

Prior to his enlistment he was employed at the Rockledge Products Company.

The deceased was born in Portland on April 4, 1944, the son of Carl and Emily (Journay) Ludy.

In May 1942 he was married to June Atha, who survives together with the parents and the following brothers and sisters: Carl Jr., Leslie, Max, Iva Lou and Sallie Sue, all of Portland.

The youth attended the Portland schools.

Citation for Silver Star Awarded to Lieutenant Jesse M. Harrison

AWARD OF THE SILVER STAR

"JESSE M. HARRISON, 0-675587, First Lieutenant, Air Corps, 77th Troop Carrier Squadron, 435th Troop Carrier Group. For gallantry in action on 19 September 1944. Lieutenant HARRISON piloted a Troop Carrier plane towing a glider loaded with troops and artillery on a critical mission to an objective in Holland. Flying through a hail of flak and small arms fire, the aircraft managed to escape serious damage until it was within five miles of the landing zone, where it was struck and set afire. Although the blaze spread rapidly and became increasingly intense, Lieutenant HARRISON, with heroic determination, continued on course. Near the landing zone the plane was again struck by flak and fresh fires swept through the cabin. Lieutenant HARRISON ordered the crew chief and radio operator to bail out while opportunity was available and continued over the landing zone where the glider was released for a safe landing on the objective. Then, mission accomplished, Lieutenant HARRISON and his copilot crawled through the blazing fuselage, suffering severe burns, and managed to parachute to safety before the aircraft crashed to earth. The undaunted courage displayed by Lieutenant HARRISON in the face of great personal danger and his solicitude for the members of his crew, combined with his determination to complete the mission, are in the highest traditions of the United States Army Air Forces. Entered military service from Missouri."

Jerome J. McLaughlin

Text of the 9th Air Force Distinguished Unit Citation presented to the 435th Troop Carrier Group on August 23, 1944

General Orders Number 212 Extract

Battle Honors

1. Under the provisions of Section IV, Circular No. 333, War Department, 1943......

The 435th Troop Carrier Group. For outstanding performance of duty in action against the enemy on 5, 6 and 7 June 1944. On these dates, members of the Group Headquarters and the 75th, 76th, 77th, and 78th Troop Carrier Squadrons of the 435th Troop Carrier Group participated in 95 powered aircraft sorties and 50 glider sorties in the Troop Carrier vanguard of the Allied invasion of the European Continent. All aircraft undeviatingly pursued their course at minimum altitudes and air speeds, in unfavorable weather conditions, over water and into the range of harassing enemy antiaircraft fire, with no possibility of employing evasive action, to accurately unload their paratroops and release their gliders over pin point objectives, thus making an immeasurable contribution to the success of the greatest airborne operation in military history. The courage, skill, efficiency and heroic scorn for personal safety with which the personnel of the 435th Troop Carrier Group struck this devastating blow against our enemies exemplify the noblest qualities of the finest tradition of our armed forces.

By Command of Major General VANDENBERG: V.H. STRAHM B r i g General, USA   Chief of Staff

Letter to Ray Geddes from Don Castona

April 4, 1945

(A typewritten version of Castona's deteriorated 1945 handwritten letter. At the time Castona was with G/501 in France and Geddes was serving as a military policeman in Baltimore, Maryland.)

Hello Ray,

Just read your letter to McVay and decided to drop you a line. Things aren't going too bad now though of course I'm still in the Army. Can't help but think that you are getting a tough break in not getting a discharge. Belles...did get to see my mother while home on furlough and I hope he eased her mind a little. Wish you could have tasted some of the stuff I was drinking last night. Words can't describe how the stuff tasted and smelled. Know you would like to know how things are in the outfit, but I guess you'll have to wait for a reunion. We had a pretty easy time in Holland - nothing like Normandy - but Bastogne was pretty bad. There was snow and real cold weather all the time we were there. I have never been hit (knock on wood) and hope the war is over before another chance comes along. Dougherty was killed at a small town near Bastogne, and of course you have already heard about Captain Kraeger. I was right there when he got it and it seemed like the bottom dropped out when I saw he was dead. There just won't never be another "Pop" Kraeger. You probably remember Purcell - he gives me just as bad a time as you did. I don't begrudge him his beefing as I guess I deserve it.

Boback and I got a seven-day furlough to the UK and spent it all in London. What a time we had! I had a pass to Paris once too - that was before Bastogne. Wish you could have been with me then as Paris is about the next best thing to the States. Sometime I hope to get a chance to tell you about my experiences there. Maybe you can get some idea of how things are now when I tell you that Sgt. Jones, McVay, Satterfield, Reudy, Boback, Ireland, Purcell, Turk, Miszaros, Ingalls, Kane, Raffailli, Evans, Parrish, Morin, Milakleave(?) are still around. I'm going to have to close now - Hope to hear from you soon.

Your old arguing mate,

Don

Jerome J. McLaughlin

Charles S. Darby

Staff Sergeant, Radio Operator

77th Troop Carrier Squadron

Although the role of Staff Sergeant Charles Darby is not significant in the story of the 77th TCS and G/501 on D-Day, the author would be doing the reader a disservice if he did not include some comment regarding Darby and his personal place in history. One of the oldest men in the 77th, at age 36 on D-Day, Darby had been Jesse Harrison's original radio operator, since Baer Field, Indiana, in October 1943. He is undoubtedly the man who named and painted the picture of the Urgin Virgin on the nose of Harrison's C-47 in England.

Amy Whorf-McGuiggan, from Higham, Massachusetts, wrote her Master's Degree thesis in 1992 on a mystery that she discovered during her early years when vacationing on Cape Cod with her family in Provincetown, Massachussets. She has permitted the author to use portions of the material from her thesis to relate the story of Charles Darby here. While some of the details of Sergeant Darby's death, as understood by his family and friends, are incorrect, the story of the reaction of his friends is quite moving.

What follows are Amy Whorf-McGuiggan's words:

"Charles Darby was probably too handsome to be a disciplined painter. Had he been less attractive, his easel time might not have been so…interrupted. Photographs of him show a man in his early thirties with that wartime matinee-idol look, a cross between Errol Flynn and Clark Gable, someone you'd expect to meet in the mist on Waterloo Bridge. Women, even in the pre-sexual liberation days of the thirties and forties, were just too attracted.

"But that wasn't why I became interested in his too-short life. It was the cross.

"As a girl, summering in Provincetown on Cape Cod, I knew of the cross. It was always there, across the harbor, on the dune, weathering gales, blistering heat, numbing cold. When I first saw it up close, its plaque had been removed and I assumed it to be a tribute to all in peril on the sea. Until one afternoon, sitting on the waterfront patio of Sal's Place, a West End restaurant, looking out to the cross, it eddied its way into the conversation. Sal Del Deo, a member of the artist's fraternity known as the Beachcombers, explained that the cross was a memorial to Charles Darby, fellow Beachcomber, killed in action during World War II.

"In early November, 1944, word reached the Beachcombers that their friend Charles Darby would never return. First details were brief, a Western Union telegram from Charles' father to John Whorf (Amy's grandfather):

'MY SON DIED ON THE 17TH SOMEWHERE OVER HOLLAND, WILLIAM R. DARBY'

"Within days, a more detailed letter from Mr. Darby arrived at the Hulk, the dilapidated fish shed the artists used as their clubhouse. Pregnant with sadness, the letter contained a pained request, that a plaque might be fastened to a stone and set, overlooking the ocean, in the lonesome sand dunes of which Charles had spoken incessantly, a memorial to an unsung soldier. 'I only thought it would in some small way tie Charles more closely to his beloved Provincetown,' wrote Mr. Darby.

"Recorded in the minutes of the Beachcombers' November 18th meeting is Dr. Frederick Hammett's suggestion: 'That we agree to select a spot upon which to erect a monument *to an unsung soldier who loved the dunes.*' Phil Malicoat, at the next meeting, 'moved that a cross be made for Darby....The motion was seconded by Whorf and carried.'

"At six bells, on a clear afternoon in October 1946, a cross built of old railroad ties by Phil Malicoat, Rober Rilleau, and John Whorf, with a bronze plaque fashioned by Bill Boogar, was dedicated by the Beachcombers on the lawn of the Provincetown Art Association, steps from the Hulk where Charles had shared the espirit of Saturday evenings.

"Some years later, the cross was removed to Long Point, the sea-girt strand that is the Cape's end. It was set into a sand hill, liberal with wild roses and impervious dune vegetation, facing Provincetown a mile across the natural harbor. Mr. Darby's wish for his son had been fullfilled.

"Today, every summer, Beachcombers too young to remember Charles make the pilgrimage to Long Point, climb the loose dune and reposition the Darby cross. Like their Club, the cross is about continuity, about keeping a memory from toppling. It is about the significance of each life, the brevity of life. If the Beachcomers do not remember Charles, who will? Only they and the dwindling ranks of the 77th hold any memory.

"A new enamel plaque has been fashioned for the cross with this simple epigraph:

Charles Darby

Gallant Soldier

Killed in Action

October 17, 1944

"Charles Darby did not set out to become the gallant soldier, but achieved that by dying for his country. In being too often romanticized, the life of the vagabond artist is not unlike that of the fallen soldier. And there, in the formal photograph of Charles in uniform that still hangs in the Hulk, is that ultimate romantic notion—the artist as soldier.

"In the end, we are remembered as circumstances have made us."

Charles Darby's cross as it appears today.

The Artists Association of Cape Cod, MA made, erected, and maintains the cross dedicated to Charles S. Darby that is mounted on the tip of Cape Cod, MA [Jesse Harrison].

Charles Darby.

Jerome J. McLaughlin

Vernon Kraeger

Captain, G Company
501st Parachute Infantry Regiment

When you speak of the men of G Company, 501st PIR, there is constant reference to the man who led them from the training grounds of Toccoa, Georgia, until his death midway through the Holland campaign. If a generational reference can be made, the loss of Vernon Kraeger was similar to the loss of President Roosevelt for the young men of G Company. They had never had another company commander, and most of them did not remember another President.

When asked to remember their Captain, they often speak of his death first, then tell stories that show their respect for his leadership, and for the man. According to Jack Urbank, Kraeger was from St. Louis, Missouri, and began his career in the Army, prior to WWII, as an enlisted man, where he served with a coastal artillery unit in Panama. When the war started, Kraeger, like many other bright young men serving in the ranks, was offered the opportunity to go to Officer Candidate School. When Urbank first met his future company commander, in December 1942, Kraeger was a Lieutenant serving as the executive officer of a "casual company" where new recruits to the 501st were administratively brought into the regiment. Eventually, he was promoted to Captain and given command of G Company.

Jack Urbank - "The first time I had anything to do with Vernon Kraeger he was demonstrating to us recruits how to put a pup tent together. There were three of us, Hellinger, Mythaler, and myself. Every step of the way something went wrong: the button holes were sewn together instead of being holes, a hinge on one of the tent poles was broken, and the tent pegs were substandard, and broke every time you hit one. After forty-five minutes Kraeger was so frustrated he just stopped and we all sat on the ground and laughed."

Kraeger was a small man. Virgil Danforth, in his description of the action on the advance to Pouppeville describes Kraeger as walking down the road shooting at Germans in the ditch with a "carbine that was almost as big as he was."[1]

Ray Geddes - "The last time I saw Captain Kraeger was the day I was wounded. He was on his way to the medics with his second wound. I learned later that they didn't let him return."

George Koskimaki, in his history of the 101st in Holland, included several references to Kraeger by another G Company runner, Pvt. Jesse Garcia. He quoted Garcia regarding action that took place in Holland, "We had a skirmish with Krauts in a woods. The captain was naturally at the front line (if not ahead of it) and I was about 20 feet away. He received his first wound (in Holland; he had been wounded twice in Normandy), a bullet in the arm. The medic told him to go back to the rear medical unit; he refused. I remember he stayed at his position firing steadily with his carbine since we could see the Krauts not very far away."

"PFC James Mongahan added another story. 'One day we were moving up a road and came under some very accurate artillery or tank fire. I noticed earlier a burned out Sherman tank that had received a hit in the turret. This convinced me it was tank fire. Warren Reudy and I were down in a very small ditch when a shell exploded so close it covered us with dirt. After seeing that neither of us was hurt, I looked up and there on the road, just as calm as could be with not a care in the world, was Captain Kraeger. I said, 'Hey Captain, when are we going to get out of this mess?' He replied very calmly, 'Don't worry Monaghan, I got you in and I will get you out.' Well, that was all I needed, and he did get us out. He was one of the greatest leaders I ever met."[2]

Jack Urbank - "We were in Eerde, Holland when Captain Kraeger got killed. The company was set up with the rifle platoons in line and my mortars behind them. Kraeger was in the line with the riflemen and machine gunners. A mortar round exploded near him and he got a small wound in his temple. One of the medics looked at him, and put a Band-Aid on his wound. Ten minutes later he crumpled over, dead. I helped carry him back to the aid station, where we undressed him, thinking that he had been hit more than once. We couldn't find another mark on him. He must have died from internal bleeding from that small wound."

Don Castona - "I was right there when he got it. It seemed like the bottom just dropped out. He just slumped over and said, 'Well, goddam' and died instantly."

Warren Purcell - "As his runner, I was right near him when he got hit. It was a small wound in his head. A while after he was wounded he just sat down and said, 'Well, goddam,' and he keeled over and died."

Jack Urbank - "Kraeger was a fair-minded leader of men. He would walk 50 miles with you with blisters the size of half dollars on his feet. One time he took us on a ten-mile run to sober us up from an all-night drinking party. He was a professional soldier. He also had dreams. He wanted to retire from the Army some day and have a cattle ranch."

Jack Urbank paid Vernon Kraeger the ultimate compliment when the war was over, by naming his second son after him.[3]

Don Castona - "There will never be another 'Pop' Kraeger. It was hard for us old-timers to take. He was replaced by Lieutenant Stanley from H Company. Also a good leader and a good man."

[1] Koskimaki, *D-Day With the Screaming Eagles,* p 168.

[2] Koskimaki, *Hell's Highway,* pp 236-237.

[3] *While I was compiling this book, Claudia Urbank frequently took notes while her father described his memories, and then forwarded Jack's thoughts to me via e-mail. After talking to her father about Vernon Kraeger, and compiling much of what you have read, she added this comment, "I wish you could have seen Dad's face when he was summing up his feelings about Captain Kraeger. Huge tears welled up in his eyes, and the respect and love he had for the man was very apparent, deep in his heart and soul, to this day."*

Honored Dead of the 77th Squadron

In Memory of Our Fallen Comrades
Officers and men who gave their lives
serving with the 77th Squadron
435th Troop Carrier Group in World War II.

Captain John H. Schaefers
First Lieutenant Richard J. Burr
First Lieutenant Harry H. Claussen
First Lieutenant Richard C. Forbes
First Lieutenant James J. Hamblin
First Lieutenant Joe W. Herriage
First Lieutenant Paul L. Hurney
First Lieutenant Joseph J. Sullivan
Second Lieutenant Thomas Ashworth, Jr.
Second Lieutenant Andrew C. Jordan
Second Lieutenaut Joseph P. Kowalski
Second Lieutenant Herbert S. Mullan
Second Lieutenant William J. Niland
Second Lieutenant John H. Starbuck
Second Lieutenant Howard P. Wilson
Second Lieutenant John B. Keiser
Flight Officer Dale R. Code
Flight Officer Howard M. Davis
Flight Officer John W. James
Flight Officer Everett R. Jones
Flight Officer Irvin S. Odell
Flight Officer Willard Van Eyck
Technical Sergeant Melvin Isserson
Technical Sergeant Milton E. Jones
Staff Sergeant Walter C. Cassiday
Staff Sergeant Charles S. Darby
Staff Sergeant David MacKenzie
Staff Sergeant Christi D. Truitt
Corporal David W. McMahan
Corporal Clarence A. Reverski

A Locomotive on the Roads

The following narrative is a chapter from a book entitled <u>Picauville se souvient...</u>, that relates tales of residents in the area of Picauville before, during, and after D-Day. It tells of the adventures of two young boys in Normandy during that time. The aircraft that the boys discovered on the late morning of D-Day was Captain Schaefers', next to the Simone farmhouse. Translation of the chapter was difficult, and resulted in my having to make some interpretations of what the translator "guessed" was the original meaning. The specific area relating to the Schaefers crash site has not been altered, and is highlighted with bold print. I am at a total loss as to the meaning of the chapter title. There is reference to a body located away from the wreckage—DoD Memorial Affairs records indicate the body was that of Schaefers' copilot, Thomas Ashworth.

In the country, it is well known that everyone gets up early. For Rene, during May 1944, it was a necessity. Not to work in the fields, but because of school. Since the Germans had commandeered the boys' school, all the classes took place in the girls' school. The boys' teachers taught in the morning and the girls' in the afternoon. Coed education was not yet in fashion. Rene Couppey rather enjoyed this situation. He was 14 years old and, well, girls started to be interesting. Shared lockers were used as mail boxes. Corresponding with the girls had become an important activity.

In Montessy, the war was not physically present. No soldiers, no apartment requisitioning. Montessy was not a strategic location. Since the flooding of the marshes, the Germans believed the village could be left alone. Still, you could feel the repercussions of the war. Frequent requisitioning of food, workers, and transportation. Obviously, Rene, who was only 14, did not feel directly affected by these measures, but once in a while he had to drive a cart to transport goods from the occupying troops staying at Chef du Pont to the hospital Bon-sauveu.

Times were hard, even though getting food in the country was not as difficult as in the city. Some products were totally unavailable; some appeared on the market intermittently. Bread was the big obsession. Even though people did not die of hunger, the food they ate was not well balanced and some weird illnesses appeared, such as the "bread mange."

The new school hours had a great advantage. As soon as they were finished with farm work and school, Rene and his friend Desire Lebrenne would spend their time at their favorite occupation: picking up everything that lay around.

Our two friends were not picky; they would take anything that had been stolen from the German army as well as what came from the air. After all, wasn't it a certain kind of resistance?

Even though these "thefts" had some value due to the danger involved in getting them, they were not as prestigious as everything that came from the other side of the Channel. Thus, in 1942 or 1943, the two friends went to Coigny to take everything that could be dismantled from a British plane that had crashed there. With the pieces they brought back, they built a still that worked! Desire was great at this kind of game. Nothing frightened him.

June 5 in the evening was the beginning of the historical night. Rene and Desire were at Desire's house sitting by his fireplace. You could hear shooting everywhere. The loud roar of the plane indicated there was a lot of them. For the two boys, it was the greatest opportunity for picking up scraps. At 6:00 in the morning, they left for Clainville, where they thought they had heard a plane crash. They had to cross some fields to get there. While crossing Grandes Mares, they noticed two large canvasses. When they got closer to them, they realized they were parachutes. A detail worried them: a sort of triangular package with a red handle was attached to the harness of one of the parachutes. Red was the color of danger. The two boys did not know it was an emergency parachute.

They decided not to touch this red handle and went on their way until they found in the grass a foot and a hand with two very large rings. They were now scared.

Then they reached the plane, which was lying on its back. The plane was still smoking, and they could hear the detonations of ammunitions in the background. They were probably exploding because of the heat. At the time, the two boys saw only one thing: the plane was on its back and the wheels, highly desirable objects, were of easy access. They climbed on the fuselage to get to the wheels and noticed seventeen Americans who had died, burnt, inside the plane. A ghastly detail made them feel sick: the bodies were black, but their hair was intact. Their helmets must have protected it. An eighteenth body was lying nearby in the grass.

By then, the boys were completely panicky. All they wanted to do was to get away as fast as possible and return to Montessy. They took nothing that

day. They learned later that three passengers were alive and that two of them were hidden at Paul Lebruman's home, from which they had already left to look for German troops.

For Rene it meant "to go hunting."

From Montessy, you could not see anything but you could hear everything. You could hear the difference between the German Mausers and the American U.S. M-1. Since the noise came from everywhere, you could not figure out what was happening. As soon as they heard artillery, they would hide in the shelter dug in the backyard. They even had installed electricity; unfortunately, it was cut; they had not thought about it.

Our two pack rats had found American C rations everywhere. The sweets were quickly eaten; they hadn't had any for so long. But what could be this black powder that smelled like coffee? When you ate it, it did not taste good at all.

The first refugees were arriving from the town of Eglise. They were the first of a large number of refugees who came to our town, most of them from Pont L ' Abbe. Our farm had up to 120 refugees in this first week of freedom. Each day brought a new bunch of refugees, while some left in a hurry to find out what tomorrow would look like. Everyone who lived in areas easily targeted chose to come to this sheltered area, next to the marshes and far from the road. The bridge between the Tripettes marshes and Beuzeville had not been finished.

Desire and his friend decided to go see what was happening on the Chef du Pont road. A group of seven or eight parachutists controlled the area. The two boys were welcomed and given sweets. Suddenly, one of the soldiers behaved strangely. Sticking his ear to the ground, he listened attentively; when he got up he said something to his friends and told the boys to go away as fast as possible. The boys fled all the way to the Clainville crossing where they stopped, held by their curiosity. The Americans were hiding behind bushes when a group of Germans approached. There were shots, some soldiers fell; this was the first time Rene saw men being killed.

During another of their "scavenger" trips, the two boys and another friend, Roger Scelles, went to Hates Portes where, supposedly, there was a stack of abandoned German bicycles. When they arrived, there were no bicycles, but a cart with a dead horse and a dead driver.

The boys took the horse's harness and discovered in the cart some back packs. Each took one and they came back home pretty happy with their loot. They stopped in a field to rest. A few turkeys were walking by; all of a sudden a shell exploded, a turkey kept on walking beheaded. Up until now, Rene and his friend had not realized that death could befall them at any time. And on all fours they crawled all the way home.

Back home, in spite of the loot, Rene was severely punished by his mother, who had been terribly worried. Another day Rene and Desire were questioned by a German soldier who asked them, "Tommies?" "Tommies?" Since about twenty parachutists had landed in the region, Desire thought he could get rid of this soldier by sending him to those men. The German, who did not trust them, made them walk in front of him to where the parachutists were located. The two boys were very frightened. What would the parachutists do? They coughed and made other "natural" noises in order to warn the parachutists. The latter aimed and shot the German. This was the first time Rene saw death so close to him. He was never able to forget the look of this dying soldier.

Rene's grandmother, who had a farm in Pont l' Abbe, arrived to tell the family that Pont l' Abbe was burning. When she left, her house was still intact. The boys offered to go there to bring back some of her belongings. When they reached the village, it was empty; only a few people were trying to find some remnants of their lives. When they arrived at the house, nothing was left; it had burned down. Two-thirds of the animals had been killed. While looking for the last third, they came upon a dead German soldier still sitting on the ground in a hole. Six months later he was still there. Finally, the mayor had him buried to be found again unearthed; somebody must have wanted his boots. This time the body was evacuated.

Around the 12th of June, Rene and Desire were dying to see where the trucks were coming from. Everybody knew they came from Sainte Marie du Mont. They decided to try to go there. The boys knew the Americans liked strong drinks; they took with them a bottle of "goutte" (Calvados) and bicycled toward the sea. At the forges crossing the Military Police stopped them and forbade them to go further. They rode back to the Galais house. There, they hid their bicycles and this time tried their luck hitch-hiking. At the sight of the bottle they were waving, the first truck passing by stopped. This sudden stop created a series of collisions with the trucks that were following. But who cares! The GMC and the Dodge were very strong, and when the trucks started again, the boys were sitting in the back of an empty truck on their way to the sea. At the forges crossing, they hid and were not discovered. At some point a train engine was coming toward them on top of a truck that had at least 40 wheels. The two boys were dropped off shortly before reaching the coast. They finished their trip on foot.

What they saw stunned them. Where was the sea? As far as the eye could see, boats were arriving waiting to unload or moving out to go back to England. Little boats came back and forth to amphibious "ducks" that transported the cargo to the dunes. The sky was black with *sausages*, balloons held by cables.

The return trip was easy. A truck took them back to Galais, where they found their bicycles. At the MP post, no one checked the truck.

Jerome J. McLaughlin

Shovel and Pick

Also from "Picauville se souvient...," this narrative describes the crash of Lieutenant Hamblin's aircraft on what is now the Bisset farm. The translation was done by Nadine Hanguehard-Turmel.

I remember the 5th, June 1944, when I was 19. I was with Michèle Avoine, the grocer's daughter of "Le Hamel au Sort," our little village, often named "L'Angle" (*The Corner-*). We both were riding our bikes to Carentan along the usual way. But, when we wanted to come back, there was no question of taking the same road because the Germans forbade any civilian to cross the Douve bridge: that's why we went back through Baupte and Beuzeville-La-Bastille, where we barely crossed the bridge. Our occupying forces seemed to be very tense.

In the middle of the night from the 5th to 6th, I couldn't sleep because of the noise of the planes and particular violent fires: I lied [*sic*] face down on my bed which was just in front of a window. I was examining the sky. DCA shells were exploding and exploding. I could see some kinds of big dark flakes which became rounded and fell down on the ground. At once, I realized that paratroopers were jumping at low altitude. It was the D-Day (Normandy landing). Then, there only were astounding noises of planes, DCA fires, and also rockets that were lighting up the sky, and I could watch like in broad daylight. Panic-stricken cows were mooing and trying to run away; their chains were dragging on the ground. Suddenly, I saw a plane on fire, at low altitude, and I could clearly hear its occupants' cries of pain or terror. A little later, I was told that plane crashed on the ground near Mr. and Mrs. Noel's house, in Founecrop village. In the morning, my parents and I found blackened faced American paratroopers. One of them had injured his leg: so we took him to our house and offered him an invigorating drink—as he refused it, we drank first to show him there was no risk.

We could feel those paratroopers were very tense. They had to slap their hands to show us their headquarters map in order that they stopped shivering.

Their mission was to join "La Chasse Pierre" in Etienville. A little later, we heared [*sic*] of the fact they never could reach that place because of too violent fights on the way.

The injured paratrooper and both able soldiers who were with him were hiding in a hayloft, but they soon had to move away. In fact, frightened neighbors came and insistently asked my father for stopping sheltering those soldiers because they feared German reprisals. So we took them to a trench we made for us, and we regularly provided them with fresh supplies. But one day, a great danger arose: Germans were lurking around the area. So, a very courageous and fearless man, named Jean Ferey (son), led our American soldiers to a surer shelter (a wood pile) far from 200 meters (0.12 mile).

On 6th June 1944, Dèsirè Luce, who was living in L'Angle village, was killed without any warning by the Germans, as he was crossing the lane to go and see his neighbor, Auguste Lelodey.

On 7th June, we became demoralized above all because of the fires that were coming from the sea. At any moment, marine shells might explode and immediately destroy a house. We only had one sign to avoid the worst: a little plane, called "Le Mouchard" (*The Spyplane*) that was flying and controlling the exactness of the fires between each salvo.

On the same day, Mrs. Juliette Marion's house in Founecrop was destroyed, and then Mr. Alphonse Pinel's one. This man, aged 36, was living in L'Angle village. He was seriously injured and unfortunately died two days later. Let's note that Mr. Luce and Mr. Pinel were temporarily buried in their gardens.

With three American soldiers,
Mrs. Juliette Marion
and Mr. Maurice Quertier (from Cherbourg)
who first took refuge in
Mrs. Marion's home in Founecrop,
then in Mr. and Mrs. Paul Leconte
in "Hamel au Sort"
and was injured with a shrapnel,
and finally in "Montessy."

On the same day too, the same occurred to Mr. Emile Morin's house (L'Angle). But fortunately, Mr. and Mrs. Morin had just gone away. Mr. Morin, who fought during World War 1, thought the barrage fire might reach his house. That's why he decided to leave some minutes before: he was right....

From that day, people were afraid of the situation; they were gathering—we were forty-six persons around in a thick-walled cowshed with a hayloft which had to ward off danger. Precautions (which today might seem to be derisory) were taken: we put a bucket of water, a shovel, and a pick just behind the door to clear it if necessary. When we felt a danger, we were getting closer to heavens, praying God as hard as we could. I had never felt such a fear on my life!

During those days, several families (Noël, Marion, Hardy, Quertier, Hulot, Avoine, Dibonnet, Vaulor, Lepourtois, Minerbe and Mesnage) took refuge at home.

We quickly lost all notion of time; we didn't know what day it was. We also rapidly caught lice because we basically hadn't a wash, and we didn't take off our clothes even when we rested. We were sleeping in staw [*sic*], mainly ate pancakes and meat we cut up from animals which were killed by the fires. We cooked that meat in big cast iron pots full of water. We weren't very hungry. When there was a break, we went and milked the cows: the most courageous among us made the sacrifice! I for one went once with Mrs. Juliette Marion. A shell fell down in the field where we were; needless to say we immediately cleared off. I wanted to jump the slope at the same time as Mrs. Marion. But in the rush, I knocked down and spilled the milk. I didn't feel very proud because we needed this milk to prepare the pancakes.

All those who knew the D-Day and that period, could relate their stories. As far as I am concerned, and in spite of the atrocity of war, I must admit that at that moment of my life, I could realize how strong human solidarity and fraternity were....

Marguerite CATHERINE nèe LECONTE

Table of Organization and Equipment

G Company, 501st Parachute Infantry Regiment
101st Airborne Division
Circa June 1

Total Personnel
8 Officers
119 NCO and Enlisted
Company Headquarters
2 Officers
14 NCO and Enlisted
1 Captain - Commanding Officer
1 First Lieutenant - Executive Officer
1 First Sergeant
2 Sergeants - 1 Commo, 1 Operations
5 Tech NCOs - Radio Operators
8 Pvt/PFC - 5 Riflemen, 3 Messengers
3 Rifle Platoons (Each)
HQ Section
1 1st Lieutenant - Platoon Leader
1 2nd Lieutenant - Asst. Platoon Leader
1 Staff Sgt. - Platoon Sergeant
1 Cpl. - Signal, radio, code
1 Tech/5 - radio operator
2 Pvt/PFC - messengers
2 Rifle Squads (Each)
1 Sergeant - Squad Leader
1 Corporal - Asst. Squad Leader
7 Riflemen
1 Machine Gunner
1 Assistant Machine Gunner
1 Ammunition Bearer
1 60 MM Mortor Squad
1 Sergeant - Squad Leader
1 Gunner
1 Assistant gunner
3 Ammunition bearers

Briefing Sheets

Briefing sheets on the following two pages were reproduced for 77th Squadron aircrews prior to the D-Day parachute mission. Additional comments have been added, post-mission, author unknown. (*Identical copies were provided by Walter Lake and Joe Flynn.*)

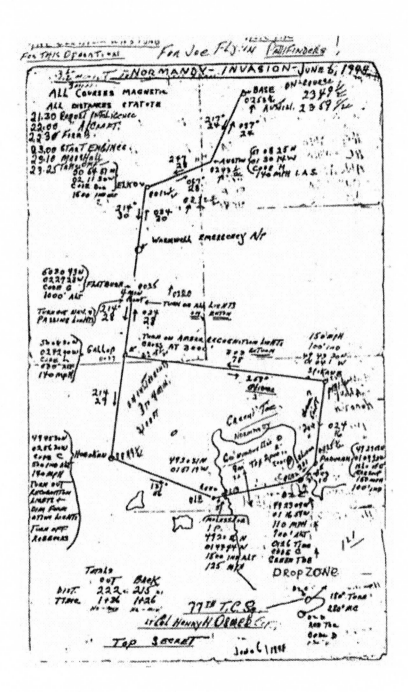

RADIO SILENCE   RADIO SILENCE

HQ RADIO STATION -- EASTCOTE   HABILE
HQ RADIO STATION FLATBUSH   PIERHEAD
ALL AIRCRAFT -- SANDBAG
OUR WING -- LEGEND
AIR SEA RESCUE LAUNCHES - SEAGULL

VHF   MP/IP SECTION N
A- AIR SEA RESCUE   FIRST DISTRESS MESSAGES
B- ESCORT   CALL FC7   FREQ 363 KC
C WING COMM
D- COMMAND COMM   FIXED BEACON FOR RADIO COMPASS
                             HOMING
                             CALL 7J7   FREQ 845 KC

EUREKA DOPE   DZ LIGHTS
SET TO B RED LOW   DZ C GREEN TEE CODD CHARLIE
EXPO CODD DOG   DZ D RED TEE   DOG
FLATBUSH " GEORGE
GALLUP "   LOVE
HOBOKEN "   CHARLIE

TURN OFF AT THIS POINT
SET TO A RED HIGH
DZ C CODD CHARLIE
TURN OFF IMMEDIATELY ON
PASSING HOBOKEN

IFF OFF ALL THE WAY EXCEPT FOR DITCHING.
                    LEAD FORMATION

SPARE
DROPPED PARATROOPERS ON THE OTHER TWO.

Letters Between Mrs. Katherine Sullivan and the Department of Army

Following is typed copy from aged original.

Mrs. Katherine Sullivan
8015-85th Drive
Woodhaven, New Jersey

The Adjutant General,
Casualty Branch,
Munitions Building,
Washington 25, D.C.

Dear Sir:

I would appreciate additional information regarding 1st Lt. Joseph J. Sullivan, O 811 795, Plot CC, Row 2, Grave 48, United States Military Cemetary, Neuville-en-Condroz, Belgium, before advising the Office of the Quartermaster General of my wishes as to the disposition of his remains.

The only information I have ever received is that my son was missing in action. After a year, he was classified as dead, although his status as missing had not been changed. Now I received a request regarding the disposition of his remains.

According to information received, the plane he was in was shot down on the 6th of June, 1944, over Normandy, France. In October, 1944, I received a list from the Air Corps giving the names and family address of the members of the crew. In contacting them I found out that they had all received word that their boys had been killed in action. I did not. One of the families advised that the boys were buried in Blosville, France and that their information was that there were unknown graves there too. I presume that one of these might be my son's grave. Now I get the notification regarding the cemetary at Neuville-en-Condroz, Belgium.

Jerome J. McLaughlin

I would certainly appreciate it if you could advise me how my son's grave happens to be in Belgium and how it is that he is identified after all this time. This information would help me to understand what has happened and assist me in answering the Office of the Quartermaster General, which I will have to do in another week.

Sincerely,

/S/

KATHERINE SULLIVAN

cc -   Office of the Quartermaster General
        Memorial Division, War Department
        Washington, 25, D.C.

*(Following is a typed copy of an aged original Department of the Army letter
to Mrs. Katherine Sullivan concerning the remains of her son, First Lieutenant
Joseph J. Sullivan. The letter was never delivered, but was located by the author
in Lt. Sullivan's Memorial Affairs file in 1981.)*

10 March 1948

Mrs.. Katherine Sullivan
80015 85th Drive
Woodhaven, New York

Dear Mrs. Sullivan:

Your letter pertaining to the remains of your son, the late First Lieutenant
Joseph J. Sullivan, has come to my attention.

I wish to advise you that Units of the American Graves Registration Service
overseas are constantly engaged in intensive searching operations and they
expend every effort to locate the remains of deceased Americans. The remains
of your son were found in the wreckage of the plane in which he met death in
Picauville (Manche) France by a Disinterring Team of the American Graves
Registration Service. The identification tags of your loved one together with other
identifying articles were found at the time his remains were recovered.

In accordance with the "Return of World War II Dead Program," the remains
of our heroic dead are placed in well established military cemeteries closer to
the lines of transportation. In view of the fact that the United States Military
Cemetery Neuville-en-Condroz, Belgium, was the closest established American
Military Cemetery to the area in which your son met death, his remains were
interred in that cemetery on 17 September 1947.

With sincere regret, I must inform you that it is not possible to grant your
desire to postpone your decision for the final disposition of the remains of your
son.

The Department of the Army will, if at all possible, comply with the wishes
of the next of kin in accomplishing The Program for the Return of World War
II Dead. You will understand, I am sure, that the magnitude of this world wide
Program requires close adherence to predetermined schedules for exhumation,
supplies, labor, transportation and weather.

This Program is already underway. The cemetery in which rest the remains
of your beloved son will be exhumed in the near future. It is vitally necessary,
therefore, that your decision be recorded with us by the return of the completed
Disposition Form at your earliest convenience to enable us to reserve grave space
in a National Cemetery, if you so desire, while it is still available.

Jerome J. McLaughlin

Please be assured of my continued sympathy in your great loss.

Sincerely yours,

/s/

RICHARD B. COOMBS
Major, QMC
Memorial Division

Telegrams

(Telegram #1 dated June 26, 1944, informing the family of Raymond Geddes that he had been wounded on June 8. Telegram #2 dated July 8, 1944, from Ray Geddes to his brother-in-law, announcing his return to the U.S. and pending arrival in Baltimore.)

Telegram #1

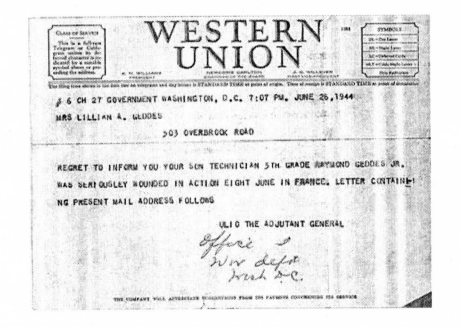

Telegram #2

WESTERN UNION

9 CH 36 NEW YORK 5;07 PM JULY 8 1944

MR LEALAND C TINSLEY
503 OVERBROOK ROAD

DEAR BUD ARRIVED IN NEW YORK YESTERDAY BY WIRE WILL REACH BALTIMORE VIA PENNSY R R AT 8;40 PM WEST YOU MEET ME YOURSELF AS YOU WILL HAVE TO BURNTON THE SHOCK AM OK HAVE WEEK END PASS

RAYMOND

Eisenhower Letter

SUPREME HEADQUARTERS
ALLIED EXPEDITIONARY FORCE

Soldiers, Sailors and Airmen of the Allied Expeditionary Force!

You are about to embark upon the Great Crusade, toward which we have striven these many months. The eyes of the world are upon you. The hopes and prayers of liberty-loving people everywhere march with you. In company with our brave Allies and brothers-in-arms on other Fronts, you will bring about the destruction of the German war machine, the elimination of Nazi tyranny over the oppressed peoples of Europe, and security for ourselves in a free world.

Your task will not be an easy one. Your enemy is well trained, well equipped and battle-hardened. He will fight savagely.

But this is the year 1944! Much has happened since the Nazi triumphs of 1940-41. The United Nations have inflicted upon the Germans great defeats, in open battle, man-to-man. Our air offensive has seriously reduced their strength in the air and their capacity to wage war on the ground. Our Home Fronts have given us an overwhelming superiority in weapons and munitions of war, and placed at our disposal great reserves of trained fighting men. The tide has turned! The free men of the world are marching together to Victory!

I have full confidence in your courage, devotion to duty and skill in battle. We will accept nothing less than full Victory!

Good Luck! And let us all beseech the blessing of Almighty God upon this great and noble undertaking.

Dwight D. Eisenhower

- 7 -

A55

Jerome J. McLaughlin

Cowan News Article

(Following is a portion of a typed copy of a news article written by Howard Cowan, an Associated Press reporter who spent a great deal of time covering the 435th Troop Carrier Group.)

Wounded Sky Trooper Leaps Into France Ahead of Mates

"Let Me at Them," He Shouts as He Tears Loose From Crew and Jumps With Machine Gun— Troop Carrier Command Does Its Job Well.

A NINTH Air Force Troop-Carrier Base, June 8. (AP)—The troop-carrier command did its job.

Its men went into France at little better than 100 miles an hour unarmed and unarmored and within bow and arrow range of German machine-gun and flak emplacements.

They delivered an army with weapons and supplies behind Hitler's Atlantic wall.

Take the case of Lieuts. Theron Anglemyar of Dodgeville, Wis., and Jeffey Harrison of Centreville, Miss. Clouds obscured the area where they were supposed to let the troops drop and they missed it.

They circled and headed back into withering fire. This time they placed the paratroops right on the button.

The Joes they fly are amazing—hard bitten, unfearing men whose trench is the sky.

Disappointed Bunch.

One paratrooper riding in a C-47 of the squadron commanded by Lieut. Col. Henry Osmer of Elmhurst, Long Island, shouted "Let me at them," tore loose from the crew who tried to restrain him and jumped with his machine gun.

They found a jagged bullet hole in the bucket where he had been sitting. Nobody knows his name. He wasn't much for talk.

Wounded Sky Trooper…cont'd

A tow rope broke while one group was forming up over a base and one glider had to land in a pasture several miles away while the rest of the outfit went on to France.

"When they went to pick them up in a jeep, the profanity was something terrible," said Capt. Frank Coffey, Lincoln, Neb., tow ship pilot. "The paratroopers had filed out and were stomping around giving us hell. 'Blankety blank blanks of blanks, they can't even get us where we are going,' one said."

The paratrooper doesn't use blanks in conversation anymore than he does in a tommy gun.

They Arrive in Daylight.

Coffey delivered them safely in daylight yesterday to the air-borne army on the Cherbourg peninsula.

Sergt James Lilly, Holly, Mich., repaired a C-47 landing gear in the air during the second movement of troops and supplies.

"He didn't have anything but a Scout knife but he practically took the ship apart in the air until he had those wheels fixed," said Maj. Tommy Nunn, Austin, Tex.

Jerome J. McLaughlin

A Very Special Reunion

(Following is the text of Joe Flynn's monthly column published in the El Dorado County, California, <u>Mountain Democrat</u> on June 5, 2000.)

It was a dark and stormy night 56 years ago, and this story could well be fictional. But it wasn't. Today and tomorrow, June 5th and 6th, in Baltimore, Maryland, the five or six people involved will for the first time in all these years get together and share their memories. Five men were paratroopers in the 3rd Platoon, G Company, 501st Parachute Infantry Regiment (PIR), of the 101st Airborne Division. One was a fellow pilot in my own 77th Troop Carrier Squadron, a unit of the Ninth Air Force, and one is the person primarily responsible for getting them together.

Our Preparation in England

We had five months of intensive training in both night and day paratroop missions. We also learned that there were limits in how low a formation flight leader can fly and still make turns. It was discovered that 250 feet above ground was too low! We practiced takeoffs and landings until we could launch and later land fifty-four C-47's, the military version of the DC-3 civilian airliner, on one runway in fifteen minutes, on average of one every fifteen seconds!

Many practice flights were in less than ideal weather conditions. Once, in a large night formation, we passed through an unexpected German bombing raid on the edge of London. We were picked up in the searchlights and discovered what "friendly" ack-ack really looked and smelled like.

Another night after a practice mission with the drop zone on the Salisbury Plain, near Stonehenge, we found our home field had been covered with fog. Looking for another place to land, our flight leader discovered the English trying to assist three Spitfire fighters in landing near the city of Bath. They concentrated searchlights, creating a bright spot on top of the fog above the center of their airfield. In addition, they fired red rockets up through the glare. By circling the light spot and rocket fire, we were able to circle through the fog and all nine planes from our squadron

landed OK. The Spitfires never made it, their pilots parachuting after pointing their planes out to sea when their fuel was low.

Getting Ready

Just a few days before D-Day the 501st PIR moved into our airbase at Welford Park in Berkshire, between Oxford and Reading, in southern England. Among these were Capt. Kraeger, Lt. Crouch, Lt. Barker, Sgt. John Urbank, Sgt. Charles Word, T/4 Ray Geddes, Pvt. Arthur Morin, and PFCs Don Kane and Lucien

"Lew" Tetrault. On this eventful night, giving the final preflight inspections to the Douglas C-47's, were pilots Capt. John Schaefers, Lt. James Hamblin, and Lt. Jesse Harrison, of "B" Flight, 77th Troop Carrier Squadron. Word was passed around that General Eisenhower was on the field chatting with the troopers. Harrison and Geddes remember Harrison having given a final briefing to the paratroopers saying, "This is for real tonight." How true that was to be.

Then at the last minute, Lt. Crouch, originally scheduled to board Harrison's plane, decided to board Hamblin's plane, and so changed places with Kane. At about the same time, just outside of the French village of Picauville, on the Cherbourg peninsula, the vehicle-mounted antiaircraft of the German 81st Division parked for the night on two hills just on the east end of the area where the 501st PIR was to drop.

All being ready, the men of the 501st boarded the C-47's. Flight B taxied to the runway, took off and formed with the other flights into formations of three and then nine ship elements in what we referred to as a *V of V's*. Time of departure was about 10:30 PM on June 5th. "Private Ryan" and a few thousand others were already on landing craft heading for Omaha and Utah Beaches. Flight B and the rest of the big Douglas airplanes, some 950 in all, from airfields all over Southern England were assembling in their formations and flying their assigned routes to the "drop zones."

Into Battle

All went well until just a few minutes after midnight when the west coast of Cherbourg peninsula was reached. To the dismay of the flight commanders, an unpredicted fog bank lay along the coast and inland along the course. A decision to descend into the fog was made, causing some disruption of the formations. Breaking out of the clouds about 500 feet above the ground and just minutes from the drop zone, severe antiaircraft fire was encountered. Just a few seconds after the "stand up and hook up" order was given, both Schaefers' and Hamblin's planes were hit by flak and exploded. Standing ready by the open door, Sgt. Word and Lew Tetrault, along with Art Morin, jumped clear and were the only ones surviving from Schaefers' plane. No one was able to get clear of Hamblin's and all perished. Pilot Jesse Harrison, after consulting with the paratroop officer on board his ship, and because of the burning planes below, elected to make a complete circle and come around to the drop zone again, where all his jumpers landed on their assigned spot. At about the same time, Capt. Theron Anglemeyer's flight of three, also from the 77th Troop Carrier Squadron, missed the drop zone and they, too, made a complete circle back around to the drop zone and successfully put their paratroopers on the landing spot. In all, thirty-eight C-47's and some 788 men were lost that night and day, putting about 14,500 soldiers on the ground behind the landing beaches.

Jerome J. McLaughlin

Fast Forward About Forty Years

Jerry McLaughlin, nephew of Joe Sullivan, my good friend and roommate and the navigator of Schaefers' plane, wrote to me. He lived in Alexandria, Virginia. Jerry and Philippe Nekrassoff, a former French paratrooper had become interested in the events having to do with Flight B on that historic night. Jerry, who was born in 1944, wrote to me in 1984 wanting to get the real facts about his uncle's death and why he was reported missing in action for a couple of years. Philippe, who was locating and documenting the exact spots where all thirty-eight planes crashed wrote to me (in French) in 1990. Locally, Mrs. Denise Worthington translated Philippe's letters for me. Jerry had my address from correspondence I had with Joe Sullivan's mother just after the war ended. I was able to put Jerry in touch with Philippe. Jerry later traveled to France to meet with Philippe, and between the two of them assembled records of the soldiers in each of Flight B's planes.

Then with a great deal of effort, Jerry located pilot Jesse Harrison of the 77th Squadron. Though he made it through D-Day, Harrison's luck ran out later when he barely escaped, badly burned, from his crippled plane over Holland. Also located were Ray Geddes, Don Kane, John Urbank and Art Morin, Jr., son of one of the troopers who jumped safely from Schaefers' plane. Now it is planned that these and others surviving from Flight B will meet on the 56th anniversary of D-Day. To the credit of the Boomer generation, there is a growing interest in the history of World War II and the veterans who survive. My thanks for his special interest and dedication in the research and follow-through go to Jerry McLaughlin for making the reunion of the survivors of my squadron's Flight B a memorable occasion. I am told that we are losing about 30,000 World War II veterans each month, not surprising when we consider that about sixteen million of us served in the war that ended fifty-five years ago.

Newspaper Article Depicting
Ray Geddes' Return to U.S.
After D-Day

(Copied from faded originals.)

Sergt. Raymond Geddes Is Among First
Wounded To Reach Home

As he was preparing to jump from his plane over Normandy on the third day of the invasion, Paratroop Sergeant Raymond Geddes, Jr., of 503 Overbrook road, Anneslie, saw two planes filled with other American paratroopers blown to bits by enemy flak before the men even had a chance to bail out.

Sergeant Geddes' left eye was badly injured by shrapnel from a German 88-mm. shell near Carentan, France, two days later. He is among the first American wounded to return home from the invasion battles.

The son of Mr. And Mrs. Raymond Geddes, Sr., the sergeant who is 19, said yesterday that he felt by being wounded so soon he had somehow let down the men who were killed, often within his view.

Reluctant To Talk

Reluctant at first to talk, he consented only after he was asked about the quick service rendered by the army to wounded men and how his own return home from the front within a month had been accomplished.

Paratrooper Tells of Leap in Normandy, cont'd

"The brave men did not come back," he said, "and I am among the lucky ones. When you see your friends killed before your very eyes, the war becomes awfully personal. The men who died—and the casualties were very heavy among the paratroopers—were those who stuck out their necks and who really went after the Nazis."

Geddes recalled that his major was killed by a sniper's bullet intended for himself. The bullet whizzed past his head and struck the officer alongside him.

Carried Walkie-Talkie Outfit

"I have jumped from planes 15 times in all, but the time I leaped from the plane into the moonlight over France was the most thrilling," the sergeant said. "I landed in a pasture field where there was a large herd of cattle. Everything was quiet. I carried a walkie-talkie outfit, my Garand rifle, rations and canteen.

"At first I lay still and listened for the sounds of my friends who were to gather at a particular signal whistle. Finally I heard the signal, then used my radio equipment. I was the captain's radio operator, and there were two other platoon operators to be contacted."

Germans Anticipated Landing

"The Germans were waiting for us; later a Nazi prisoner told us that we had been expected at this point. The German intelligence service is very good.

"After we got our group together, at least those of us who were left, we started to attack the town of Carentan. At times I fired with the rest, but I had my job of communications to do, so I was kept pretty busy.

"The Normandy countryside consists of a lot of fields, with hedgerows between them. We had to advance across this terrain, and the Germans did well with their 88s and machine guns. Let a man show himself through a hedgerow and he was dead.

"Well, we captured some prisoners, and most of them were seond-line Nazi troops. A lot of the enlisted men were Poles and White Russians

Paratrooper Tells of Leap in Normandy, cont'd

who had been pressed into the German armies under penalty of death to their families if they refused.

"We found one Pole sitting under a tree with an unloaded rifle, which had not been fired in the battle; he was waiting for us to capture him.

"The enemy laid down their artillery fire with accuracy; three shells landed in one spot among our men. One exploded close to me, and I went down."

Treated By Captured Doctor

"I was first treated by a captured Nazi doctor, who sprinkled sulfa powder over the injury; then I had to wait for a hospital ship.

"Other wounded men were being taken back to England on landing boats, and the like. The hospital ship was wonderful, but I was not operated upon until I got back to England—one of the first wounded Americans to return there. It was an aluminum timer from the shell which shattered the nerves and blood vessels around my eye, according to the doctors.

"From that time on the treatment I received was wonderful. I was shipped back to New York, and last night given a pass from Mitchell Field."

Sergeant Geddes is a graduate of the Towson High School. After finishing his studies there he was a laboratory assistant for a contracting firm in Baltimore county.

Jerome J. McLaughlin

Legere Letter

The letter on the following pages was provided to the author by Edwin Hohl's nephew, Arthur Couchman. It was prepared by Laurence Legere after many years of searching to find the family of the man who had died attempting to save Legere's life.

UNITED STATES MISSION
TO THE
NORTH ATLANTIC TREATY ORGANIZATION
(USNATO)

APO New York 09667

3 March 1980

Mrs. Florence Russell

4364 Westwood Road

Harris Hill, New York 14221

Dear Mrs. Russell,

Your address has come to me from Mr. George Koskimaki, Executive Secretary of the 101st Airborne Division Association, presently located at P.O. Box 101 AB, East Detroit, Michigan 48021.

It will be 36 years on June 6 since your brother, Eddie Hohl, was shot and killed while attending to me as I lay severely wounded in the middle of an exposed crossroads in the village of Pouppeville, just behind Utah Beach in Normandy. Hours later I was being evacuated across the Channel to a hospital in England from which, after about six weeks, I was evacuated for a further seven months' hospitalization in the United States. In the late winter of 1945, I left the hospital to serve on "limited duty", and thus was out of touch with the 101st Airborne until it was deactivated after the war.

Later, beginning in about the late 1940's, I started trying to find out who the soldier had been who was trying to help me with medical attention on "D-Day" 1944 when he was killed. None of my former associates in the Division Headquarters group knew because, as we later found out, Eddie had belonged to the 501st Parachute Infantry and had just fallen in with our group accidentally on that morning, after we had all landed by parachute during the early and confused hours.

Not until the late 1960's did I learn that the soldier in question had been a medical corpsman from the 501st named Hohl, and not until later than that did I learn he probably had a married sister living in or near Baltimore. Nothing came of my attempts to follow up on that lead. In fact, nothing much further happened until I read in a recent issue of the

Jerome J. McLaughlin

101st Airborne Division Association's bi-monthly newsletter that George Koskimaki had visited Eddie Hohl' sister in upstate New York. I immediately wrote George, who, after a determined search of his files, found your address and sent it to me.

Since 1974 I have been serving here in Brussels, Belgium as Defense Advisor to the US Ambassador to the North Atlantic Treaty Organization (NATO). In July 1978, Ambassador and Mrs. Bennett and my wife and I took a five day trip by car to Normandy, and for the first time since 1944 I found myself in the area of our D-Day airborne operation. I had thought that the nature of that whole area would have changed after so many years, but in fact it had changed not at all.

With very little trouble, we found the village of Pouppeville, the crossroads at the entrance to the village, and the roadside ditch from which both Eddie and I had leaped: me to dash across the open space and Eddie to come to help me when I was shot down in the middle of it. He had started to take some of his medical supplies out of his carrying cases and was on one knee beside me when a shot rang out and, without a sound, Eddie fell dead beside me.

He was wearing prominent Red Cross markings on his sleeve and on the front of his helmet, and was, of course, unarmed. We will never know whether he was shot maliciously in spite of his medical markings or whether a nervous and ignorant enemy soldier just did not know the rules of war in such cases. Many of the enemy soldiers in that coastal sector were actually Polish prisoners of war who had been impressed into the German Army, and I think it could have been one of them who was maybe less aware of the special protection accorded personnel than professional German soldiers themselves would have been.

In any event, Mrs. Russell, your brother Eddie's act that morning was one of tremendous bravery. No human being in his right mind wants to risk the only life he has, and yet he did just that for a fellow-American he did not even know, and the risk failed. For all of us who took part in the events of that historic day, the memories of it have been with us ever since and will continue to be for as long as we live. In my case, those memories will continue to be headed by my clear recall of the heroic act of your brother, Eddie Hohl.

With best wishes,

Sincerely,
Laurence J. Legere
Defense Advisor

Other Stories

These brief descriptions did not find a niche in the overall narrative, but they are poignant individual statements.

Frank Blaisdell – *During the time that the 77th was stationed at Welford, many of the officers became acquainted with the flight nurses that would eventually fly with the 77th when they brought wounded back from France. Several of these relationships resulted in wartime weddings between two commissioned officers. Pappy Rawlins described one romance in his history of the 77th Squadron (In May 1944):* "Squadron Executive Officer Frank Blaisdell met a lovely young nurse at the 98th General Hospital, and they immediately fell head-over-heels in love. They wanted to get married, but where would they live? They certainly did not want to live apart, each at their own station. Besides, the 98th was not too far from Welford Park. Frank discovered that the GC-4A gliders were shipped in sizable crates to our base. He arranged to 'rent' some farm land halfway between Welford and the 98th General Hospital, and proceeded to take several of the glider crates and build a sizable, and liveable, home for himself and Marge. Where does a hospital nurse in wartime and overseas find a suitable wedding dress? Trust the saying, 'Necessity is the mother of invention!' Somewhere, someone found a discarded parachute, and the silk panels were sewn into a lovely white wedding dress. Their wedding was attended by one and all, and they began a comfortable life in their 'little glider crate bungalow.' "

Bud Busiere - "One of my most vivid wartime memories was when we flew the second mission with gliders on D-Day afternoon. I looked out the door as we were flying across the channel, and it was like there were two bridges that went as far as you could see in both directions. We were in the bridge flying towards France, and there was another bridge with all the planes coming back. It was amazing."

Art Couchman (nephew of Edwin Hohl) - "Last year I got a letter from my old high school gym teacher, Don Puff; [he] grew up in Williamsville, [NY] and was one of the young men greatly influenced by my uncle Edwin. My uncle introduced him to football by knocking him on his butt the first time they met on the field. The two became good friends, and my uncle's influence eventually led Mr. Puff into teaching. However, before that, he joined the Marines and served in the Pacific during the war. He was in the first wave at Iwo Jima, and was wounded in the head there. He was a tough, tough gym teacher, and he always pushed me hard. I believe his influence, among others, led me to the Marine Corps. He was devastated by my uncle's death, and never really recovered from it. He told me, in his letter, that he visits my uncle's grave several times a year and puts an American flag on it. He was upset because the gravestone had become weathered over the years and was getting hard to read. He wanted my permission to replace the stone, at his own expense. I told him that it wasn't up to me, but my aunt, who was the closest relative, and that I would be glad to help pay for the stone. To make a long story short, my aunt was thrilled, and the stone was replaced with a new one. Mr. Puff wouldn't take any money from me, but my sister and I both contributed money to a scholarship fund [in his name]. I have since gone to see the stone. It is very nice, with a little American Flag waving in the breeze. I called my old teacher to thank him, and he became all choked up when he began talking about my uncle.... I find all these little interrelated turns of chance and the quirks of fate very interesting. War is the greatest disrupter of the human race."

Joe Flynn - "I can't speak for the other troop carrier groups, but I got really mad, as did others, when we read Stephen Ambrose's D-Day book and he referred to us on page 198 as being untrained in night flying, or in dealing with bad weather. The 77th completed their D-Day mission successfully, and we certainly were trained well by our leaders. I joined the squadron as a replacement pilot, in England, in December 1943. My log shows that I flew more than 25 hours of night practice missions before D-Day. One night we had a mission where we flew without lights of any kind and we encountered weather of every kind. We learned how to tighten up our formations when things got tough. That's why our guys did so well in Normandy. They held formation through flak and weather."

Ray Geddes - "On the morning of June 8th we moved out prior to an attack on Carentan. A bombing raid was in progress and the concussion was considerable. We were in the outskirts of the town of St. Come du Mont, which is a little above Carentan. All of a sudden, I found myself flat on the ground from an incoming artillery round, with a small wound in my left leg. Shortly afterward Lieutenant Colonel Julian Ewell, our Third Battalion CO, came along. His radio operator had just been wounded, so I took over. He was calling in artillery fire on Carentan. We moved behind a house (which is now known as *The House at Dead Man's Corner*) which at the time was a German aid station, with a big red cross on the roof. A shell came in and a piece of it hit me in the left eye. It did not hurt, just felt like someone might have slapped me. I went down to the basement of the house, where the aid station was located. It was filled with wounded Germans. I guess I was the only American there. A German medic looked at my eye and said, 'nicht kaput', poured some kind of powder into my eye, and applied a dressing. Then someone spoke to me in English. It was a Luftwaffe medical officer (who I am now sure was a member of the German Sixth Parachute Division). I commented on his excellent English. His answer was, 'I took my medical education in England.' When I left I took a hat, which must have been the doctor's, and some German binoculars. I still have them."

Ray Geddes (another story) – "Some things one remembers well, and this is one of them. Before we jumped in Normandy they made us turn in all our U.S. money for "invasion money." I kept a ten-dollar bill and hid it in the butt of my M-1 rifle. After I was wounded, and was told I was to be evacuated, I took the money out of the rifle and put it in my pocket. A month later I was flown back to Mitchell Field, near New York City—one of the first D-Day wounded to return to the U.S. The people there told me I could have a weekend pass and report in on the following Monday. I knew that my parents were frantic, having received a telegram saying that I had been 'seriously wounded' with no further explanation. I had to get home. It was that ten bucks that got me a train ticket from Grand Central Station to Baltimore."

Ray Geddes standing outside his hospital quarters and wearing the hat of the German doctor who treated his wound in Normandy.

Don Kane – "I learned a lot about the reality of war early on in Normandy. We were advancing on Carentan and I came across a wounded German officer and a private. The private was obviously terrified, and the officer looked in pretty bad shape. I didn't have time to waste on them, and I couldn't take them prisoner, as the officer couldn't walk, so I just continued on my way. A short time later I heard two shots—the guy behind me had killed both of them. He caught up to me later and asked me if I was crazy, leaving those guys behind me like I did. I told him that the private looked too scared to do anything, and that the officer had appeared to be a goner. He told me that the officer had given his pistol to the private, who was aiming to shoot me in the back when he had killed them. I learned a real lesson that day, and I never had any problems with prisoners from then on."

Henry Osmer - "Not many people know this, but I got it from Frank McNees' copilot on the D-Day drop. He was a fellow airline pilot, from TWA. He told me that when we flew into the clouds just before the drop, General Taylor got worried. He told McNees' crew chief to go up to the cockpit and find out what was going on, that he (Taylor) was worried about a collision with the cloud conditions. The crew chief went to the cockpit, and in the stress of the moment forgot to mention he was speaking for General Taylor, and not himself. He asked Colonel McNees, who was under quite a bit of pressure himself at that moment, "Isn't it kind of dangerous flying in formation in these cloud conditions?" McNees was incredulous, and told the man to "get the hell out" of the cockpit. By the time the crew chief returned to the cabin, the plane had emerged from the clouds and General Taylor was looking out the door waiting for the green light."

Jack Urbank - "When we were in Holland there was an incident where we used a 50-caliber machine gun to clean some Germans out of a gulch-like area. We went in after the shooting stopped to see if there was anything worth claiming as a souvenir, or that the intelligence people would find interesting. I was going through an officer's personal effects and found out that his name was Urbank. The guys told me I had

Picture of German officer named Urbank, found by Jack Urbank when looking through the officer's wallet [Urbank].

probably killed one of my own relatives. In the wallet was a picture of the guy with a small child. I kept the picture, and still have it. Later we were commended because the officer had some papers that Regiment thought were valuable."

George Winard - "My most vivid memory of the war is the first mission we flew dropping supplies to the guys in Bastonge. Some of the bundles didn't even have parachutes, they just contained winter clothing and boots. We came in really low, and looking out the door it was like a moonscape, all white. I vividly remember the 101st guys getting out of their foxholes and waving. I can see the faces today. Every time I think of those men, and their faces looking up at us, I start to cry, even today."

Where They Are Now

Busiere, Marion F. "Bud" (77TCS) - Returned to the United States with the 77th Squadron and was discharged in 1945. He continues to remind his fellow 77th comrades that no airplane on which he flew ever received a single hit. He reenlisted in 1946 for one additional tour with the USAF, during which he served with the occupation forces in Japan and with the maintainence forces in Europe that supported the Berlin Airlift. He was once again discharged, in 1949, and married Louise in 1950. He began a career as a civilian employee with the United States Army in 1954, from which he retired in 1978 as Director of Product Assurance for the Army Aircraft Maintainence Facility in St. Louis, Missouri. Bud and Louise raised two children; they live in Collinsville, Illinois.

Castona, Donald (G/501) - Twenty-three years old when he landed in Normandy, Don prepared notes for this book during the week of his 80th birthday. He is retired in San Lorenzo, California. He wrote to me after reading an early draft of the chapters on G Company, saying how much he had enjoyed reading the comments of his friends from a half-century ago. He also said that reading the comments of Toccoa men Ray Geddes, Don Kane, Jack Urbank, Charles Word, and Art Morin—and good friends he made later, to include Lew Tetrault and Warren Purcell—"brings out emotions I thought were pretty well forgotten. These were a hell of a group of guys; we had a special feeling of comradeship after all we did together for so long; maybe it's because misery loves company."

Flynn, Joseph (77TCS) - Flew with the 77th Squadron until the end of the war, completing missions to Normandy, Holland, Bastonge, and the final major airborne drop of 17th Airborne Division across the Rhine River. After the war Joe completed his degree in Forestry at Oregon State College. He remained in the Reserves as a pilot, and retired in 1967. He also had a 37-year civil service career working for the United States Forest Service, during which he was Forest Supervisor of the El Dorado National Forest. He retired as the Federal Assistant Regional Forester for the state of California. Joe is the father of six children, grandfather to eleven, and has three great-grandchildren. He is a member of United Flying Octogenarians (UFO), an association of licensed pilots who are at least 80 years old, and continued to fly his own airplane, along with his wife, Halmar, to the annual 435th TCG reunions until the year 2000.

Fosburg, Gene – After receiving his discharge in 1945, Gene returned to his native Galesburg, Illinois, and entered the insurance business. He attended both the Universities of Iowa and Illinois, married Pat Stephens, and had two children. After several career changes he formed and managed the Customer Relations Department for the Dick Blick Company, an art supply company. He retired in

1988. After 33 years of marriage, Gene lost Pat to cancer in 1984. In 1985 he married Flo Hendricks after she lost her husband under similar circumstances. On November 4, 2003, Gene's good friend from the 1943 Atlantic crossing, Ed Clark, called to wish him a happy birthday on the 60th anniversary of the day they arrived in England.

Friedman, Abraham (77TCS) - Returned to his native New York after the war, and retired from the U.S. Treasury Department in 1978 as Chief of the Intelligence Division of the Brooklyn IRS District. He later worked for the New York Stock Exchange. His first wife died in 1970. He and his wife Selma were married in 1975. They left their native Long Island to retire in Colorado and be near their children and grandchildren.

Geddes, Raymond (G/501) - Returned to the United States in July 1944 and served as an instructor and a military policeman until the war's end. He attended the University of Maryland on the GI Bill and graduated in 1951. Ray and his wife Shirley have two sons and are retired from a family school supply business. They live in Baltimore, Maryland, in the house in which Ray grew up. Ray remains in contact with General Ewell, for whom he was operating the radio when he was wounded. He describes Ewell as "the finest officer with whom I ever served."

Harrison, Jesse (77TCS) - After returning to the U.S., and marrying Shelia on March 17, 1945, Jesse spent another nine months in various military hospitals recovering from his burns. Released from medical treatment in January 1946, he and Shelia returned to Connecticut to start a family. He worked for the Johnson Control Corporation for forty-five years as an engineer, turning down several offers of airline pilot positions because he did not want to be away from his family. He maintained his pilot's license until 1995. Jesse and Shelia live near their two children, five grandchildren, and one great-grandchild, in Rocky Hill, Connecticut. Since regaining contact with each other, after fifty-six years, Jesse and Jack Urbank remain in close touch. As a result of his renewed contact with wartime comrades in the 77th TCS, particularly Henry Osmer, it was discovered that Jesse had been awarded a Distinguished Flying Cross in 1944 for his heroic actions and pinpoint flying and navigation on D-Day, but that the award had been lost in the wartime bureaucracy. Thanks to the efforts of Colonel Osmer, he receied his DFC in June 2003, presented by his local congressman, 59 years—to the day—from which he earned it.

Ingalls, Wilber (G/501) - Drafted in December 1942, he volunteered for the airborne and served with G Company from Toccoa until the end of the war. He maintains that he does not regret a minute of the time he spent in the Army. He took part in every major G Company campaign, being seriously wounded during the German attempt to retake Carentan in June 1944, and again by a sniper firing from a windmill the following September in the "Sand Dune" battle. He returned to his native Cuba, New York, after the war and had a forty-year career as a railroad signalman. He and his wife Alberta retired to Little Rock, Arkansas, to be near their grandchildren. Alberta passed away in 2003. Wilber's only regret about WWII is that President Roosevelt did not live to see the victory.

Kane, Donald (G/501) - One of the very small group of men from G-501 to serve during the company's entire WWII history, from the time it was formed in Toccoa, Georgia, in 1942, until it was disbanded in Austria in 1945. He was present for duty on every one of the company's 150-plus days of combat, and rose to the rank of Sergeant, earning two Purple Hearts, and two Bronze Stars, one each in Normandy and at Bastonge. He married Sue Richards, the girl who had waited for him during the war, and graduated from the University of Vermont School of Engineering in 1950. Don had a successful career as an engineer and plant manager while he and Sue raised four children, all of whom became medical professionals. Today, they have nine grandchildren and live an active retirement life in Purceville, Virginia, with a dog named Duke and two cats. Don and Sue returned to Normandy for both the 40th and 50th anniversary celebrations. More recently, Don completed a four-hour video history of his WWII years with the 501st PIR.

Krause, Paul (77TCS) - One of the few men in the 77th squadron to remain in the service when the war ended, Paul did not become a civilian until 1947. He was recalled at the rank of Captain a year later and served in the Strategic Air Command as a combat crew radar operator in B-50 and later B-47 aircraft until 1954. Deciding to remain in the military, he served in staff positions until 1958, when he was converted to Regular Air Force status. He next served in the B-58 bomber maintenance program. His following assignment was to SAC headquarters from 1966 until 1970, when he assumed command of the 321st Strategic Missile Wing, in Grand Forks, North Daota, an assignment that earned him promotion to Brigadier General. The final years of his career were spent at the Pentagon, working with the Joint Chiefs of Staff, and in Europe. Paul retired from the USAF on July 1, 1975, with thirty-three years of service.

Morin, Arthur, Sr. (G/501) - Returned to his native Massachusetts, retiring from a career with General Motors Corporation with more than thirty years of service. Arthur Morin died of cancer in 1995. His son, Arthur Jr., was located by the author in 2000 and participated in the development of this manuscript. Art, Sr. maintained that the movie "Battleground" (the story of a 101st Airborne Glider Infanty company at Bastonge) was the most realistic Hollywood movie he had seen regarding his experiences in Bastonge.

Orlowsky, Fred (G/501) - Born and raised in Brooklyn, New York, Fred returned home after the war and became a policeman in his native borough. He completed the war with G Company, missing several months after being wounded at Bastonge. When talking to the author, Fred had two points he wanted made clear regarding his time with the 501 PIR: he believed that the senior officers, particularly Colonels Ewell and Kinard, were the finest men—and leaders—he ever met, and that the 501st never got the credit it deserved for its efforts, compared to the other 101st regiments. He also feels strongly that many of the men in the regiment were not recognized individually for what they had done. Specifically, he remembers his squad leader, Virgil Danforth, who received the Distinguished Service Cross at Pouppeville but "did a whole lot more" later in the war. Fred is retired and lives in Pennsylvania.

Osmer, Henry (77TCS) - Hank Osmer returned to Eastern Airlines and his home in the borough of Queens in New York City when he was released from active duty. He remained a pilot with Eastern Airlines until his 60th birthday, in 1973, when he was flying as a Captain on 747 aircraft. He also retired from the military as a pilot in the reserves with thirty-five years of service. Colonel Osmer told the author the story of how the pilots of Eastern Airlines who were members of the military reserves at the time of Pearl Harbor attempted to enter active duty as a group to fly B-17 bombers. They knew nothing of the concept of troop carrier aviation. The Army Air Corps, in its infinite wisdom, saw the need for troop carrier units and the concept of airborne operations with paratroopers and glider infantry. This was the reason that Osmer and his airline comrades, with thousands of hours flying the civilian DC-3, were assigned to the newly forming troop carrier units, flying the same airplane under the military designation of the C-47. Henry Osmer proudly states that, "My current flight time is 36,250 hours, civilian and military. At age 80 I passed an airline pilot physical." Henry Osmer lives in Florida.

Purcell, Warren (G/501) - Fought in every one of the 501's battles in the dangerous job of the company commander's runner, and finished the war, amazingly, without a scratch. After the war he started his own trucking business, married Madeline, and raised two children. Today he is retired in Petersberg, Virginia, where he has lived—except for his time in college and the military—for his entire life. He stated to the author, "When it was over I hadn't had a scratch, through Normandy, Holland, Bastonge, and all the rest. The longer I was in combat, the more I felt like the law of averages should be catching up to me."

Rawlins, Phillip (77TCS) - A Regular Army officer, "Pappy" remained in the service when the war ended. He was selected for the Air Command and Staff College in 1947, and was then assigned to the U.S. Army Infantry School at Ft. Benning, Georgia, in 1948, to teach Air Force doctrine to aspiring second lieutenants (an assignment he loved, having begun his military career in the Army as an infantry officer). He next served as the Director of Instruction at the Air Ground Operations School in Southern Pines, North Carolina, and in 1953–54 was on a covert assignment in the Far East with the Central Intelligence Agency. He returned to flying in 1954, with the 4th Fighter Interceptor Wing, stationed in South Korea, where he became a member of the select group of 1950's pilots who had broken the sound barrier. In 1957 he graduated from the National War College and served for the next three years in staff positions with Air Force Headquarters at the Pentagon. After several additional overseas and Washington assignments, he was named Commander of Clarke Air Force Base, Republic of the Philippines in 1967. He retired from the USAF in 1970, with the rank of Colonel, and thirty-one years of service. Pappy retired in San Antonio, Texas, and continues to live there today.

Tetrault, Lucien (G/501) - In 1996 author Mark Bando found Lucien Tetrault living in Florida and called me with Tetrault's address. I sent a letter with a Xerox copy of the pages from Mark's book that mentioned Tetrault's name. "Lew" Tetrault called me when he got the letter, and we talked for some time. He was happy to have the material, he said, because his children thought that his stories about the war were all made up. He told me a version of his stay at the Lebruman farm that was more complete and differed in several ways from Charles Lebruman's memory. Tetrault concurs that Charles did visit the crash site of Schaefers' plane before dawn on the 6th, and that he returned with dog tags, which he had taken from the bodies he had found. Tetrault said that he was angry with Lebruman because when they both visited the site later in the morning, Tetrault realized that the burned bodies would be very difficult to identify without the dog tags. He also told me that he believes that he and Morin only remained with the Lebrumans until June 9th or 10th, and that they left with a passing 82nd airborne patrol. Within an hour the group got into a firefight and Tetrault was seriously wounded in the shoulder and became seperated from Morin and the 82nd men. Unable to move, he hid in a wooded area for four days until he was found by a young boy who fed him and assisted him to a nearby American field hospital. The remainder of Tetrault's WWII career continued to be, as he says, frustrating and difficult. He was hospitalized in England from his wound in Normandy, and missed the September–November campaign in Holland. He finally returned to G Company in time to travel with them by truck to Bastogne, where he was wounded again in the company's opening moments in that battle. He believes he was placed on the last ambulance to leave Bastonge before the town was surrounded. He never returned to G Company.

Urbank, Jack (G/501) - After being discharged from the Southhampton Military Hospital, Jack returned to G Company in time to participate in the Bastonge campaign and the remainder of the company's wartime exploits. Discharged in 1945, he returned to Ohio, where he went into business with his brothers while he and Edna reared four children. His youngest son, David Vernon Urbank, is named after two G Company comrades who did not survive the war: David Mythuler and Company Commander Vernon Kraegar. Jack has been very active supporting authors and researchers who have documented the WWII service of the 101st Airborne Division and its 501st Parachute Infantry Regiment.

Vollbrach, Earl (77TCS) - Returned from the war and opened an automobile parts business in his hometown of Canton, Missouri. Earl Vollbrach died of a heart attack on March 9, 1986.

Winard, George (77TCS) - Had the unusual experience of flying from the U.S. to England, going through all of the 77th's combat missions, and returning home having flown with the same crew and on only one airplane. After the war he returned to his native Long Island town of Islip. He eventually moved to California and started a clothing business with his brother. He and Mikki were married in 1951. They raised two children and are the proud grandparents of four. The Winards have lived in the same house in Sherman Oaks, California, since 1955. They missed the 2001 trip to Normandy in order to celebrate their 50th anniversary with

their children and grandchildren.

About the Author

Jerry McLaughlin is a native of Queens, New York. Raised on Long Island, he graduated from Lynbrook High School and Long Island University. He began a career with the federal government by serving in the US Army from 1969 until 1971, and retired from the Central Intelligence Agency in 2003 as a senior training manager. Mr. McLaughlin began research for this book in 1980, including several trips to Normandy. The most recent visit took place in 2001, when he and other family members and friends dedicated plaques commemorating the bravery of 40 men, including his uncle, who lost their lives on D-Day, June 6, 1944. Mr. McLaughlin and his wife, Denise, currently live in Alexandria, Virginia, along with a Wheaten Terrier who goes by the name of Murphy.

Printed in the United States
30274LVS00001B/2